A Time to Mourn or a Time to Dance

Vera Inice

PublishAmerica

Baltimore

First printing

ISBN: 1-59129-391-X
PUBLISHED BY PUBLISHAMERICA BOOK PUBLISHERS
www.publishamerica.com
Baltimore

Printed in the United States of America

This book is dedicated with love and gratitude to men in my life, Jack and Joe, who nagged, browbeat, and shamed me into putting my IBM Selectric manuscript into the computer. Thanks, guys.

There is a time for everything
And a season for every activity under heaven:
A time to mourn
And a time to dance.

—Ecclesiastes 3:1 and 4b

CHAPTER 1

The bonds on her wrists and ankles seemed to be getting tighter. Lately her ankles began to swell when she sat for very long. How long had she been here? Six hours? Ten hours? There were no windows in this warehouse and the only light was a bare bulb over the dilapidated metal desk where the massive black man sat with his back to her.

The big thug suddenly turned to stare at her and barked, "Don't you try nothing, lady, or you're dead meat." With his duty thus fulfilled, he turned back to his comic book and sat perfectly still, except for an occasional silent chuckle which made his rickety chair wobble and the floor boards groan with the shaking of those enormous shoulders.

Hillary couldn't suppress her own silent chuckle at the preposterous statement. Try something, indeed! What could a matronly lady like herself possibly try, sitting here gagged and bound with every joint in her body going stiff and painful? She had to think of something. It was not in her nature to give up. The greater the challenge, she often told herself, the greater the ingenuity she would have to summon and then the greater the satisfaction in a job well done.

It was her own fault, of course. She should not have stuck her nose into this shady transaction; at least not without being in direct communication with her backup. And where was he now?

Another shoulder-heaving chuckle and creaking floor boards turned Hillary's eyes back to the black man. He looked familiar. He seemed to resemble Rosie Greer, the gigantic football player. She looked at him closer. He WAS Roosevelt Greer! No, that's ridiculous, Hillary told herself. Rosie was one of the good guys, not the kind to associate with thugs who'd capture and tie up a sweet little old lady. Besides, he wouldn't be sitting there reading comic books. Somewhere she had read that he liked to do handwork in his spare time, knitting maybe, or needlepoint.

Think, she told herself sharply. You got yourself into this and only you can get yourself out. What to do? For starters, where are we? She listened to the muted noises coming from outside the warehouse. Perhaps she could detect some pattern if she put her mind to it and just maybe she could pinpoint this warehouse once she got back to the office. To her left she could hear traffic at a distance punctuated with the sound of a train nearby at intervals of fifteen or twenty minutes. To her right, she knew, was the waterfront. Now what would she, a woman from Waco, Texas, know about a waterfront? She could hear a clanging buoy far in the distance, sometimes the long hoot from what she imagined was a tanker or freighter. Ship sounds came from directly behind her, then moved out to the right, and faded away into the distance directly in front of her. Other ships would then reverse this course. That could only mean this warehouse was out on something of a peninsula, or even a pier, jutting out into the waterway.

Well, Hillary, she chided herself, now that we know EXACTLY where we are, what are we going to do about it? An idea was forming, not the whole escape plan, but a beginning.

Hillary began stamping her feet as loudly as possible to get the attention of the black giant. He turned around slowly to look at her from under heavy brows. "What is it now, lady? I just took you to the john. You got some kind of bladder problem?"

Hillary stamped her feet again till her captor came over and pulled down her gag. "Have you ever heard of Roosevelt Greer, the famous football player?" she began.

Surprised and offended, the black man answered, "Are you kidding, lady? What do you take me for, some kind of dummy that don't know what's going on in the world?"

Gently Hillary began to explain how he resembled the famous man and greatly exaggerated the needlepoint stories, building them into heroic feats of daring and bravery. The big man listened politely, nodding from time to time when Hillary made a carefully executed point. When she knew she had his attention and hopefully his cooperation, she continued, "I'm having some trouble with this afghan I'm working on and, well, I shouldn't ask you, but..."

"What is it, lady, maybe I can help you. Just tell me what you need." He squinted at her suspiciously and added, "But I ain't gonna untie you, if this is some kind of trick."

"Oh, thank you, uh, Josh, isn't it? I thought I heard someone call you Josh while I was blindfolded." If he will only bring over my purse and knitting bag, Hillary plotted, and if he isn't too curious why a knitting bag would be so heavy. The .32 caliber automatic was tucked neatly into the false bottom

of the knitting bag with quick pull-apart velcro tabs, loaded and on safety. On past occasions it only took seconds to retrieve the weapon and reverse an uncomfortable situation. With her small stature Hillary liked to think of the pistol as her "equalizer" and, even so, was considering her co-workers' suggestion that she graduate to a .38 caliber, or larger.

"Okay, lady, here's your sewing stuff. But I ain't going to give you your purse. You might have some mace or a gun or somethin' and I ain't gonna fall for no tricks."

"Well, if you won't untie my hands then I'll just have to use your hands, won't I?" Hillary explained to Josh how he should hold the yarn in his left hand, wrapped around his little finger to stabilize it, over the index finger for the correct tension, and the thumb and middle finger holding onto the afghan-in-progress. "Now, with your right hand hold the crochet hook kind of like a spoon. You see, there are already some stitches on the hook, so don't bother them. Now dip the end of the hook under that next stitch. That's right, and reach up for the yarn and pull it through. No, not so tight. It's so dark in this corner that I can't see very well."

Reluctantly Josh put his precious afghan back into the bag and picked up Hillary, bag, and purse and walked over to the lighted desk where he deposited them all on the top of the desk. He settled himself in the chair and carefully reached down into the bag to retrieve the afghan. He wound the yarn around his fingers as before and dipped the end of the crochet hook under the proper loop, hooked the yarn, and pulled it through. As he breathed a deep sigh Hillary realized he had been holding his breath during the intricate exercise. She was surprised at the gentleness with which those huge fingers worked the soft yarn. The bag, with her only means of escape, was so near, just below her left elbow, and she couldn't move far enough to reach it. And even if she could reach the gun she could never make her escape with her hands tied so tightly together. Her only chance was to somehow persuade him to untie her hands and then...

Suddenly the door beside the desk was thrown open. "What the...!!" The hoodlum who was obviously the ringleader stood mesmerized by the sight in front of him: the gray-haired woman on top of the desk, and his biggest henchman sitting literally at her feet with yarn wrapped around his fingers and actually knitting, or whatever.

"What do you think you're doing? I give you a simple job to do—just watch one old lady—and look at you," he spluttered, red in the face with this outrage.

9

"Boss, I think you got this old lady wrong. She couldn't possibly be onto our operation. She's just someone's grandma and in the wrong place at the wrong time."

The ringleader peered at Hillary with his squinty eyes for what seemed a very long time while she tried to maintain her wide-eyed innocent expression.

"Yeah, you're probably right, what could she do? Okay, get rid of her," he barked. "And I don't care how!"

Josh replaced Hillary's blindfold and untied her feet and then her hands. He picked up her purse and knitting bag and gently led her out of the warehouse and down a broken concrete sidewalk to what seemed like an ancient van. He started the motor with difficulty and began driving down a pot-holed street. Hillary counted the blocks—only three—before he parked the van and led her down another sidewalk, not so broken. As Josh untied the blindfold, Hillary noticed they were just outside the Water Street Metro station. He really doesn't suspect me, she thought. What a sweet and simple guy he is, to be in such a despicable business.

"Okay, lady, you just forget everything you seen or heard if you know what's good for you." And, as an afterthought, "I just might try some of that knittin'." The train doors were closing as he shoved her on board.

"Crochet. It's crochet."

Hillary was poised to jump off the train the second it stopped at the next station and raced to the public telephone. When she recognized the voice of her superior officer, she quickly related the events of her capture, the residence she suspected and where she was picked up, the description of the abandoned warehouse where she was held, just three blocks from the Water Street Metro Station. All of this she rattled off, professionally she hoped, hardly stopping for a breath.

"Hillary, you're alright. That's the important thing," the Chief told her, obviously relieved. "Once again you've done us an outstanding job. Now go home to your hot bath and a well-deserved rest. We'll be depositing a sizeable sum in your account, as usual."

Hillary massaged her wrists and ankles and opened her eyes. She realized she had been sitting too long with her ankles crossed and her feet were, indeed, beginning to swell. The handles of her purse were tightly wrapped around her wrists and making deep ridges. She glanced over at the bed where her husband lay, and was startled to see that his eyes were open, staring suspiciously at her.

"Where's Harry?" he asked.

"I'm right here, Darling."

"No, you're not Harry! She's pretty and young. You're not young," he said evenly, his eyes narrowed. The words stung, and she knew it was true that she had become very gray and held little resemblance to the girl that Pete had met in college. She just had to consider his condition. Some days he knew her immediately and laughed and joked about his poor memory. Other days were hard to bear.

Hillary hated self-pity in anyone, but hated it more so in herself and wouldn't give in to that type of self-indulgence. She couldn't tolerate despair and tried every kind of mind control she could devise to keep herself out of the doldrums. She had experienced the paralysing hold of depression and refused to let it control her again. And she prayed, oh, how she prayed.

Pete lay very still with his eyes tightly closed, but Hillary knew he was not sleeping. She wondered what, exactly, he was thinking. He may have been wondering how he got to this place, wherever it was, and who was this gray-haired woman pretending to be his pretty little "Harry" with her black hair and almost black eyes.

Hillary held Pete's hand firmly, not only to comfort him, but to comfort herself. She was needing desperately to feel some continuity with her past. With their past. Here, in this man who would not open his eyes and look at her, was her life, her reason for being, and she could see him slipping farther and farther away from her.

"Pete, know what I was thinking about?" she started, hoping to get his attention and interest. "Remember that day at the university when I flirted with you, thinking you had a newly broken heart?" She chuckled, remembering. Pete's expression didn't change but maybe he was following her line of patter that she often used to reorient him to his past and to his present.

What a good-looking old man he had become! His gray hair and mustache were very dignified, Hillary thought. His lanky frame had a few more pounds on it, but he still appeared to be a tall, thin man, and his bearing made people take a second look at this authoritative person.

Hillary leaned back in the recliner, careful to elevate her feet and making sure nothing was restricting her wrists. She was aware of her fantasies, and loved them. When things around her became painful she could easily slip into an adventure which would, for a few minutes, let her be a heroine, save a life or a country, in short, make the world a better place in which to live.

She smiled, wondering what a psychiatrist would make of her Walter Mitty episodes. Being a registered nurse herself, she was familiar with psychological jargon and sometimes envisioned herself trying to convince a psychiatrist that she was still in touch with reality and had *insight* into her condition.

"Do you remember, Pete, that day at the Sub when I practically threw myself at you?" Hillary smiled remembering the morning she dropped by the Student Union Building, or Sub, as they called it, to pick up a cup of coffee before English class. How surprised she would have been to know that her life would be changed forever that day. "I thought you'd been jilted by that beautiful Alicia and then I find out she's your cousin.

"Do you remember how much we talked about airplanes in those days, Dear? I didn't know the first thing about planes then. But you taught me so much." She kept holding and patting his hand, hoping he was listening to her. During that long-ago semester, Hillary came to know a lot about Pete. He had been a pilot and as a veteran still enjoyed flying single-engine private planes when he could afford it. She could still remember some of the details of the airplanes he told her about. In World War II, Pete's dad flew in the Air Corps, which was later to become the Air Force. Pete grew up intrigued by the five-passenger Staggerwing Beech, or Beech Model 17, that took the Air Corps brass from field to field. As a teenager he had studied all he could learn about this unique aircraft. For the longest time Hillary remembered the aircraft's airspeed and the horsepower of the Pratt & Whitney engine because those were the things that Pete was interested in. She also knew that he had longed to fly the fighters, and when the Korean conflict began heating up, he got his chance with the newer models of jets.

Hillary had to know if he was listening. "Do you remember all those things you used to tell me about that Staggerwing plane that you used to fly? The Beech something or other, Model 16 was it?"

"Seventeen."

Thank you, God, she said silently.

After they were married, Pete coaxed her into taking flying lessons, just so she'd be comfortable when they flew together, he persuaded. To please him she became a licensed pilot, and had ultimately enjoyed her flying lessons and had become what she considered a pretty fair pilot. Reading aerial charts was easy for her and she could help Pete with the navigation, but she felt panicky and tongue-tied when she needed to speak on the radio. Pete would just chuckle and remind her that there was no secret language she had to learn, just to state simply and concisely what it was she needed to request or convey. He also reminded her that she didn't seem to have any trouble talking on the telephone.

"Pete. I think that if I hadn't been so forward you might never have gotten around to speaking to me, and certainly not ask me for a date." He smiled slightly and covered her small hand with his big one. Pete had begun calling Hillary Harrison "Harry" simply because it was so inappropriate.

The shadows were getting long, and Hillary knew it was time for her to leave. She held Pete's hand and prayed a short and simple prayer that Pete would understand readily, asking for God's protection for them both and for his care givers to be skilled and gentle.

Driving home from the Four Seasons Nursing Home, Hillary realized she felt very tired and sad. Sad because once again she must go home alone and she knew that nothing would ever change that. And some days she felt guilt, too. She was always anxious to leave as early as possible on days like today had started out, when Pete was antagonistic and didn't seem to recognize her. Maybe if she worked harder at the "Time, Place, Person re-orientation" that was ingrained into her nursing behavior, he would begin to improve. But not likely, she admitted to herself.

"I'm not going to be this depressed. I'm going to do the best I can for Pete, and I'm going to do the best I can for me, too."

Hillary's spirits quickly changed when she remembered the surprise she had planned for the bridge party tonight at her house. She laughed out loud thinking of the expressions she expected to see on her friends' faces. The sound of her own laughter startled her since she was so accustomed to the monotonous drone of her engine. Hillary switched on her radio to a country and western station and began to sing along with the heartbroken cowboy who regretted his wild ways and the loss of the only real love he had ever had.

Hillary loved music, any music, all music. It made her feel good and she wished that she had real musical talent like Jane. Jane could play anything she wanted to, classics or rock and roll, and didn't even need the sheet music. Hillary knew that both Jane and Sharon would be delighted with the surprise she had for them. Once they had recovered from the initial shock.

Hillary changed into her casual clothes, brushed her hair smooth and went into the kitchen to finish the food for the party. The game was designed to be happy and cheerful because, for different reasons, they each needed a time to be free of all other cares. "Endorphins," she said aloud.

Jane had been the one to suggest and name the "Gritch Kitty," a collection of money forfeited by saying a negative word about anything. Anything, that is, other than a bad bridge hand. They planned that the money would take them out to dinner at their favorite restaurant on the lake. So far it didn't have many dollars in it.

Hillary had two pans of stuffed mushrooms ready to pop into the oven as soon as Jane and Sharon arrived. Lady, her aging black Lab, suddenly sat up listening for a familiar motor which Hillary couldn't hear at all. Finally Hillary did hear the car pull into the driveway and a door slam. Lady began to bark a happy welcome. She loved Sharon and Jane, and having company was very exciting to her, so Hillary didn't scold her for barking and dancing through the kitchen begging to be let out the side door. When Hillary opened the door, Lady bounded out to greet Sharon, who was equally happy to see Lady.

"What on earth happened to your grass and that bush by the driveway?" Hillary didn't want to discuss that subject tonight. She didn't want them to know how disturbing it was to her, and she was afraid she couldn't talk about it without giving away the frightening feelings she had experienced. And they had pledged to each other to keep bridge party night a happy time because of their need for some happiness in their lives.

"Well, I don't know. It looks like someone might have lost control of their motorcycle there. I can smooth it out tomorrow. Oh, Sharon, that outfit is even cuter than the others." Hillary laughed and made a face. "I don't think even Dale Evans would have worn a dude getup like that."

Sharon, the proud owner of Partners, the two child care centers that were the favorite of many parents with young children, always wore flashy western clothes when she went to work. The children loved it and were always eager to be dropped off. The parents also loved it, and Sharon herself was happier than she had been in many years.

"Where's Jane? She usually beats me here." Sharon sprawled on the recliner, tossing her mauve hat into a corner and putting up her mauve booted feet. Lady lay down close enough to be patted occasionally.

"I guess she'll be along soon, she hasn't called." Hillary put the first pan of stuffed mushrooms into the oven, sure that Jane would arrive by the time they were done.

Lady lifted her head again, and although Hillary was sure there was no sound of a car nearby, she did hear a vague thump, thump, thump. Lady repeated her excited barking and dancing around the kitchen until Hillary opened the side door. Jane stood on the porch in her sweat suit, spinning the basketball deftly on her index finger, waiting for the admiration that she knew Hillary would offer. Jane's dark hair was pulled neatly back into one long braid down her back and was crowned by a thick gray streak that rose from the right side of her forehead.

"I'll never know how you do that, Jane. Come on in. I've got your favorite snack in the oven, stuffed mushrooms. You didn't drive?"

"Would you believe I dribbled all the way from my house?"

"Well, June Allyson says we don't have to be embarrassed by that sort of thing anymore," Sharon answered with a smirk.

Jane feigned a shot with her ball at Sharon's head, catching it easily in her other hand. She then walked over to the frig and found a can of soda she knew would be there, just for her. She opened the freezing compartment and found a frosty mug which she also knew would be there, knowing it, too, was just for her. Jane turned back to Sharon, taking in the outlandish mauve western outfit.

"Well, I see you've had another hard day on the range, Tex." And turned back to Hillary to ask, "How's Pete?"

"He wasn't that great today. Accused me of being an imposter because his Harry is young with black hair," she answered truthfully. But since that bordered on the unpleasant, she added, "But I sweet-talked him back into the present and we had a good walk. He's gotten interested in the crafts room and showed me the pottery and sculpting he's doing. I never dreamed he'd be interested in anything like that. He's hardly ever had any hobbies or other interests outside of the bank."

"Well, he spent his life working for the bank and you could tell he loved it," Jane offered. "Except for his family he seemed to love that bank better than anything. I wouldn't be surprised but what the lake house and roping club membership were for business development purposes for that bank."

"Yep, you're probably right. The kids and I knew that whatever we did might reflect on the integrity of the bank. I don't know if that's good or bad, but at least they never got into any trouble. And, of course, I never got into any scandalous affairs, either," Hillary added with a mischievous grin.

"I can't see you getting into any *scandalous affairs*, even if Pete had been business manager for a bawdy house." Jane turned back to Sharon. "Why are you so quiet, tonight, Roy Rogers? And where did you get that outfit? You look like Dolly Parton with a chest reduction. Or is that one of those subjects we don't talk about?"

"Dear Jane," Sharon laughed, "I've never known you to stay away from any subjects that 'we don't talk about.' Actually I was kind of re-hashing my day. My new saddle stools came today and we should get them installed this week. But mainly I was just drinking in this...this atmosphere. They call it *ambience* in those fancy restaurants—the comfort of this room and listening to you two talk. Even if you're both a little crazy. But it's nice to be able to say what we feel without having to worry that something will be taken wrong and having to qualify every statement." She sighed and continued her nostalgia. "I can't remember being so comfortable with anyone since the sorority house, when I was in college. I was kind of a clown and loved it. But poor Harvey always acted so embarrassed when I tried to be funny that I decided maybe I wasn't that funny after all."

The three of them finished their snacks and took their drinks over to the game table where the cards and score pads were waiting. They drew for high card to determine who would deal and Sharon won with a Jack of Clubs. "We play three-handed so often that I forget how to play real bridge," Sharon complained. "Why don't we get a fourth? How about Martha?"

"No, not Martha," Jane answered. "I love Martha. I owe her my life even. But if she were here I couldn't cuss, know what I mean?" She paused. "What I'm trying to say is, I couldn't be myself. She's even worse than Hillary, here, for expecting the best in someone. Besides, if we got a fourth maybe they wouldn't know how to play like we do and we'd have to teach them. I can't stand to spend an evening teaching someone how to play bridge." The three of them concentrated on their cards, each of them a skilled tactician and each of them extremely competitive. They finished a party rubber and Hillary went back into the kitchen to pour decaf coffee. She smiled to herself, thinking of the surprise she was going to pop on them and wondering whether she could pull it off. But first, Harvey.

"Sharon, did you know Harvey is in the hospital? I worked today and visited with him on the GU floor." The genito-urinary unit was often just called Urology by lay-people, but Hillary was still very much the nurse even though she had retired and was now a volunteer. She took pride in her duties as a Pink Lady and spent two mornings a week at the hospital where she had worked full or part-time most of her adult life.

Sharon looked up at the question, surprised. "Really? Is he sick?"

"He's having some tests run and may have surgery. They think he may have BPH, that means benign prostatic hypertrophy, it's an operable condition. Men usually do fine after surgery. He's really anxious, though, sure that it's probably cancer. He told me a lot of things, I'm sure, so that I'd tell you. Do you want to hear it?"

"Well, of course. Not that I can do anything about it. I haven't even seen him in months. I don't even know who his current bimbo is." Sharon was not bitter; they just always referred to Harvey's current affair of the heart as a bimbo, which in truth was usually accurate.

"Harvey seems to be feeling his mortality all of a sudden. What it boils down to seems to be this: Harvey once had a beautiful wife that he slaved for and gave her everything she could possibly want, and now, when he needs her most, she's left him for a bunch of snot-nosed kids. His words, not mine. He thinks you tricked him into the divorce and he only gave it to you to make you happy. I didn't want to fight with him while I was on duty, but I couldn't help observing that it didn't seem to me that *all* his activities were just for your happiness. I'm sorry, Sharon, maybe I shouldn't even have mentioned this."

Sharon was looking down at her hands, palms down on the table. She began to absently rub the back of each hand as if to erase the age freckles, or liver spots as so many people refer to them. "No, Hillary, that's alright. I'm used to Harvey and the way he can twist things. He's the world's best manipulator. Maybe he's even partly right. Maybe I did trick him, but it was the only way I could get out." Sharon smiled faintly. "Actually, Harvey's big problem is similar to mine." She hesitated, trying to think of a way to phrase her thought. "We've got to determine whether an old businessman who's lost his business and an old beauty who's lost her looks have any right to go on taking up space and air."

She knew her joke was not really funny and looked pensive for a brief moment. "But let's talk about something besides Harvey, okay?"

Jane had walked over to Hillary's small grand piano and had been playing soft music and had listened quietly to the conversation. But now she looked up at Sharon and said, "He really did a job on you, didn't he?" Sharon didn't answer, knowing it was not a question but a statement. "You know, Sharon, I used to watch you two before we knew each other very well and I wondered what you saw in Harvey. He seemed so cocky, always had to be the center of attention and let everyone know what his opinions were on every subject. And I thought you had so much class, not to mention being the most gorgeous woman in town." She added with a wry smile, "Even if you did dress a little flamboyantly."

Sharon's eyes were moist with tears but now she laughed. "Oh, Jane, you always make me laugh. It's like I was saying awhile ago, you two make me feel so good. The clothes were always Harvey's idea. I don't know any other woman whose husband buys all her clothes. He always chose such expensive things and he liked bright colors. Sometimes I felt more like his showhorse than his wife."

"Yes, but you looked like a movie star every year at the Charity Ball. Remember that yellow outfit with the big bow on the shoulder? Very few women can wear yellow."

"Do I ever remember it! It was the year of my mastectomy and the right shoulder was bare but the left shoulder strap covered my scar and had that big bow on it. I told Harvey that I felt like a giant chrysanthemum, which I thought was kind of funny, but it made him mad. He never laughed at my jokes, as I mentioned before. But, please, let's don't talk about poor Harvey anymore. Hillary, next time you see him just tell him we all wish him a speedy recovery."

Hillary placed the dessert and coffee in front of her friends, feeling grateful for an excuse to use her fine china and silver. It had become one of those things she had come to think of as "feel-good" things. She had too many anxiety attacks and days of depression lately and had begun her counter-attacks. She made many plans for her week now instead of just drifting along. Most of the plans included outings with her friends and other things which lifted her spirits. Like her fantasies, she admitted. Like riding Queen, especially when Sharon and Major could join them.

She found herself looking forward to her work at the hospital and visiting with her old friends, staff, and the patients. She sometimes enjoyed her visits with Pete, but all too often the visit left her blue and worried. Hillary wished she enjoyed spending more time with her daughter's family, each of whom she loved dearly, but she frequently came home from a visit feeling very old and old-fashioned. She really couldn't identify her discomfort. She just knew she came off second best in a contest she didn't understand. She prayed privately about this and yet couldn't help feeling guilty as though it might be her fault. She wondered if other mothers ever felt that way but never mentioned it.

Ah, but lately she had been feeling very good, and now it was time to spring the surprise on her two very dearest friends. "Ladies," she announced in her Master of Ceremonies voice, "for your pleasure and amusement, or AMAZEMENT, we have planned the following extravaganza!"

Hillary ducked into the next room while Sharon and Jane looked at each other shrugging their shoulders. When she returned she was wearing black tap shoes with a bow on the strap and carrying her recorder. She rolled back her Oriental rug to expose waxed hardwood floors and turned her recorder to "PLAY."

The tape came on loudly, as planned, and Hillary began her tap dance routine. The music was country and western, all about "she used to be somebody's baby" with a rhythm that forced one to tap his toes, snap his fingers, or sing along.

But Jane and Sharon were still sitting dumbstruck with their mouths open. Sharon giggled and then Jane. They were at first embarrassed, and then they began laughing until tears rolled down their cheeks.

When the music and dance routine were done, Hillary turned off the recorder and asked, "Well, what do you think?"

Jane was wiping her eyes with a tissue she had pulled from her pocket and apologetically replied, "Oh, Hillary, I'm so sorry we laughed. It's just that, well, you're so BAD!" Sharon said nothing but was still trying to catch her breath and stifle her laughter.

Hillary was radiant. "That's just the point! You see? I made you laugh and it makes me laugh, too. I don't care if I only know four steps and I'm behind the music at least half a beat. I've only been practicing a few weeks and I am getting better. Really. But isn't this fun? When have we laughed so hard?"

Sharon jumped out of her chair and went over to the uncovered wood floor beside Hillary. "I don't know any tap dancing but I've spent enough years in aerobics and Jazzercize to know about a thousand routines. Let's do it again."

Jane turned back to the piano. "And I can add a little something to the music with a boogie beat."

Together they went through the music again, and Hillary picked up her tempo to match the music. Sharon, with her usual grace and agility, performed a bizarre dance routine in cowboy boots. Jane's long, skilled fingers ran the catchy rock beat up and down the bass keys of the piano with some appropriate improvisation on the treble keys. The Gatlin Brothers had never had a more appreciative audience.

The second and last tape that Hillary had prepared was Hank Jr. singing "Born to Boogie." The three gray-haired women laughed at themselves until the music finished, and Hillary and Sharon flopped down exhausted on the sofa. Sharon was holding her aching sides. "I don't know when I've had this much fun. Maybe never. You know, at our age we just might laugh ourselves to death."

To which Jane answered, "Yeah, and what a way to go!"

Sharon glanced at her watch and exclaimed, "Would you look at the time! And we didn't even finish our bridge game. I'd better get home and feed my animals. Do you want a lift, Jane, or would you rather dribble back?"

Hillary handed Jane her basketball while Sharon went to find her hat. Hillary said quietly to Jane, "I understand what you're going through, but just remember, it's not forever, and you really are doing them a big favor."

"I wish I could be sure it's temporary. It's been almost two years now. Oh, I miss Max. He'd know how to handle this."

Lady was standing beside the door waiting for her pats. Sharon put her hands on each side of Lady's head and put her cheek next to Lady's cheek. Her instinct was to give nice people a big lick, but early in her training Lady learned that humans didn't like that. So she sat down and favored her people with big, adoring brown eyes. Jane walked past and patted her head and talked some baby talk to Lady, which made the dog wag even faster and appear to smile.

The women repeated their good-byes and thank yous while Jane and Sharon climbed into the Suburban, still chuckling about their evening.

After her friends had gone, Hillary took the dishes to the sink and cleared away all signs of her party, pleased with the evening. She had been studying her tap dancing for only a short time and, although she knew she would have to practice a long time before she would actually be a dancer, it was fun and good exercise.

"Thank you, Lord, for sending me these beautiful friends. Thank you for the tough-talking Jane with the heart of gold, and for sweet, sensitive Sharon. They've added so much to my life." Lady cocked her head, watching Hillary wash the dishes as she hummed a happy song and shuffled her feet to the rhythm.

CHAPTER 2

The drone of the engine made conversation all but impossible. But at this point conversation was no longer necessary. The landscape down below was that of unending desert hills with a small range of mountains in the distance. An occasional shepherd's hut was seen but no villages or major highways since crossing over Highway 40 connecting Saltillo and Torreon. They were both relieved to be flying CAVU: clear air, visibility unlimited. There was slight turbulence due to thermals but they had not been uncomfortable. After filing their flight plan in Del Rio, their course was west of Super Highway 57, ostensibly the shortest course to Guadalajara, but they needed to see some landmarks southwest of Zacatecas. Most flyers on holiday would have preferred to fly IFH (I Follow Highway) down Highway 57 to Saltillo and then Highway 54 through Zacatecas and on to Guadalajara, if for no other reason than to have some signs of civilization nearby in case of mechanical problems.

"We're almost opposite Durango, Sam. We'll be seeing Zacatecas before long. Do you have your aerials in order?" Sam was a terrific medical doctor but a very mediocre navigator. Sam and Hillary had spent many hours planning their trip and each of them were plagued with doubts and fears that they may be forgetting something. All their check lists indicated nothing had been left to chance. They were fairly confident that authorities would not suspect a middle-aged couple on holiday of smuggling anything INTO Mexico. They had no trouble at the airport filing their flight plan to Guadalajara. They were just two happy vacationers, and no one questioned why the woman was flying left seat. However, if anyone had asked, they were prepared to say that this was a training flight. She needed extra time as pilot in command; therefore, she did all the flying, flight plans, dealing with customs and immigration, everything. A younger woman might not even be noticed piloting a plane, but women in Hillary's age group usually deferred to their husbands when it came to flying, and they took a more conventional role, possibly helping with navigation or just preparing snacks en route.

Sam was not a relaxed passenger. His entire experience with private, single-engine aviation was flying with a few other doctors to a hunting camp years ago. He had been so uncomfortable that he gave it up forever. He was as surprised as Hillary when he made up his mind to undertake this trip and he masterminded the strategy, with a little fine-tuning from Hillary.

Sam had his map case in his lap and began to take charge of the navigating. Jesse had made the maps by hand and they were very accurate. Every ranch, mountain and waterhole were just where the maps showed. "When we get to Zacatecas, turn right to a heading of 240 degrees, which will just about follow Highway 54. When the highway turns back to a more southerly direction, we will continue this heading until we reach the big river, about fifteen minutes. The aerials start where we leave the highway. Lord, I hope I can read them and don't get us lost."

Sam had his homemade aerials marked in big numbers and sat tensely while Hillary approached the town, still flying at altitude. She made her righthand turn and rolled out on 240 degrees on the magnetic compass. She also was tense but felt that she knew the maneuver by heart, they had been through it so many times.

"Look there, up ahead! The highway is veering back toward the south. We keep on this course and start descending to 6500 feet. The terrain around here is mostly about 4500 feet but he has the major peaks marked. Some are well over 6500 feet but they aren't on our course. We should be able to see them off in the distance," Sam shouted over the engine noise.

Sam studied aerial #1 and looked ahead at the terrain. "Wow, this is great! There's a stock tank directly ahead of us and another up ahead that will be off our left wing and those two peaks over there to the right are 5000 and 5500 feet high and they're just where they're supposed to be." Sam was surprised and pleased with his navigating, thanks to Jesse's good maps.

Hillary smiled. Dead Reckoning and Visual Flight Rules (VFR) were a lot of fun as an exercise, but there were things that could go wrong. The most obvious problem would be rain or a heavy cloud cover, which was not a concern today. Also, if one were using the clock and a pre-determined wind setting to fly from point to point, a change in wind velocity could blow one badly off course.

Sam was studying aerial #3, which would lead them to the big river. Over the river Hillary banked and made her left turn to 160 degrees which, with luck, would take them directly over the rancho and also be their heading into the city of Guadalajara. "Jesse said we'd be flying over the barranca, which

22

is rough country. But I had no idea the air could be this rough. I guess I have this macho thing about throwing up in front of lady pilots who appear to be so cool and completely in control," Sam teased. It was the first relaxing they'd permitted themselves since they started into the progressively turbulent air in northern Mexico.

Hillary laughed and admitted, "I'm a little worried myself about becoming incontinent in the company of a well-known physician." They both laughed. "When we buzz the ranch house and we make sure we've been seen, then we can climb back to altitude and hopefully it'll be a lot smoother."

The rancho was in the center of aerial #5, and even before starting her low turn around the place, people began pouring from the house and barns and waving frantically. Hillary didn't see Jesse himself but knew he'd get the message from one of these people.

Hillary completed her 360 degree banked turn around the ranch headquarters and continued her original heading, climbing back to a cooler, smoother altitude to head into the beautiful city of Guadalajara. Miles from the airport, Hillary contacted Approach Control, who then directed them to the south side of Guadalajara and into the busy international airport.

After having "powdered her nose" and practically holding her breath during a perfunctory examination of their luggage with customs, Hillary was delighted to be back in the mile-high city of fountains and roses. They picked up their rental car and made their way back toward the city. Sam was pilot-in-command of the rental car and Hillary was navigating this time. "You'll see El Tapatio on a hill on the right. It's a bunch of Spanish-style buildings winding up the hill. It's charming."

Registering at the front desk, Sam and Hillary played their tourist role with much animation. They made a special point of asking for maps of the city, of Lake Chapala, Puerta Vallarta, and mentioning that they did so want to see as much as they could in the short time they'd be here.

The phone call came as planned late in the afternoon, and the next morning as the sun came up, Hillary and Sam were traveling north through the barranca in their rental car. After driving the prescribed miles from the outer limits of Guadalajara, they found the gate they were searching for, well-marked with century plants. The sun was high in the sky when they turned off the pavement onto the single lane dirt road. They were still following Jesse's well-done maps. After more than an hour of driving almost due west, Hillary begged, "Let's make a pit stop up there in those trees and have some of that lunch we packed."

Hillary picked up a large stick and walked over to the cluster of trees saying, "Shoo, snake. Shoo, snake." Minutes later she rejoined Sam, who was watching her, very amused.

"What's this 'Shoo, snake' business?" he asked, laughing. "However, it must have worked, so let me borrow your stick and I'll excuse myself, too." As he walked away into the thicket of trees, Hillary could hear him saying, "Shoo, snake. Shoo, snake."

Almost an hour later, bumping along the dirt road, Hillary reported, "According to this map we're almost to the meeting place. It seems to be a low-water crossing on a small river just ahead." Hillary had her finger on the route they were taking and could see the rise in the road ahead, which presumably would descend to a creek below. Topping the hill they could, indeed, see the beautiful creek with cottonwoods towering on each bank. But there was no one there to greet them.

"Oh, dear. What will we do now? Our map stops here." Just as Hillary finished speaking the words, the trees came alive with vaqueros, whooping and spurring their horses toward the car. In the lead was Jesse, their old friend and patron of one of the larger cattle ranches in Mexico, Esperanza, meaning 'Hope.'

"Ah, Muñeca, even with silver in your hair you are as lovely as ever!" Jesse then turned to Sam and said, "Well, old friend, what are you going to charge me for this house call?" and laughed at his own joke.

The vaqueros descended on the rented car and carefully took all the luggage and supplies. One of them drove the car into a clump of small trees where it could not be seen from any direction. "From here we go horseback. There is a road but it would take hours and break all the springs in your rented car. Horseback we will be there in less than two hours. You both still ride, do you not?"

Hillary did ride frequently, but Sam just shrugged his shoulders and said, "¿Como no? Who could forget how to ride a horse?" However, he looked very anxious when the big black gelding was brought for him to mount.

"For you, Muñeca, this beautiful palomino stallion. We call him Don Juan. He loves the ladies, as do we all." This he translated into Spanish for his vaqueros and they all laughed.

The trip to the rancho was actually longer than two hours and Hillary suspected that they were trying to make it easier on her and Sam. Much of the ride was at a slow lope, except for the times they were climbing loose shale or crossing shallow streams. The sun was low in the west when they *rode into the yard of the Spanish Colonial ranch headquarters.*

Exhausted, Sam and Hillary could hardly be polite to the many ranch people who wanted to meet them and thank them for coming. After dinner they were both dozing over dessert and were relieved when their host thoughtfully offered to show them to their rooms.

At breakfast the next morning Jesse was very serious. "Sam and Hillary, my dear friends, there was no one else I could turn to for help. You know from my letters how bad it is in this state. It's not the official position of the state to sanction Communism, but still it is allowed, and no one will protect us from their propaganda. We, at the Esperanza, are not given medical treatment, not allowed in the public schools, even our churches have been infiltrated. I can't tell you how many restrictions they've put on us. If only we will cooperate, they say, we can live like kings. Pero, anyone who goes against the public interest, they say, should not share in the bounty of the state. Pero, village after village has fallen to this small but powerful faction, and they are not better off, but ¡que verguenza! have given up their freedoms. What I'm going to ask of you may seem a little melodramatic, but please trust me. Appearances, or symbolism, if you will, are very important to these simple people. I say simple, but not ignorant. There are many wise, intelligent souls among them." As they finished their coffee, he added, "Who would have thought those three children playing cowboys and Indians would be now planning a game of such intrigue?" He chuckled. "I want you to know that I got very tired of always being the Indian!"

They all laughed, remembering. Hillary recalled those happy days when Jesus, or Jesse as they called him, had lived with his grandmother in Texas to attend school. Later they all attended the University of Texas together in Austin, shared their studies, criticized each other's dates and were almost inseparable until their respective careers took them away. They had stayed in touch at least at Christmas time, but when Jesse's letter came crying out for help, Sam and Hillary didn't stop to ask whether it could be done, just how, and how soon.

"Well, my friends, I have some costumes for you. Believe me, it is very important." At this a young Mexican woman came from a back room, bringing Hillary a large white hat and white jacket with fringe flowing from each sleeve and across the back, amply studded with silver conchos. "You have your own riding pants and boots, Querida, which are more comfortable than any we could provide. In this costume and riding our beautiful Don Juan, you will look like the angel of mercy that I know you to be.

25

"And you, Don Samuel, should wear this black sombrero and black chaqueta. You will be very dashing on the big black. We will call it 'dressing for success', no? We will always be in a hurry. Our plan is to visit seven villages in these five days. We have arranged our clinics in the home of trusted friends, but there are always spies who will run and tell, for money or for favor. These filthy traitors! Traitors to their own family and friends! So when they get back with the officials we will be long gone, verdad?"

Sam and Hillary were excited and anxious to be off. The masquerade began as fun but when they entered their first makeshift clinic their hearts were broken at the pitiful conditions they met. Children and adults blessed them as they sped on their way: "¡Vaya con Dios!"

Flying home at the end of the week, Sam was still excited. "I wish we had a video of what we did. I hope we can come back. I'd like to see how that compound fracture heals. Remember those two Indian children that came in toward the end of the week? I know they were suffering from vitamin deficiencies and I sure would like to see how they respond to those multi-vitamins."

The roar of the engine was so loud Hillary had to shout. "You were a real Pancho Villa, Sam, quite dashing in your outfit. You'd break lots of hearts in Dallas in that getup," she teased.

Sam smiled. "I don't know about Pancho Villa." He patted his ample belly. "I felt more like Sancho Panza!" Hillary smiled as the engine droned on.

When the engine sound suddenly turned off, Hillary gave a startled jump. She looked around and there was Jane's big Cadillac, not six feet from where she was sitting on her weeding stool repairing the damage made by the motorcycle. Jane was getting out on the opposite side, and as she walked around the front of the car, she said, "Penny for your thoughts, or are they private? You had a big smile on your face, you know, and didn't even hear me drive up."

"No, I didn't. The airplane engine was too loud," she said without explaining. "Do you remember my telling you about my friends, Sam and Jesse? We were the three musketeers from elementary school and into college. I was just thinking what fun we had. Want some tea or something?"

"Thanks, no. I was just on my way to rehearsal and had a few minutes. Just wanted to thank you again for last night."

"It was fun, wasn't it? We need a few laughs every now and then. Are you singing or playing an instrument?" Hillary asked. "And what group is this?"

"It's the Waco Symphony, and I'm playing the cello but they've also asked me to do one of the solo parts in the chorus, so they're pulling me out of the orchestra for that one song."

Hillary knew Jane to be very modest about her musical gifts, but she not only played cello and piano but had a deep, well-trained alto singing voice. If Jane had not chosen to be a basketball coach, she would certainly have become a professional musician. Now that Max was gone, Jane sang in the church choir and played piano for one of the special ensembles at the church.

"Look, Hillary, I know you've been depressed lately. And certainly you have a reason to be sad. I saw the music on your piano last night. Hymns. You play hymns when you're stressed."

"Well, would you look at the pot calling the kettle black!" Hillary laughed. "At least I didn't dribble a basketball over a mile to a bridge game!"

"Yes, well...Touché! Anyway, keep your chin up, and if you ever need to talk, I'm a good listener, and I don't give advice." Jane walked back to her car, and Hillary once again thought that Jane must have more genuine class than anyone she knew. Not only her talents, and not just her tall, regal bearing, or her sincere warmth, or even her sometimes bawdy sense of humor. But whatever Jane's many attributes, Hillary knew she was fortunate in having her for a friend. And now, their great losses both bound them together in friendship and comforted them.

Hillary looked around at her work. She had filled the ruts with sand and sprigged some grass throughout. Now she would turn on her lawn sprinklers and turn the rest over to nature. She rubbed her aching hands, looking down at her gnarled fingers as if they belonged to a stranger. When had the knuckles become so enlarged? And they hurt so much the pain would sometimes awaken her in the night and she would have to take medication. What kind of pain? her doctor might ask. Well, she might answer, they ache most of the time and sometimes the pain is a burning pain. Doctors know so much about arthritis, she reminded herself, except how to cure it or make the pain go away.

She could feel the familiar anxiety rising, like butterflies in her stomach and like blushing, with her scalp prickling. Hillary, even in her discomfort, was analytical. If she understood these attacks maybe she could prevent them. But for a moment she gave way to the paralyzing fear that she had been hoping to squelch with her fantasy.

What kind of mind does a fourteen-year-old boy have when he finds pleasure in tormenting an older woman who lives alone next door? Why would he drive through her yard and tear up her shrubbery? He must know that gardening was one of her favorite pasttimes. Who would believe her if she told of the catalog of things he had done to her and to Lady? The truth was she didn't know exactly what it was he did to Lady, but several times the dog had yelped and whined as if hurt, but when Hillary brought her inside she didn't seem to be injured. *Maybe he's shooting her with an air rifle*, she guessed. And who would believe how many nights he had aimed his speakers at her bedroom and blasted her out of a sound sleep? And who was it that smoked those cigarettes she found near the bench at the back of the garden? *What kind of a little sociopath is he, anyway, and what will he do next? Maybe he plans to hurt me.*

And money. Always the money, or lack of it, rather. The thought of it paralyzed Hillary with dread again. She was often so paralyzed with fear that she was unable to perform even her simplest chores. The thought kept returning: *what will happen when it's all gone?* Hillary begged God not to punish her for her unbidden fear, thanked Him for His bountiful provisions, and willed herself not to think about neighbor boys or money but to go into the house, shower, and get ready to go spend the afternoon with Pete.

Hillary stepped out of the shower and in front of the full-length mirror, remembering the speaker she had heard years before who advised, "Start the day with a brisk shower and then stand naked in front of your full-length mirror and have a good laugh."

The phone began ringing and Hillary was pleased to hear Sharon's voice. She said she'd meet Hillary at the Four Seasons. She wanted to visit with Pete and a couple of others that she knew there.

Pete didn't speak when Hillary came into the dayroom and kissed his cheek. He, along with several other residents, was pretending to watch the television screen. Hillary noticed the channel was on a talk show that Pete had always particularly disliked. So, he was having one of his silent days. She classified his days by the apparent mood he was in: surly, animated, hostile, sociable, and sometimes a combination of moods.

Hillary made small talk with Pete for about fifteen minutes before he would take his eyes away from the screen. *If I can only get him to look into my eyes*, she thought, *he'll respond to me.* She knew that when he looked at her as a whole, like when she first walked into the room, he only saw a gray-haired woman, slightly thick through the middle—someone he did not know. But when he looked into her eyes, those same nearly black eyes with the thick black lashes and eyebrows, a flash of recognition would show in his expression and many times he would call her by his pet name, "Harry."

She placed herself directly in front of Pete so he would have to look at her and not at the television set and said, "Pete, dear, it's Harry, I've come to visit with you. Let's go for a walk. Would you like to see the puppies?"

Pete re-focused his eyes and looked into Hillary's. "Harry." He smiled. "Harry, I've been waiting for you." He looked down at his left wrist where there was no wristwatch and teased, "You know you're late again, I don't know what I'm going to do with you."

He pulled himself out of the chair with more effort than Hillary had noticed before and together they walked down the hall toward the side garden where the cocker spaniel had her five puppies. Pete had been six feet and two inches tall to Hillary's five feet and three inches. They had fallen into a comfortable habit of walking together with his right arm around her shoulders and her left arm around his waist. How many hours, how many miles had they walked like this, sharing thoughts and feelings, discussing personal, civic, or world affairs? This is what Hillary missed so acutely, talking with someone, sharing ideas. No, not just someone, talking with Pete, because he wasn't like anyone else she had ever conversed with. He was wise and objective. He could be funny, always interesting. She could disagree with him and he wasn't offended. She could tell her secret feelings and not get a sermon or lecture. And he could tell her his innermost fears, disappointments, or pride in accomplishments without any worry that his vulnerability might be used against him in some future argument. The main thing they liked to share was funny stories or just happy events. But now Pete didn't always understand the jokes she told him and just stared when she delivered her punch line.

As soon as she heard the door opening, Blondie came bounding toward the chain-link fence to be patted. Her puppies were now three weeks old and kept with her, fenced off from the residents for fear that one might injure the other. Even a small dog jumping up to be patted could knock an elderly person off balance and perhaps break a hip. All the residents had taken an interest in Blondie's pregnancy and delivery. Chairs were placed in front of the kennel and under the shade of the trees so that residents could watch the puppies feed and frolic.

Pete and Hillary were sitting lazily in the shade of the elm trees watching the puppies nap when Sharon found them. Sharon had stopped by the dining room and poured three lemonades into plastic glasses and carried them out on a small tray. "I thought I'd find you two here. Would you look how those

29

puppies have grown! Blondie is such a good mother."

Pete stood cordially as the handsome gray-blond woman approached. Hillary noticed that Sharon was not in western attire but dressed simply in skirt and blouse with multi-colored sandals appropriate for the heat of the late summer afternoon. Pete took the glass of lemonade and began making small talk beginning with, "How have you been, you're looking good." Pete volleyed answers to questions and offered short phrases: "It sure has been hot. We need some rain."

Hillary had heard Pete many times making conversation such as this while knowing he didn't actually recognize the person he was speaking with. She thought of it as "faking conversation." He was responding to the questions he was asked but not voicing an original thought. Hillary was relieved when she heard Pete say "Harvey." Her shoulders relaxed as she realized that she had practically been holding her breath. Glances passed between Sharon and Hillary as he continued, "How is Harvey?"

Sharon enjoyed talking with Pete and still did, either in dementia or lucidity, and could keep up the conversation even when it switched back and forth between the two. "Harvey's fine, Pete. Well, maybe he's not so fine," she said, remembering what Hillary had said about his being in the hospital. "He's having some problem with his prostate, might have to have surgery." Sharon laughed, trying to keep the conversation light. "We used to talk about 'female trouble.' Maybe I should just say 'male trouble,' but that seems to be a little bit Victorian, don't you think?" Pete smiled politely as his gaze went back to the puppies and he said nothing more.

Sharon noted his withdrawal and said quietly to Hillary, "I want to visit with a couple of people. I'll be back in a little bit and say goodbye."

Hillary sat companionably with Pete until the shadows were becoming long and coaxed him back into the building so that he would not be missed when supper was announced. As she was leaving the parking lot, she noticed Sharon's Suburban still parked nearby and wondered who else she knew in the Four Seasons to visit for such a long time.

CHAPTER 3

Lady, as always, was delighted when Hillary's car pulled into the drive and the automatic garage door opener hummed its announcement that her mistress had returned. Hillary changed into her summer "uniform," baggy shorts and oversized shirt, before inviting Lady into the house. Lady's exuberance had soiled lots of Hillary's clothes in the past, so now she tried to wear indestructable clothing for these reunions, even though she had only been gone a few hours.

After a light dinner snack, Hillary decided not to watch the television but to start the new book a friend had recommended. Only a few pages into the book, Sharon phoned to see if Hillary could join her at the roping club to ride their horses together.

"Yes, yes! I'd love to. It's been so hot lately. I've been out to curry Queen a couple of times but didn't have the energy to put the saddle on. She actually seemed disappointed when I left. Let's start early, okay?"

"That's what I was thinking. I'll have to get back to work by noon. They feed the horses before seven every morning, so why don't we meet at seven-thirty and we'll have plenty of time to ride before it gets too hot."

Hillary felt light and cheerful. She knew that she could ride every day if she chose to, but it just didn't seem as much fun alone. Pete had loved to ride, too. He even joined the Sheriff's Posse, which was very much a social organization, and good publicity for the bank. Pete and Hillary had enjoyed short trail rides with other couples and had always planned to do one of the big ones, in New Mexico maybe, or even Colorado. How many times had they talked about this big trail ride: sleeping in tents, hobbling the horses at night, cooking over a campfire?

Ah, but that was then, and this is now, Hillary reminded herself.

The horses were finishing up their alfalfa hay when Hillary arrived at the roping club. As she turned down the lane where Queen was stabled, she saw that Sharon was already there and brushing Major. She was not dressed in her usual flamboyant western attire, which was her work uniform, but had on a large cotton tee shirt with jodphurs and boots. So, thought Hillary, this is an English saddle day. Sharon had an enviable assortment of saddles and changed them as a man changes his ties. She owned a hand-tooled Western saddle which she rode more often than the others but also had a large colorful Mexican saddle with tapaderos covered with silver conchos and leather thongs hanging down almost touching the ground. More than once she had dressed Mexican style and ridden in parades on the beautiful work of art. Her other saddles were an Australian rancher's saddle and the two English types, one called a forward seat saddle, used primarily for jumping.

Hillary opened the back door of her station wagon and Lady bounded out, rushing over to greet Queen and then running at break-neck speed to greet Sharon and Major. As soon as she received her petting from Sharon and friendly sniffing from Major, she quickly returned to Queen's stall where she plopped down to watch the grooming and saddling.

"Let's go ride down by the creek, if it's okay with you," Sharon proposed. The club was fortunate to own many acres of pleasant trails, some on the creek, some rough country, and lots of open fields. Near the stables there was a large arena and a round pen for training.

The trail was wide enough to ride side-by-side and the women could chat. Lady was on every side of them at once, sniffing all the exciting smells. Once long ago she found a rattlesnake and barked her warning until Hillary came back and ordered her to come away.

Both women were exhilarated with the early morning freshness, Sharon posting and Hillary riding western style to a brisk trot. They were reminded of the time when low hurdles were set up in the arena and they tried to coax their horses over them. "And do you remember when we tried to play polo with broomsticks and a beach ball?" Sharon asked. They both began laughing, remembering. The horses were spooked with the broomsticks flying around their head; Major began rearing and Queen tried to buck. And besides, the beachball went flat from sticker burrs in the field.

"The first time I ever saw Harvey, he was practicing for the polo team at New Mexico Military Institute. He was riding this big liver-red bay with four white stockings and he was just as cocky as his horse was flashy. I guess I fell in love at first sight, maybe as much with the horse as with Harvey. I'm sure I've told you this story before, though."

Hillary smiled and said nothing. Yes, she had heard the story before, and not just once. She realized that as they got older they repeated their stories;

she did it herself. There were things that they needed to say again, over and over. And feel the things that they felt at the time. Young people were very intolerant of this repeating, but they just couldn't understand. Young people thought it was because they were losing their memory. But it wasn't the loss of memory causing it. It was the acuteness of remembering that forced the words out even when there was no one around who wanted to hear.

"Harvey was so full of himself that he didn't even know I was alive in those days," Sharon laughed. "But the next year I was elected cheer-leader for the Roswell Coyotes and finally he noticed me. Every year the state basketball tournament was held at NMMI, and even though there were hundreds of people in the gym, I was watching just for him. When I finally spotted him he had a date, naturally. But I was kind of brazen and when he got up to go to the concession stand I started that way at the same time. When he turned and went into the men's room, I felt like a fool. Well, he finally came out and I was standing in such an obvious spot that he almost had to step over me. Then when he noticed my uniform, he had to tease me about our chances of taking the tournament and I teased him back. NMMI wasn't doing well that season. Then I told him, 'Well, good luck, anyway,' and turned around and walked off real cool. I was so excited, though, that I could hardly lead yells." Sharon realized that she had been rambling and became embarrassed. "Oh, Hillary, listen to me rave on. I don't know what made me think of that just now. I don't really want to think about Harvey at all. I have so many mixed feelings. Sometimes I think I should have stayed with him and been a dutiful wife to the end. Do you think I should have, Hillary?"

"You know I couldn't say what's right or wrong for you, Sharon. But I will say this, from what I observe, okay? I used to think of you as a beautiful, reserved or withdrawn, showpiece of a woman. And now you seem to be happy and self-confident. Maybe something of a kook." Hillary glanced at Sharon's serious expression as she said this and put her heels into Queen's sides while shouting to Sharon, "And you can't ride a hoss!"

Major sensed a race even before Sharon, and she almost lost her balance when he bolted ahead, trying desperately not to be left behind by the palomino mare. The horses had begun to slow before the curve in the road which led downward toward the creek, and both women had high color in their cheeks from the gallop.

After a little more than an hour, the day was becoming very warm and the riders were walking slowly back up the hill toward the stables. They had had a satisfying ride and the horses' coats were glistening with sweat. Sharon realized she was in a talkative mood. Hillary was such a good listener and her ideas or advice were appreciated by Sharon. "I think I've fallen in love," she began.

"Anyone I know?" asked Hillary, suspecting she knew the answer.

"Actually I think I'm in love with two young men. Tony, over in the north school and Sean in the south. They're both crazy about me," she smiled and became very serious. "I think Sean may be an abused child and I don't know how to prove it, but I'm going to watch very closely. It seems to be more of a psychological abuse than physical. I hope I'm wrong, it's just a hunch I have. But Tony, he's just a doll and nobody has ever abused him, I'm sure. He'll probably grow up to be President, he's so smart and self-confident. And did I mention that he's nuts about me, too? His parents are having a hard time keeping jobs and may have to pull him out of Partners, but I hope not. They live in a run-down house in a bad neighborhood so Partners is about the only nice thing that ever happens to him. His folks are trying very hard, but they haven't been able to keep steady jobs since they've been in the states."

Hillary turned in the saddle to look at Sharon. "Sharon, Partners is the only nice thing that has happened to a lot of those children. I've heard from many of them, especially over on the north side, that Miss Sharon is wonderful. But you realize that the others on the south side don't all have an easy life, even when their parents are affluent. Like your friend Sean, there are many of them whose parents don't want to be bothered with them for one reason or another. You've been a Godsend to them."

"No, Hillary. It's just the opposite. It wouldn't take much of a psychologist to diagnose that my life had a terrific void which the pre-schools have filled. No, they're a Godsend to me and I do love them. Most of them, anyway." They rode on to the stables feeling warm and lazy and looking forward to a cool shower and getting on with their day.

After giving their horses a good brushing, Hillary and Sharon said their goodbyes. Lady had plopped down wherever Hillary happened to stop. She had first jumped into the water trough to cool off and shook a large volume of water all over Queen and Hillary.

Sharon decided it might be a good time to go by the vet's and get some kind of vitamin supplement for Major. "Old Boy," she said to him. "You're getting to be some kind of hypochondriac. I need to go by the vet's office pretty regular." She laughed at herself.

Charlie Hoelscher was such a good-looking guy and he always made Sharon feel special. She hoped he didn't know that she felt like a teen-ager with her first crush everytime he was around. Logically, she knew, he probably not only did not know but also did not care. He was several years younger than Sharon, and middle-aged men, in her opinion, were always interested in the younger women. At least Harvey always was and she knew that since Charlie's disastrous second marriage had ended women of all ages were vying for his attention. Charlie's rugged good looks were nothing at all like Harvey's well-groomed and manicured appearance. Charlie was tall with heavy shoulders, weather-beaten, and had a permanent grin on his face anytime Sharon was in his clinic with the pets or with Major. She knew that he flirted with her but supposed he did with all his customers and that was good for business. Anyway, she knew the age difference would disqualify her for his interest.

The veterinary clinic had a good business. In the parking lot there were several cars and around to the side there were two pickups with stock trailers hooked on behind. Somewhere there were several calves bawling.

Since Charlie's daughter, Jenny, finished her degree at Texas A&M, their business had steadily grown. Jenny took care of most of the small animals while Charlie and his assistant tended the horses and cattle. When Sharon entered the reception room, there was no one in sight, but she could hear Jenny's friendly and knowledgeable conversation with a patient's mistress. Soon she came out to the desk and noticed Sharon. "Mrs. Butler! How are you? I hope you haven't been waiting long. What can we do for you? I don't see any animals with you this time."

"Major's a little bit off his feed. I'm sure it's just the heat but Charlie mentioned that a vitamin-mineral supplement might be helpful." Sharon tried sounding concerned but knew that Jenny could probably see right through her weak excuse.

Jenny was delighted for the chance to throw her dad and Mrs. Butler together. Jenny had long since decided that Sharon was about the neatest lady she had ever known. She also knew that her dad had been very lonely and disappointed since her mother died a few years ago. And then his miserable re-bound marriage. Jenny wrinkled her brow, thinking, and finally said, "I'm not sure what Dad would recommend, Mrs. Butler. He's still the expert in large animals, you know." She hesitated. "I'll be through here in a few minutes and I can go out back and ask him. Or if you'd like you can go out in the barn

35

and find him."

"Sure, Jenny, I'll just step out back and ask him myself. I don't mind at all." She was already moving toward the door that connected the clinic with the barn hospital. The air was cool and breezy in the tall metal building. It was designed to catch any breeze and on the hottest of days was quite comfortable. And in the winter, closed up, it was warm and cozy.

Sharon heard loud banging and horses nickering, almost in panic. She became afraid that something or someone was hurting them and she shouted, "Charlie! Dr. Hoelscher?"

Charlie came around the end of a partition and looked very pleased to see her. "Sharon! What's this 'Doctor' business? Are we getting formal now, after all we've been to each other?"

Sharon laughed. "I guess all that noise startled me a little bit. I thought someone was killing some horses."

"No, on the contrary. Those two horses are making each other very happy, they just do it loudly. Have you ever seen horses bred? Would you like to watch?"

"Thank you, no. That's a pleasure I've never had. And I think I'll just leave it that way. Actually I need to know what kind of mineral supplement I should give Major while it's so hot and he's off his feed."

"I have just the thing for him, and it's half price because the supplier is promoting it." Just then there was another series of banging and squealing from the stall where the horses were held. Charlie laughed. "That old mare is a lot older than that young stud, in fact more than twice his age and I've never seen him more excited. Just goes to show that love really is blind."

Sharon felt her face flush. *He knows*, she told herself. *He knows what a fool I'm making of myself.* "Well, I'd better go and let you get back to work." She said this over her shoulder as she fled out the side door to the parking lot.

When she reached her car, she was out of breath and could feel her pulse pounding. As she tried the door and found it locked, she realized she didn't have her purse with her. But where did she leave it? If only she had her keys she'd just leave the darned purse. She stood there, beside the car, feeling more foolish than she could remember. She would have to walk back in there and get her purse. Maybe Charlie had gone back to the horses, surely he had.

Sharon walked back to the side door and peered around. There was her purse on a utility ledge where some medications and syringes were kept. She couldn't see Charlie so he must have gone back to work. Sharon tiptoed over to the ledge and picked up her purse carefully so that she didn't make a sound. As she was about to turn and sneak away she saw through the corral panels that Charlie was still there, near where they had been visiting.

Charlie was sitting on a bale of hay, elbows on his knees, slapping his gloves into the palm of his left hand. He didn't look at all like a smug fellow who had just had a woman make a fool of herself over him. *In fact*, Sharon thought as she tipotoed away, *he looks pretty awful.*

Jenny found her father just like that when she came out to see how things were going with her match-making. "Where's Mrs. Butler? Did you scare her away?" she teased.

He smiled up at his pretty daughter who always brought a smile to his sun-burned face. "Your old dad is a real klutz when it comes to pretty women. I think I did scare her away and I don't even know what I said." He got up and stretched with both hands on the small of his back and started back to the breeding pens. "I sold her some of that mineral supplement, half price, $11.95."

"Dad, it's a good thing you asked me to go in business with you. Half price of a $35 item is NOT $11.95," she scolded, then grinned at him. "I didn't even know the supplier had a half-price promotion on that stuff. You must be pretty fond of that old gelding. Hmmm?"

Charlie paused before he rounded the partition. "Anyway she forgot it, she was getting out of here so fast. Why don't you stop by and take it to her on your way home tonight. Do you mind?"

Jenny rang the doorbell, admiring the stylish townhouse perched high above Lake Waco. It seemed to fit Sharon perfectly; in fact everything about her was so neat, so appropriate. Jenny wondered if there was any place in her life for a big good-natured guy, her dad specifically. Maybe Sharon's life was already custom-tailored to her liking and maybe her dad wasn't polished enough to fit in. No, Jenny didn't really believe Charlie was coarse or unpolished; she only wanted so badly for him to be happy again.

"Jenny!" Sharon said, surprised. "What brings you out to this part of town?" She took note of the can of supplement. "Come on in. Would you like something to drink?" They moved into the high-ceilinged living room with tall windows overlooking the lake. Jenny couldn't take her eyes off the view. The sun had gone behind some towering cumulus clouds sending rays of light outward in brilliant colors of silver, gray, and blue.

"Wow!" Jenny took a deep breath. "You've got a front row seat to the best show in town."

Sharon smiled, pleased to hear someone appreciate the view as she did. "It gets better and better at this time of day, Jenny. If you don't have to rush home we could sit out on the deck and watch the sunset. Every day it's different, of course, but there will probably be all shades of reds and blues and the sun rays are either silver or gold. And today those big cotton-candy clouds will make it even more spectacular."

Jenny knew the invitation was sincere. "I'd love to, Mrs. Butler. That is, if you have the time. Tonight the law firm is having their monthly business meeting and Dick has to stay for it. They serve supper, too, so I don't have to cook."

"I've got tea, coffee, sodas, and some of those flavored mineral waters that seem to be the fad right now," Sharon said over her shoulder as she started toward her kitchen.

"Iced tea would be great, thank you."

As the last of the pink tinges began to fade from the sunset, Sharon said quietly, "It's so nice to share this time of day with someone, Jenny. It's special to me and I sometimes feel like I'm being selfish with all this, like a hoarder, maybe. But I realize that not everyone would enjoy it like I do. And I wouldn't want to share it with just anyone, either."

"Sure am glad you shared it with me, Mrs. Butler." Remembering why she came, she added, "Oh, I put that feeding supplement down by the door in your entry hall. Dad was sorry he let you get away without it. He said you were in a big hurry." Her voice trailed off into a subtle question.

Sharon had regained her composure and her sense of humor. "That father of yours is really a considerate guy. I'm sure that if I were younger and prettier I just might set my cap for him. Anyway, Major and I are lucky to have him for our vet."

Jenny opened her mouth to blurt out the fact that she wished more than anything that Sharon would like Charlie and... But she didn't say what was on her mind, knowing it might embarrass Sharon and if that happened she wouldn't feel comfortable coming around the clinic. Instead she thanked her hostess for the sunset and the snack and went home.

There had been Hoelschers in Central Texas as long as anyone could remember. Some said they had landed at Indianola with other early German pioneers. Many stayed along the coast and others settled in the hill country around Fredericksburg. A few wandered up to the panhandle of Texas and settled in small farming communities such as Nazareth or Umbarger. Charlie's family, his grandparents, parents and uncles had been farming south of Waco on numerous farms, and now his many cousins were living on those same farms. Some of the German families had intermarried with the Czechs around Zabcikville. One thing the Hoelschers excelled in was farming.

Charlie had been the third son in his family and knew that his chances of inheriting any land were pretty slim. Since he was an exceptionally bright child and good student, he had been encouraged to prepare for college. When he went off to Texas A & M, his father told him, in German, how proud he was, for Charlie would earn the first college degree in their family. In English he added, "And you can be our very own Aggie Joke. Ha, ha, ha." In Texas the Aggies accept a lot of good-natured bantering from grads of other colleges. Nevertheless the high quality of their education and the traditions they uphold make the Aggie ring a symbol of a very select fraternity.

During his undergraduate years, Charlie kept his old pickup on the roads back home visiting Olga Doskocil, the prettiest girl in the county. When Olga graduated from high school she took a job locally and saved her money until Charlie graduated and they were married in the big old church in Westfalia. After the formal ceremony there was the typical celebration, barbecue, and dancing till way past midnight when the happy couple slipped away, unnoticed by the revelers.

While Charlie was in graduate school, Olga worked for a family-owned company in Bryan, and after he became a Doctor of Veterinary Medicine, she was content to stay at home awaiting the birth of their children. After several miscarriages, Jenny was born to the Hoelschers, and life was good.

Olga never wanted anything more than to be a homemaker, and Charlie's veterinary business was growing. He frequently teased her for being slender. "Cows breed better on the gain, you know."

"Well, maybe you should have married some fat, bovine type. Who knows, by now you might have raised a whole herd of Hoelschers," she responded.

Charlie always laughed when Olga pretended to be mad. He knew she could no more stay mad than fly, and Jenny was growing up with the same sunny disposition.

Just seven months after being diagnosed with cancer, Olga was gone, and Charlie fell into a bottle and could not climb out. Jenny came home from college to try and help but felt that she was wasting her time, utterly failing her dad and getting behind in her college work as well. Bills were piling up, and Charlie's animal practice was almost gone.

A painful year passed, and Jenny went back to school. Charlie's small clinic had a few regular customers who kept his bills paid. It was not until he met a voluptuous young divorcee that Charlie became fully alive. She was everything that Olga was not. She loved to party at the clubs, had no interest in cooking or making a home, and Charlie didn't care. They went out every night, and Charlie had finally learned to moderate his drinking, not needing to anesthetize himself against an unbearable pain.

His wife loved to dance, and not only with Charlie. Sometimes he came home from the clinic to find that she had already gone out to a club and was several drinks ahead of him when he arrived. Charlie tried to stop the pattern of destruction his marriage was falling into but could not. His beautiful young wife found younger men to entertain her, and she became bored with monogamy.

When his second marriage failed, Charlie quit drinking altogether. He knew there were worse things than loneliness, and he had experienced one of those things. He began to build up his business in earnest, hoping Jenny would join his practice when she became a vet. And she was hoping he would ask her.

Charlie and Jenny were a winning combination. People loved their friendliness and concern for their animals. Jenny's wedding was attended by several hundred people—many were relatives—and Charlie beamed his happiness.

"Dad, do you ever think of marrying again?" Jenny asked one evening as they were locking up.

"Think about it? Yes, I guess I think about it sometimes. It sure would be nice to share things with the right person. But who could be the right person? That's the tricky part. I sure don't want to make another mistake." He laughed. "Last time just about broke me, so maybe I'd better not go looking for trouble."

Still, Jenny could not help but wish for a companion for her father. She was so happy now in her own new marriage that she wanted everyone to find that kind of happiness, maybe she would play Cupid if she could find the right person. She knew several women who flirted with Charlie and would welcome his advances, but he didn't encourage them and she didn't think they were appropriate either.

Jenny had a list of requirements for her father's companion. She must be close to Charlie's age, attractive, or at least well-groomed. The most important requirement would be a good sense of humor. Maybe she should have her own money; that would rule out gold-diggers. Then Jenny laughed at herself, wondering where this perfect woman was—probably not in Waco. And besides, if she were all that perfect maybe she wouldn't be interested in Charlie Hoelscher.

CHAPTER 4

Hillary backed her car out of the garage and put the door down with the automatic control. She left her car windows down to enjoy the cool evening breeze for her drive over to Sharon's. Fall was definitely in the air, and Hillary felt rejuvenated now that the temperatures no longer climbed into the mid-nineties. Darkness was coming earlier now, and on Sunday Daylight Savings Time would end. Also on Sunday Hillary would have lunch at the cafeteria with her daughter's family after church.

Pete had always enjoyed the Sunday visit with his interesting son-in-law, his precious, if moody, daughter, and their sons. Since Pete was no longer around, the Sunday lunch was all the more important to Hillary because of the continuity of life it provided. Hillary smiled to think of her grandson, Greg. At fifteen he was unbelievably handsome, thought his grandmother, very predictably. Greg was tall and thin, but beginning to fill out. His hair was dark blond like his father's, and he had the same comfortable smile Hillary had always admired in Tom. Damian was younger but very different from Greg. He was so very serious, an intense but loving child. Yes, she always looked forward to Sunday lunch. And always hoped her daughter would be in a good mood so that they could enjoy one another.

Why did she feel so different about meetings with her son's family? Pete Jr., or Pedro as they had always called him, was low-key and cheerful, always fun to be around. His family had taken on his relaxed, undemanding quality.

Hillary chided herself for the circuitous route her reverie had taken her. Bridge at Sharon's house was always a treat. The view was spectacular and Sharon was a superb hostess without seeming to put forth much effort. *Maybe that's the secret of hostessing*, she mused. She herself felt that any party was a success if the guests seemed comfortable with each other and ate all the food.

Sharon finished her party preparations in time to sit out on her deck and enjoy the sunset. The cool weather brought back a flood of memories: football games, cheering and traveling with the pep squad, dating, after-game dances. Sharon stood up and paced the length of her deck. *Even good memories are bittersweet*, she realized, *because those times are gone, forever*. Admittedly, she'd had lots of successes, more so than most women, she felt. She'd been "popular," had lots of dates, awards, friendships—all backed by lots of snapshots to document that they actually happened. But then most women had husbands, children, and grandchildren around them, and what better documentation of success could there be?

Sharon recognized her nostalgic mood and was happy to be interrupted by the doorbell announcing that Hillary or Jane had arrived. She didn't really think that Jane had dribbled all this way but was amused to think that she might. She consciously shrugged off her restless mood and determined to have a good time tonight and make sure Jane and Hillary did too.

Hillary bustled into the entry hall and into the kitchen, making small talk and complimenting the table settings and flower arrangement that was so beautiful and yet understated, typical of Sharon.

"Am I early? I felt so peppy with this cool weather that I couldn't stay home any longer." She put her cardigan on the back of a chair. "I always feel as if I have come out of hibernation in the fall. I usually start two or three big projects, too, like painting or digging a new flowerbed. I think it's my nesting instinct."

"I've always loved fall, too," Sharon agreed, "but the biggest thrill for me is the first snowfall of the year. We used to put a fire in the fireplace and toast marshmallows and watch the snow drift up on the windows. I still would enjoy it, but Waco doesn't have that many good snowfalls. I guess I'm still a New Mexican at heart." Sharon brightened. "Would you like to go up to Ruidoso or Santa Fe with me this winter? We could just walk in the snow and enjoy the beautiful sights."

"I would dearly love to see a deep snowfall," Hillary answered earnestly. "Pedro and his family are always asking me up to Denver and I'd love to go. But I just can't think of getting away right now. Let's just wait and see. Okay?" A part of Hillary wanted to take off and do something frivolous, forgetting her real-world cares, but she knew that she never would unless circumstances changed a great deal. And she could not bear to think of the *circumstances* that would allow her the freedom to go off and play in the snow.

The doorbell rang again with Jane's usual code. When Sharon opened the door and Jane stormed in, it was no secret that she was upset. "I know we're supposed to be cheerful and upbeat at the bridge party, but doggone it, I don't feel like it." Jane reached into her pocket and pulled out some coins. "Here's fifty cents for the gritch kitty. No, here's a whole dollar."

Sharon, trying to lighten the subject, said, "We'll be going out to a fine dinner on the lake before long. And I think that almost all the contributions so far have been yours. What is it now, the same old problem?"

Hillary said softy, "Just tell us about it, dear, if you want to. We can't offer any advice, but if it will make you feel better to get it off your chest, you know we're good listeners."

Jane stopped pacing and looked at her two friends. "I'm lucky to have friends like the two of you." She looked at her hands and rubbed her palms together, and then, as if she didn't know what to do with them, she put her hands into her pockets. "Actually, I don't even know what I'm so mad about. It's just that my daughter-in-law is so... well..." she paused, "she's just so *sweet*!"

She looked quickly at Hillary and Sharon, half-expecting them to laugh at the statement. But both were solemn, knowing Jane was very serious. "Almost every day I'm treated like a stranger in my own house. This morning I had left my briefcase in the sun room and went to get it only to find that this was Junior League meeting day. I excused myself, of course, but what made me uncomfortable was that they were all talking and laughing when I went in but they just stared at me in dead silence till I got my things and started out. And then after I left they started talking and laughing again. And later Chrissy said, 'Mother Westerman, please feel free to join us anytime.'"

"Is that all there is, Jane?" Hillary encouraged.

"No, but it's all like that, so vague, so nebulous. And I can't even explain how I feel. Like yesterday. I was practicing on the piano and my granddaughter came down from her mother's room and asked me not to play so loudly because her mother had a headache. And she calls me 'Grandmother Westerman.' She looks, acts, and sounds just like her mother, so damned sweet and proper. I know that I'm being manipulated so subtly that I can't even fight back. Chrissy is even telling the gardener what to do. Even contradicting things I've told him. And she does it soooo nicely, " 'Mother Westerman, I'm sure you'll agree that... blah, blah, blah.' Maybe I'm just getting to be a cranky old woman. Sometimes she's even right, or at least not all wrong."

Jane stopped and took note of herself and her conversation and laughed out loud. "What I'd really like to do is come down my own stairs each morning into my own kitchen and just burp! Real loud. Know what I mean?"

Sharon put on her mock-seriousness expression and said, "Yes, I think I do, although I could never have stated it so eloquently!"

Hillary, whose nature could not abide a problem without a solution, asked quietly, "And what are you planning to do about it?" She paused briefly and continued, "You know there are three possible ways to deal with this. Change them, change yourself, or leave things as they are and continue to feel miserable. I'm not suggesting that you go out and 'do something' because I don't think you know yet what you want, and I know you wouldn't want to do anything hurtful to them, either."

"Hillary, you instinctively cut to the bottom line, as we say in the business world," Sharon interjected. "Problem-solving really is something of a science. There are several steps, starting with data-collection and ending with evaluation or re-evaluation. It only seems different when it's a personal problem and you are emotionally involved. But I know you'll come up with a fair solution when the time comes, Jane." She turned back to the kitchen for the tray with a carafe of coffee and cups on it. "Want to eat now or later? Sorry I don't have any entertainment planned like Hillary did that time. By the way, when are we ever going to get a fourth for bridge? Or have I asked that question?"

Jane made a face in answer. "Let's deal the cards."

For over an hour the game was cutthroat, the way they all liked to play. At the end of a convenient rubber, Sharon suggested they put on their sweaters and sit outside on the deck. The moon was almost full and shone brilliantly over Lake Waco, sprinkling silver dust to its far corners, causing the observer to believe in magic.

Sharon brought out a hot drink and pastry hot from her oven. They ate in silence, each with her own special feelings about a night such as this.

The restlessness returned to Sharon, and although she had not intended to ever mention the subject to another living creature, she found herself blurting, "Remember when we were teenagers and we sat around wondering what love was? And now at this advanced age I'm still wondering. Tell me, what do you think love is, and what is it not?" She looked from one to the other. "And what's the difference between true love and just physical attraction, or lust? How do you know that's not love? Dear God, we did have this same conversation when I was a teenager."

Sharon felt embarrassed for having brought up the subject. "Funny thing is that when I was a teenager I was so sure I knew all the answers."

Hillary sat very quiet, looking out onto the lake. She had her hands wrapped around the hot cup, warming her gnarled and painful fingers. She looked over at Jane, who just shrugged before she started to speak. "Sharon, I just can't answer that question because I don't think there is one answer. To me love was always just Pete. It was from the very beginning. If he hadn't reciprocated I don't know what I would have done, maybe something desperate and foolish. But the fact is he seemed as if he had been waiting all his life for me to come along, and you can imagine how that made me feel."

"That's the same with me. To me love was just ugly old Max Westerman, the most beautiful person I've ever known." Tears were glistening in Jane's eyes as she looked far across the lake and into the past. "I knew I was destined to be an old maid. And I really didn't mind. I didn't know any men who could handle me, I suppose. Maybe I intimidated them." She sat up straight and tossed her long, single braid. "I really didn't care at the time. My girls were winning district in basketball and the symphony let me play the cello or sing with the chorus. My life was very full."

Her eyes softened and she smiled. "And of course, you know the rest of the story. Max came along and then I really began to live. So you see, I don't know the answer, either."

"I should have known that if I wanted an answer to that particular question I should just ask some teenagers. Or maybe some old maids, right?"

Hillary suddenly sat up straight. "I know something about physical attraction, though. I'll bet you didn't think I was a passionate, lustful person, did you?" She chuckled, remembering. "Wow, I can still see his face. We were juniors in nursing school and he had only finished his residency a few years before. He was so gorgeous that I would hyper-ventilate and think I'd pass out when he spoke to me."

She looked around at Jane and Sharon to judge their reaction, and they were nodding encouragement. "His hair was pre-maturely gray and wavy. His teeth were perfectly even and his smile, well, it seemed as if it were just for me. You see, the other doctors' visits were just perfunctory and they didn't seem to know one student from another. They never even looked at us. Maybe that was part of his charm. He looked and spoke directly at us and now that I'm older and wiser, I realize he knew exactly what he was doing."

Hillary's solemn expression was bordering on anguish. "It was my best friend that he actually took up with. She was very forward and outgoing and I understood why he chose her over me. What I didn't know was that she wrote him letters and met him after lights out and the inevitable happened.

47

She got pregnant. Her parents were furious with him for taking advantage of her, only twenty, and threatened a law suit. However, he had kept her letters and promised to have them read in court if it came to that. I don't know exactly what happened after that except that my best friend left school and never even tried to get in touch with me."

"What a cad!" Jane agreed. "But most men would have a hard time turning down a pretty girl throwing herself at him. I've seen it happen and it takes a really strong person not to be flattered into doing something foolish."

"Life and time have taken their own vengeance on him. I was back there a few years ago... no, it's almost twenty years ago already. We had a homecoming banquet and he and his wife were there. Both were fat and had sour, surly expressions. I don't know if they were unhappy but they were both very unattractive. He had a big bottom, kind of sissified, and walked sort of splay-footed and... Would you listen to me lambast that poor old soul? He might not even be alive for all I know."

"Well, Hillary, I never would have pegged you for a love-sick girl carrying a torch," Jane teased.

"I'd like to think that I'm really not, but even now I remember how I felt and if he had wanted me instead of Ginger I know that I would have been putty in his hands. But I was lucky, though I didn't think so at the time. I try to remember that whenever I start to be judgmental about something. I really believe that for every decent person there is, somewhere, another person so charming and attractive as to be completely irresistible, given the right circumstances. I don't believe, however, that someone is terribly moral just because they've never had any opportunities. Sorry, Sharon, this is still not answering your question."

"That's okay, Hillary. Maybe there isn't an answer. Jane, what in the world are you thinking with that wicked smile on your face?"

"I was just wondering how *moral* I am. You know I'd never advocate sleeping around or even moving in with someone I'm not married to. But if I should fall in love and contemplate marriage, do you think I should at least *audition* the fellow?"

Sharon and Hillary howled with delight thinking of Jane auditioning her prospect.

The bridge party was over and Hillary was driving home rehashing the evening and replaying the bridge hands in her mind. Jane had arrived edgy and irritable but had been cheerful by the time they all left. She had tried so

48

hard to help out Bruce and Chrissy when he lost his job as controller for a small manufacturing firm that went under.

Max had only been gone a few months, and Jane was feeling very lonely in the big colonial mansion and she had invited them to move in with her till they were back on their feet. At first Jane was thrilled to have children and laughter in the house again. She taught her grandson, Little Max, to play driveway basketball and was very proud of him. Her granddaughter was pretty as a picture and very lady-like. But it had not turned out the way Jane had hoped, a temporary situation. From every indication they intended to stay there, and it seemed almost as if they were trying to push Jane out of her own home. Two years had passed and it looked as if they had put down deep roots.

Jane seldom mentioned the arrangement unless she was extremely distressed, like tonight, but Hillary knew that Jane paid for all the utilities, housekeeper, and gardener, and now Bruce had been employed for almost two years by a reputable accounting firm. Bruce and Chrissy had given several parties, always inviting the most affluent of their acquaintances, and seemed to have forgotten their old friends from their former neighborhood.

Hillary sighed, thinking what it might be like to live in the same house with her son or daughter. She would, of course, offer her home if some disaster made it necessary. Pedro and his family lived in Denver with their children and she loved to visit them or have them visit in Waco, but they had a tacit agreement of non-interference, she felt. Neither stayed more than three or four days on their visits, making every moment very special and preventing any host/guest problems.

She felt happy thinking of Pedro and his group. He had never been any trouble and was very independent. He had continued to make his own decisions through college and after graduating had found a good job and lovely bride. Hillary wondered if she would have this same sweet relationship if they were living in the family home at her expense.

She chuckled to think how bad it might be to live with her daughter's family. Dear beautiful Elizabeth, who was so high-strung that she seemed to be driven by an excess of adrenalin, to whom every event was either "marvelous" or "disastrous." It might not be so bad, though, her son-in-law, Tom, was always level-headed and cheerful, and their son, Greg, a carbon copy of his dad. Damion, however, was frightfully like his mother, intense and bordering on irritable. All things considered, though, she admitted, they were a terrific group and she was very fortunate.

Hillary shivered in the cool air and rolled up her car windows. The cold snap would not last, coming this early in the season, and within a couple of days the temperatures would again climb up into the eighties but there would be no more really hot days.

She turned the corner onto her street and reached for her garage door opener when she noticed her front porch light was off. As she came even with her house she found that the side porch light was also off. Her skin prickled as she remembered deliberately leaving them lighted because she never liked coming home to a dark house.

Maybe she shouldn't have raised the garage door. Whoever was in the house waiting for her would have heard it come up and would be expecting her. She tried to organize her thoughts but felt her heart pounding in her chest and her head seemed light, as if she might faint. She glanced across the street and all the neighbors' homes were dark. Of course next door lived the boy monster and she would never go there for help. Maybe this was his doing. Where was Lady? She was always at the back door or back fence making a racket to welcome Hillary.

"Well, this is it," Hillary said under her breath. "I'm not going to cower in the garage afraid of a boy burglar. Or any other kind," she added.

Hillary touched the button on the wall that lowered her garage door and reached into the cabinet above Pete's work bench. She pulled out the gun she knew would be there and opened the door into the utility room.

There were lights on somewhere in the house but not the ones she had left burning. There was someone else in the house. She stepped quietly into the kitchen and stood there motionless, listening. From another room came the sound of a steady thump, thump, thump. And she distinctly smelled smoke! Without trying to be quiet, Hillary reached into her pantry and grabbed up the fire extinguisher in her left hand while keeping the gun aimed with her right hand.

She rushed into the next room, the big library, and there was the fire and the thumping increased as Lady welcomed her into the room without leaving the side of the man sitting in the wing-back chair.

"Harry, is that you? Where have you been till this hour of the night?" Pete leaned around the side of the chair, smiling at Hillary as if he had just gotten home from the bank. She noticed he had on his old tattered robe and some pajamas she thought had been thrown out long ago. She took a quick glance around the room and noted that he had started a fire in the fireplace and was reading the newspaper she had left on the kitchen table earlier.

Hillary put down the gun and extinguisher and gave Pete a quick kiss on the cheek as she had done so many days for so many years and tried to keep up a conversation while her pounding heart returned to normal.

When the telephone rang Hillary jumped up to answer it. "That'll be Sharon checking to see if I got home alright," she lied. She raced to the kitchen and carried the phone around the corner so that Pete could not hear.

"Hello," she whispered. "Yes, he's here. No, he's fine. No, don't send them. No, really, I'll bring him back. I don't know when, maybe tonight. Or maybe even in the morning, I'll let you know. Thanks for calling, Rose."

Hillary hung the phone back on the hook and stood for a moment wondering what to do. Should she insist on taking him back to the nursing home and would that precipitate another violent episode? He seemed so content in front of the fire with his beloved dog. But the truth, she admitted, was that she had wished, no, she had prayed, for him to be just there doing just that for so many many evenings, and if she could just keep him indefinitely she would be completely happy.

Well, Hillary, she told herself as she squared her shoulders, *you've got him back for maybe an hour, maybe all night. It's like a wish come true, so let's make the most of it.*

"Would you like a cup of hot chocolate, dear? It's still pretty cool out. Did you walk home?" she asked from the kitchen.

"Yes, I would like some of your famous hot chocolate. Nobody makes cocoa like you do, except maybe my mother. But she doesn't make it any better, you understand. Yes, I walked home because I forgot where I parked my car. You'll have to take me to find it tomorrow, if you don't mind." He paused. "I seem to be forgetting more and more things lately. Have you noticed?"

"Yes, I've noticed. But that's probably pretty common with people our age," she answered as she set the little tray on the table between their matching wing-back chairs. The little round tray was a memento of their cruise to the Virgin Islands. It was gold-leafed and came from Italy. She hadn't used it lately because it was a part of their late-night ritual and brought a painful stab to her heart.

Hillary made small talk, telling Pete about the bridge game and improvising some other home town gossip to make him feel part of the community. He listened attentively until she ran out of news, then said, "You'll have to admit that Max and Harvey and I are pretty understanding husbands to let you girls run around like this." He stood up and stretched. "Why don't we go to bed?

51

I'm so tired I could hardly wait up for you."

After taking the cups to the kitchen sink Hillary let Lady out in the back yard where she usually spent the night. But before Hillary had on her pajamas, Lady was whining and scratching at the bedroom door, begging to be let in the house. *Lady knows*, she thought, *that this is a very special night and she doesn't want to miss a moment of it.* She opened the French door, and Lady came bounding into the bedroom where she settled down on the carpet beside Pete, who was taking off his slippers. He patted her head fondly and spoke a little baby talk that Lady loved to hear.

When they turned out the light, Pete wrapped his long arms around Hillary in the familiar way of so many years and was almost immediately asleep. The lump in Hillary's throat was so acute that she knew she could easily cry. With difficulty she willed herself not to cry but to try and be happy. She wanted so badly to enjoy every minute of this night, knowing it was the last night she would ever sleep in the arms of the man she had loved so long and so well. For some reason, God, in His mercy, had given her one more night with Pete.

When Pete turned the other way, Hillary nestled in the curves of his back. She ran her hand down his wiry arm remembering when the muscles bulged with strength. She traced his hairline on the back of his neck and noticed that the hair was thinner, but she didn't think he'd ever be bald. The moles on his back were familiar—might be growing slightly. She'd have to keep track of their growth.

Memories of such nights as this came flooding back to Hillary: passionate lovemaking, tender consoling, or just comfortable companionship. All the memories were equally precious.

Sometime in the night Hillary dropped off to sleep. When she awoke with a start she realized that Pete was not in the bed. There was only a hint of light in the morning sky and he could have gone outside in the cold and become lost. She grabbed up her robe and put her feet into her slippers, calling, "Pete, Peter, where are you?" There was no answer, but she found Pete sitting in front of the blank television staring silently.

Hillary made Pete his favorite breakfast, which he ate quietly and with no appetite. She dressed quickly and coaxed him into the car still in robe and pajamas for the ride back to the Four Seasons Nursing Home. The staff came out to take charge of Pete, reassuring him and reminding him where his room was and his belongings. He gave no sign of recognition of them or of Hillary.

She stayed with him to get him settled in, and after almost an hour of silence from Pete, she went back home.

When she came into the kitchen, Lady came trotting out to meet her. The dog asked the question as articulately as only a Labrador retriever could, with her big brown eyes, tail wagging slightly, and a broken-hearted whine. Hillary got down on her knees and hugged the dog to her breast and said, "He's gone, Lady. He's gone and he'll never be back."

Then she cried until she could cry no more.

CHAPTER 5

The hospital was busier than usual, and Hillary was in her element. They needed her and she needed to be here. As a volunteer she worked mostly on the GU ward, which had been her specialty as a nurse. But she was willing to rotate whenever there was a vacancy that needed filling.

The charge nurse was a special friend. Now. She hadn't always been. At one time, when the nurse was new and Hillary recently retired, they had had some differences. Hillary had vowed to herself that she would stay out of nursing and just be a good volunteer, but when she found a middle-aged man in acute distress following a TURP (transurethral resection of the prostate), she ran out to get a nurse to help him. The young nurse she first found was surprised to have a volunteer seeming to give orders and became very defensive when the pink lady told her the catheter had clotted off and needed to be irrigated immediately. "Take the tubing and double it over and then give it a few quick twists. Sometimes that's enough to release the clots."

"Why don't you just finish filling water pitchers and find something to do on another unit? And let me take care of my patients." She stood beside the bed until Hillary left the room, and then seeing that the catheter was indeed clotted off, she picked up a portion of the connecting tubing, doubled it over, and gave it a sharp twist. There was still no fluid coming through the tubing. She checked the continuous bladder irrigation bag and found that it would not run, due to clotting. Again she doubled and twisted the tubing, several times, and when she released it she noticed the blood-tinged urine starting to flow through the tubing. When it slowed she repeated the process and a stringy blood clot snaked its way down the tubing and into the drainage bag.

She knew there were standing orders to irrigate the catheter with sterile saline, as needed, to remove clots that might occlude the flow of urine which would give the patient extreme discomfort. Following the irrigation, the urine began to flow down the tubing, bringing numerous small clots. When 500 cc of urine and saline irrigation had filled the bedside drainage bag, the patient breathed a sigh of relief and thanked the nurse as though she had saved his very life. The nurse, Mary Jane, felt the gratification she always felt after handling a crisis. But she was troubled about the volunteer, Mrs. Johnson, and needed to talk with someone about her.

Hillary decided that the best way to handle the situation was to quietly earn Mary Jane's confidence as a volunteer. If she had explained that she had been a GU nurse for so many years perhaps Mary Jane would have been embarrassed and never have been comfortable around her. She did want very much to win her friendship and not become a threat to a young and willing nurse. Over time Hillary and Mary Jane discussed many urological nursing problems, with Hillary giving input but not dictating the nursing action that should be taken. The hardest part of Hillary's firm resolve not to do any nursing activities had been the hospital staff who could only think of her as a nurse. She had been the first on the scene of a cardiac arrest in the waiting area outside X-ray and had put away her resolve for a few minutes while she was performing cardiopulmonary resuscitation until the Code Team arrived.

"Hey, Mom." Hillary turned from her magazine cart to see her tall, handsome son-in-law still in scrubs and leading grand rounds with a retinue of other professionals. He took the time to come over to her and give her a playful hug before he turned back to the chart in his hand. The others gave her a smile and she heard several say, "Hi, Hillary" or "Morning, Mrs. Johnson."

After the water pitchers were filled and she had chatted with patients, Hillary ran several errands for the unit clerk and head nurse. She didn't mind doing small tasks because she knew those things could take up a lot of the nurse's time. At the end of the day she was always pleasantly tired.

"See you next Tuesday, Hillary," Mary Jane said from the medication room. "Thanks again for cleaning up. Sorry we made such a mess."

"Good morning, ladies. Do you have any prayer requests? Any praise?" Martha asked her class as she had every Sunday for so many years. Several requests were made with sympathetic nods from class members.

Sunday was possibly Hillary's happiest day of the week. She loved her dear friends in the Sunday School class, and could always look forward to an uplifting lesson from her teacher and friend, Martha Lodge, followed by an equally good sermon from Dr. McDonald. She had not accepted Chester McDonald well at first, simply because of his youth. But over the past eight years he had proven himself to be quite a Bible scholar and even more. He had a gift of pastoring that was surprising in one so young. He talked to the rich and poor with equal sincerity and didn't dwell so much on the fire and brimstone message that was common in Hillary's youth, but delivered a sermon of love and hope. She knew she must come back every week to get her spiritual batteries recharged.

Hillary opened her eyes while the rest of her class members were still earnestly praying. There had been numerous prayer requests today for problems but too few "praises," prayers of thanksgiving.

Gravity, she thought, silently looking around the circle of her friends, trying to suppress a giggle. *Our faces have fallen into sour frowns because of gravity. All these beautiful, cheerful faces relax and look grumpy. Dear me*, she scolded herself. *It must be Satan busy in me to have such a frivolous thought, especially during the prayer period.* She again closed her eyes tightly until the amen was said.

At the cafeteria the line was already long. *The Methodists have beaten us here once again*, she thought, smiling. "Gram, over here," she heard Greg's voice. Her daughter's family was already in line just one loop of the queue away from the serving line.

After she got and gave hugs and kisses, they all tried to talk at once to catch up on the week's activities. "Mother, you've lost so much weight. Are you well?" her daughter wanted to know, with uncharacteristic concern.

"Of course I'm well. I've been exercising and watching my diet. I haven't lost many pounds, but I've cut down a few inches around the middle and firmed up some. I'm so glad someone noticed." She smiled happily. Her daughter was just about the last person to whom she would admit her tap dancing activities.

Hillary noticed that each of them was eating just about the same foods they ordered every Sunday, including herself. And once again she was astonished at the amount her grandson Greg ordered and finished. Damian, five years younger, sometimes ordered a large amount but seldom finished his food. In fact, sometimes he would take a few bites and leave most of his food uneaten. She refused to be one of those grandmothers who would mention this fact and nag the children to eat. She herself couldn't think of anything less appetizing than to have someone harping on the subject. Good conversation was the best appetizer. Besides, it was up to his own parents and not her responsibility.

"Let me tell you the scary thing that happened to me this week," she began, keeping her story light and funny. She was animated telling about grabbing the gun and fire extinguisher but did not include the deep emotions she had felt. Hillary went into detail describing how well Pete looked and how clear he seemed to be about some subjects. And then when he woke up he didn't remember again. They all grieved with her over his loss of memory, but she noticed they were smiling to hear that, for a short time, he was back to normal, almost. She did mention Lady's show of grief and knew that Greg would come over and cheer up the dog, as well as herself.

"But, Mother, why do you keep saying you would have 'nailed him' if you had caught a burglar in the house? You sound like an old B grade movie," her daughter scolded.

"Well," said Hillary sheepishly and for maximum effect, "you see, the gun I took from the cabinet, with so much confidence, was Pete's nail gun. I only realized it long after my heart had stopped racing and it seemed kind of funny to me later. I don't know if I could get a burglar to stand still long enough for me to hook up the nail gun to the compressor." Tom laughed so hard that people turned to stare from the surrounding tables. Greg and Elizabeth laughed, too, but Damion took the story very seriously. It might have been a real burglar.

"Gram, if you ever have any trouble, you just call me. Did you know I can shoot a real gun?" he asked sincerely.

"Thank you, Darling. But real guns are just to hunt with, and not to shoot people, you know. Besides, Lady would never let anyone near me. Don't you think she'd protect me?" Hillary steered the conversation away from burglars and guns.

"Gram," said Greg, "would it be alright if I came over this afternoon and took Lady to the park with me to play Frisbee?"

Hillary had hoped for just this suggestion. If he hadn't suggested it, she would have had to; she needed to talk to him about her ongoing problem. It seemed that Greg might be just the solution and everyone would come out a winner.

Poor little misfit, thought Hillary. Even though he had caused her so many sleepless nights, she had to feel sorry for the little terrorist next door. Both parents were successful professional people who had little time or patience with their son. How many times had she heard them yelling at him until he cried? If she could only talk with them, maybe she could promote some rational behavior. No, it wasn't that easy. It only *seemed* like other people's problems are so solvable. She knew that, in truth, many parents start out trying to be fair, logical, and loving, and when they refuse to overreact, the child knows how to push, bait, and goad them until they finally do overreact. *Parents also are guilty of goading their children sometimes*, she admitted. *Do I?* she wondered.

Lady announced the visitor before the doorbell rang. "Gram, can that be brownies I smell?" With a couple of brownies and a glass of milk, Greg settled himself into Pete's chair with the ease of someone who's done it many times before.

"Greg, we need to talk," Hillary began conspiratorially. "I have a big problem and I can't take it to the police because I have no hard evidence." Greg sat up straight. He had seen enough police stories and trials on TV to understand the term. "Actually, I don't want to involve the police or even tattle to his parents. I really need your advice."

She began with all the little incidents she *suspected* Patrick of: motorcycle tracks through the yard and pestering Lady. And then the things she *knew* he had done, such as the blasting speakers in the middle of the night. Hillary finished with the event that had happened just last night while she was quietly reading with Lady napping by her side. Lady sat up suddenly looking toward the French doors and began a low growl deep in her throat. The hair on her back was standing up, and as Hillary noted it, she felt that her own neck was prickly as well. She put down her book and walked over to the light switch beside the door as Lady began to bark in earnest. When the light flooded the back yard there was no one there, of course, and she didn't unlock the door. She pulled the draperies and left the lights on outside the house.

Greg listened attentively until Hillary finished and sat silent, thinking. "I think you're right, Gram. I know this little nerd and he gets into trouble a lot in school, too. He's just one grade behind me but I think he's about two years younger than me. He doesn't seem to have any real friends. Yeah, it's him alright. Patrick would do sneaky things like that."

"Yes, I think so, too." Hillary was walking back and forth with her hands in the pocket of her apron smock. "But the problem is how to get to him without making him mad and defensive. I'm really kind of scared of what he might do. Now, what do you think of this?" And then she went on to outline her plan, with Greg nodding several times and when she had finished he offered a few suggestions of his own.

The brownies and intrigue finished, Greg put the leash on Lady and went off to the park, both in high spirits. Hillary watched them out of sight, remembering her own love affair with a big mixed- breed dog who was her dearest friend for many years.

* * *

The tour bus was filled to capacity with elegantly dressed tourists, mostly couples of middle age and above. There were several older women among them, one of whom had an intelligent sparkle to her dark eyes and spoke with great wit and charm. The castle they had toured earlier had been beautiful beyond belief, and they had spent so much time walking up and down stairs that they were glad of the hour's ride before disembarking at the king's hunting lodge. Smaller than the castle, the lodge was equally splendid, every detail planned for a visual treat. The gardens and reflection pool were perfect in every way, and entering the lodge the group was almost speechless except for many oohs and aahs.

One of the older men was heard telling his wife, "Now this is what I call a nice little hunting cabin." And they all laughed. Gold was in every room, gold-leafed wood trim and furniture. Gold in the wallpaper and in the china service. And a lot of regal blues were displayed in the upholstery and bedspreads.

Hillary and her friend walked about the lodge twice before wandering back to the gardens. They sat for a few minutes beneath a vine-covered pergola enjoying a cool breeze and remarking how hot it must be back in Waco in August.

Beyond the shrubbery a brick walkway invited plant-lovers up a gentle hill to view trees and shrubs of various textures and shades of green, interspersed with flowers of all kinds and colors. From that direction Hillary heard what she thought was a groan and possibly a person falling. She stood up quickly and started that direction when she heard a woman talking loudly and then shouting for help, although not in English.

Hillary climbed through the bushes to the other walkway rather than take the time to go around the path. She found a man lying in a crumpled position, partially in the grass and quickly assessed a probable cardiac arrest as the man's face was a dusky gray color. His wife was near hysterics, still shouting for someone to do something. Hillary looked quickly to see if there was any rise and fall of his chest to indicate breathing and saw none. As she tilted the man's head back and looked into his mouth she shouted to anyone who was within hearing distance, "Get help! Call an ambulance!"

A sweep of the man's mouth with her index finger returned no foreign object, and Hillary pinched his nose shut and placed her mouth firmly over his and gave three deep breaths that caused his chest to rise and fall appropriately. Having ventilated the man's lungs, Hillary then felt the man's neck to determine if there were any carotid pulse. She felt none. On her knees beside the poor unfortunate stranger, Hillary placed the heel of her right hand over the lower end of the man's sternum and with her left hand on top of the right with fingers intertwined, she pressed down firmly and rapidly fifteen times to massage his heart. Then she repeated the puffs through his mouth twice before returning to his chest compressions, oblivious to the noise around her.

After a full minute of CPR, Hillary stopped to briefly feel for a pulse on the man's neck. She was unsure of the pulse because it was so faint and irregular and quickly resumed the CPR. As she began chest compressions again, she heard a very hesitant young American voice saying, "I know CPR," in the well-trained first-aid class manner. But then he added, "I think."

Hillary began counting out loud, "Twelve, thirteen, fourteen, CHANGE." She moved back to the man's head, tilted it back, again pinched his nose and gave him one strong puff which made his chest rise and fall before the young man began his five chest compressions, according to two-man CPR guidelines.

After another full minute of resuscitation Hillary again felt for a carotid artery pulse and was more convinced that there was, indeed, a fast, erratic pulse, but so weak that she knew it was not life-sustaining. And there was no evidence of breathing. The young man gave five firm chest compressions and Hillary gave one strong puff in each series until Hillary noticed the boy was becoming very tired. She expected him to order the change but when he didn't Hillary counted out loud his chest compressions, "Three, four, CHANGE," at the end of a series. Again feeling for a pulse and resuming the CPR with the boy giving a puff and Hillary giving five chest compressions.

They were unaware of the crowd which had gathered around them until the ambulance attendants, on their knees beside them quickly put the Ambu bag over the patient's face and gave the resuscitation with oxygen. Another attendant placed defibrillator paddles on the chest and shouted for everyone to step back before administering the shock. Intravenous fluids were started and several small ampules of medicine were infused before another shock was given.

The patient gasped for breath and began a series of ragged but effective breaths before opening his eyes and trying to understand what was happening to him. His color was no longer gray but extremely pale, and he turned on his side, retching and vomited into the flower garden.

Hillary and her young assistant stood exhausted as the ambulance with sirens screaming whisked the man and his lady off to the nearest hospital. Only then did she notice the man with the video camera filming them. She turned away clutching the boy's hand, bringing him with her through the hedge.

"Where did you learn CPR so well?" she asked, still puffing. For the first time Hillary looked at him closely, a very thin young man, probably older than he looked, maybe having a chronic illness himself. Hillary guessed rheumatic fever or another heart defect.

The boy beamed at Hillary's praise. "I learned it in Boy Scouts. In fact we only just learned it about a month ago, and I was sure I'd never get to use it." By this time the man with the camera and several others had followed them through the shrubbery and down the walk.

"Do you have any idea who that was?" someone asked. "He's probably the richest German industrialist in the world, and you saved his life!"

"He'll probably give you a million dollars," someone else added.

A million dollars, Hillary thought. And by habit began to calculate how many years and months that would pay the bills at the Four Seasons. Fortunately the bank stock had sold at a good price before Texas banks had been so devalued. And now if only the lake house will sell at a good price and before too very long...

No, I'm not going to waste this day stressed out about things that I can't solve today, she decided. Then she began to make her list of things that she could do and should do. *Tonight is bridge night, here, but I want to spend the afternoon with Pete, so I'll pick up some take-out food. I've got a couple of new tapes for the dancing.* She continued her mental list. The three women had become increasingly interested in the tap-dancing routines: Hillary with her conventional tap, Sharon with her exercise dance routines and Jane had perfected her accompaniment to the records they liked. Hillary noticed that she had lost a few pounds and felt exhilirated by the exercise.

The afternoon was a long one. Pete had been polite but withdrawn. Hillary knew he did not recognize her today, but years of public service and business development had conditioned him to be polite and tactful in any circumstance, Hillary reasoned. Sometimes even if he were being verbally abused. These skills were so much a part of him that even now, when he must wonder who was this strange gray-haired woman sitting beside his chair, he would never be rude.

The sun was very low in the sky as she walked out of the nursing home, but it was not late. Hillary felt heavy, sad, alone; she couldn't quite identify the feelng she frequently had leaving the Four Seasons, but knew it was all a part of the depression that is normal in these circumstances. Going home alone once again. It was a fact of life. She would be going home alone probably for the rest of her life and what was she going to do about it? If she couldn't make it pleasant, she had to at least make it bearable. Now the exhilaration she had felt with the first signs of fall had turned into sadness for the lost summer. Now it was just dark, cloudy, and all the world was in shades of gray. Even Thanksgiving had just been a day to endure.

By the time Hillary got home with her purchases and Lady reassured her that she was the most important person in the world, her mood was lifted several notches. The take-out food was warming in the oven, and Hillary was humming happily when Jane and Sharon arrived together.

"Something smells good. Oriental, isn't it? You spent your day over a hot wok, right?" laughed Jane while Hillary gave them each a hug and Lady demanded her own attention.

Between bridge hands Sharon asked the inevitable question: "When are we going to get a fourth to play with us?" Jane scowled and said nothing.

Hillary was quiet a moment and answered, "It's got to be someone we really enjoy, all of us. How about Jasmine?" They considered this because Jasmine was one of the most pleasant women they knew and had such a clever sense of humor.

"On second thought," Hillary said, "she's probably not ready yet. I know Julian would encourage her if she wanted to do it, but they've still got children at home. The twins will be graduating next year, and Monica is going to the university, but she's still at home as much as she is in the dorm, and usually with a bunch of her friends."

"From what I hear they may also be having grandchildren at home," Sharon added. "Julian told me last week that he and Jasmine had been up to Dallas to visit Rochelle and the children, and that football player she married didn't even come home the whole time they were there. The Cowboys were not out on the road either. I don't think I'm talking out of school when I mention that. They will probably talk Rochelle into coming home, at least for awhile."

"I'm sorry to hear that," Hillary said quietly. "They seemed so well-matched. Anyway they were the best looking black couple I've ever seen. They could easily be movie stars, both of them. And those precious children. It must be awfully hard for a young man, black or white, to suddenly have so much fame and fortune and keep his feet on the ground."

"Well, so much for our fourth for bridge," Jane concluded. "You know that we may be approaching this from the wrong angle." She looked from one friend to another. "Just what if we couldn't find anyone who'd put up with *us*? You do realize, don't you, that you're both pretty weird? Just look at you, a tap dancing grandma and a veritable vision in western clothes that defies description." They all laughed in agreement.

Jane reached into her pocket and pulled out several quarters. "I'm not going to lose my cool this time, but I would like to tell you the latest plans going on at my house." She put her money into the 'gritch kitty' and continued. "I guess it's going to be the event of the season. Bruce and Chrissy are going to have a Christmas party for the accounting firm, and I don't object to that, but I've heard them planning the most outlandish and expensive menu and entertainment. I just don't think the senior management will be favorably impressed with a junior employee putting on airs. I'm afraid it will do more harm than good to Bruce's career."

Jane reached for another dollar. "Well, tarnation! I guess what I'm really mad about is that they plan to have MY cook and her sister cook and serve. In uniform yet. And MY gardener fix up the grounds with poinsettias and torch lights. And at MY expense, of course. And what do you think they want me to do? Not just go to a movie for the evening, but they asked me if I'd like to leave town. Go visit someone or something."

Sharon and Hillary sat quietly, not offering advice or comments. They shared Jane's hurt feelings. Families can be so cruel. They also knew that Jane probably wouldn't even want to attend their company party, but that if they had coaxed her into making an appearance, it would have done wonders for Bruce with the elder members of the firm. Jane was not a doddering old senile mother, but was a stately and charming home town celebrity.

"Okay, then," Sharon began as if she had a perfect solution. "Let's just go skiing. Let's go up to Sierra Blanca and drink hot chocolate and have a great time. Who needs them?" She turned to Hillary. "How about it, Hillary? Remember we were talking about the snow? Don't you think Tom and Elizabeth can hold down the fort with Pete for one weekend?"

Sharon began to warm to the subject. "Please let me do this. I've been wracking my brain trying to think what to get you two for Christmas. Let me take care of the airfare. We can get a discount ticket to Roswell and rent a car there, and I can take you through my old stomping grounds and bore you to death with my exciting youth. We'll drive up through the Hondo Valley and maybe they'll still have some apple or cherry cider, and I'll show you where

I grew up and my grandmother's ranch, and..." Finally Sharon slowed down enough for the others to get a word in.

Hillary's first thought had been about the money it would cost, but if Sharon sincerely wanted to buy the tickets and rent the car, then the other expenses wouldn't amount to much. Sharon had several friends with condos and cabins and never ever rented a room when she went up to Ruidoso. Hillary quickly calculated the cost of meals and lift tickets for two days, maybe three. "Okay, I'm in. How about it, Jane? This sounds like it could be the high point of my entire year."

"See, you've just proved my point. You two are weird." Jane laughed. "Okay, I'll start making plans. The party's on a Saturday, so why don't we plan to leave Friday morning and come back, say, Monday night? How does that suit you?" There were nods and smiles all around.

Only then did they pick up the cards that had been dealt and happily began to play the last rubber of the evening. While Hillary was shuffling, Sharon remarked, "I had coffee with Hank and Marianne a couple of days ago. I'm amazed at the way they've bounced back after what the economy had done to them. Their life had literally been turned upside-down."

Hank Caldwell had been one of the largest developers in central Texas by volume. He had been building for almost twenty years and was highly respected for his integrity as well as his ingenuity. He was gregarious and always entertaining, sometimes celebrities and politicians, or promoting hometown projects with his time and money. Marianne was more reserved but supported him whole-heartedly in anything he chose to jump into.

"Apparently they've had several years of living hell. I didn't want to seem nosy, but they were very open about the subject and we've been friends for years. I once bluntly asked them how this all happened. Even with my business degree I haven't been able to understand what happened to the Savings and Loans and banks." Both Hillary and Jane knew and liked the Caldwells but had never actually socialized in that circle of the very rich. They had all heard unkind remarks about "those rich SOBs finally getting taken down a notch or two," by those little people who had never accomplished anything and had nothing but contempt for anyone who had.

No one picked up her cards. "He said it all started out innocently enough. His banker told him that the examiners wanted a little more collateral to secure his line of credit, so he gave them more and more every six months when he paid the interest and some on the principle, to renew his notes. Finally he had pledged his cars, trucks, boat, plane, and their lake house, all of which he had paid cash for initially. And still the banks wanted more every six months or they said they'd have to ask him to move his account." Sharon noted the sympathetic expressions on the faces of her friends and knew that they had admired Hank and Marianne and were not among those happy to see them fail.

"About that same time a Savings and Loan association reneged on a loan commitment for a project that he had put lots of money into already. They told him the examiners warned that if they made any more development loans they would be closed down."

"I remember hearing about that," Hillary interjected. "That was Federal Savings, wasn't it? And of course they got closed down anyway. And after that the whole Board of Directors was under indictment for mismanagement. How in the world could those people, who had operated a clean, profitable business for twenty-some years, suddenly become criminals? I knew many of these people and it just broke my heart. Excuse me, Sharon, please go on."

"Well, the Savings and Loan thing had cost him so much in liquidity because he had made the initial payment on the land, had paid for a feasibility study, engineering, and I don't know what all. Then the bank demanded more collateral again. Hank almost cried when he told me the rest of it, and of course, I teared up myself." She took a deep breath so that she wouldn't get too emotional and continued, "He said he knew he had been over confident, thinking he'd work things out. He always had. So then he offered his certificates of deposits for collateral. Then, of course, at the end of the next period they didn't have to negotiate with him. They already had his money, cars, trucks, plane, boat, and lake house. And then they wouldn't loan him operating money to complete the projects he had going. The very next payroll wiped him out completely and he filed for Chapter 7 Bankruptcy."

They sat quietly, remembering the pain that was prevalent at that time, wondering how this could have happened, but knew that Hank had not been the only one destroyed, and worse, discredited, during this time. "You've got to admire them, though. They took a bunch of their belongings to the flea market several times, and made enough to pay their utilities. Their income was ruined and did you know their utilities have been cut off more than once—can you imagine? Luckily their house was clear, but they've had a hard time keeping up with the taxes. They were both laughing real hard when they told me that they were the reverse Beverly Hillbillies, trying hard to adjust to poverty after having had so much affluence."

"Yes, I can imagine it, just from what I saw at the bank. When Pete first got sick we all thought he was just overreacting to new bank regulations. He used to rave and rant about how he had been required to treat some of his best customers. If they got into the least bit of trouble he had to foreclose on them instead of working with them through a hard period, until they were again current. He used to pride himself on being the best Work-Out officer the bank had." Hillary's face reflected the pain she had felt for Pete and for his unfortunate customers. "There were even *performing* loans that Pete had to write off for one reason or another." She saw questioning expressions on her friends' faces. "Performing means the loan payments were made on time and as they contracted," Hillary explained.

"I was in the bank once and Dan asked me into his office and shut the door," Hillary remembered. "He asked about Pete and then told me how the bank was doing. He said a surprising thing. Said that maybe Pete was the lucky one because he didn't have to know what was happening to the bank that they had both worked for all their adult life. He felt responsible for the whole thing since his granddaddy started the bank and it had done nothing but grow stronger until then, under his leadership. It had just always been a Williamson bank, but he knew even then that they couldn't save themselves."

"Well, it looks like our little kitty needs some more money, Hillary," Sharon laughed, reaching for coins to feed the gritch kitty. Hillary did as well.

"Sharon, how about a game of golf tomorrow after lunch," Jane asked, changing the subject. She knew Hillary did not play and had no interest in learning.

"Sure, I could play nine holes. Winter golf makes me shine." They all knew that Sharon would not play the back nine and they knew the reason why.

Jane said, "I'd kind of like to play eighteen holes; I need the exercise."

"Play the back nine, dear," Hillary said gently patting Sharon's tightly folded hands. "Maybe it's time to face the demons and put them in their place."

"I can easily be there by 12:30 for lunch and maybe we can get a tee time about 1:30. It's getting dark so early these days that we can't dawdle. Well, haven't we just talked about every subject we can think of, danced a little, and even got around to playing cards some. See, we don't need a fourth," Jane expounded. "They'd only cramp our style and we'd have to teach them to play. The gals I play duplicate with are good card players but some of them are really catty, and we sure don't need that." Jane picked up her jacket. "Well, Dale Evans, are you ready to mount up and ride off into the sunset?"

"Thanks, again, Hill. It was lovely as usual. I'll get to work on the ski trip, and you know you don't have to ski if it will hurt your joints. I'm not sure Jane and I will do much more than the bunny slopes ourselves," Sharon finished, going out the door.

After they left, Hillary sat thinking and then put on the tape again. *I'm going to ski again*, she promised herself, *and what better training program than some active tap-dancing?* Step, shuffle-ball-change. Step, shuffle-ball-change. Toe, toe, heel, heel...

CHAPTER 6

In the ladies' locker room, Sharon was changing from her western clothes to more suitable golf clothes when Jane arrived. Jane was already dressed in her sweats and wind-breaker. "I asked Mike to get our clubs and put them in a cart. Our tee time is 1:45, so we can have a leisurely lunch." Jane took a deep breath. "Isn't it a gorgeous winter day?"

A women's foursome came in just then. "Ah, Sharon and Jane. Don't forget our Golf Association Christmas party." It was going to be held at her house, a covered dish luncheon and gift exchange. She reminded them that the gifts could be gags or serious but not to exceed $15 in value.

Jane had to laugh because of the gift she ended up with last year. "Remember what I got last year? A cookbook! Now what could be more inappropriate for me than a cookbook? I kept it though. Who knows? Maybe someday I'll cook something." They all laughed about the party last year and the battle that ensued. They had each drawn a number out of the hat and when their number was called, they could take away a gift someone had already opened or take one from the tree. The person losing her gift had to go to the tree and open a new gift.

The competition always became loud and fierce over the most trivial of gifts, and good-natured threats filled the house. "Betty, do you remember what we fought over last year? Martha's home-made jam and a pair of red lace bikini panties. Didn't you end up with the panties?"

"Yes, I have them," Betty answered sheepishly. "But they're size 4 and I haven't been that size since I was 10 years old." They all laughed with her.

The foursome had just finished eighteen holes and three of them were off to other appointments, but Betty accepted the invitation to have lunch with Sharon and Jane.

Lunch was pleasant. Each of the women had some variation of salad and all drank iced or hot tea. Several businessmen in suits were in the dining room, several more in golf clothes, either just having played or just about to. Over the crowd of diners, Sharon spotted a familiar head of salt and pepper gray wavy hair and felt her pulse pound. *Dear God*, she fervently prayed. *Will I always feel like a teenager with her first crush?* She turned back to her salad, chasing a slice of mandarin orange around her plate with her fork, pretending not to notice that there was a woman across the table from him.

"So, what are your plans for Christmas, Betty?" Sharon asked, a little too brightly. Both Betty and Jane stared, open-mouthed, at Sharon, who looked from one to another, equally perplexed.

"Well, I don't know what planet you were on, but welcome back to Earth," Jane laughed, her usual loud, musical laugh. Sharon felt her face flush. "Betty here has just described, in infinite detail, their plans to go to Hawaii to spend Christmas with their daughter's family."

"I'm really sorry, Betty," Sharon finally laughed at herself. "I don't know what I was daydreaming about. Maybe I'm getting *old-timers* disease."

Sharon tried not to look toward Charlie and his date, but even in her peripheral vision she could see that they had both gotten up to leave, and she tried hard not to stare over that way to see who he was with. But Charlie and his lady didn't start out the door. And it looked as if they were heading directly toward their table.

Jane spoke first. "Hi, Charlie, Jenny. Happy holidays."

Sharon was so relieved to see that Charlie's date was Jenny that it was all she could do to keep from gushing, a trait that she thoroughly disliked.

Greetings were said all around, and Sharon noticed that Charlie and Jenny were smiling more broadly than usual, when Charlie explained, "We're over here celebrating. Jenny, here, has just given me some news. Seems she's about to make me a grandfather. I'm just wondering if I'm not too young and pretty to be an old grandpa." But he couldn't quit smiling.

"That's wonderful news, Jenny." Sharon began and then everyone was talking at the same time. People sitting at the nearby tables began to congratulate them, too. The baby was due in early July. Jenny and Dick had been hoping for this for a long time now.

"Uh, oh, Sharon, we've got about three minutes to be on the tee box. We'd better run. Jenny dear, this is the best news I've heard in a long time." She turned toward Charlie and added, just for him to hear, "Don't worry, Charlie, you're really not that pretty."

Charlie's hearty laugh filled the large dining room, causing friends and acquaintances to look up and smile. Sharon recognized that she was having mixed feelings, sharing his happiness, of course, but feeling something else that she couldn't quite identify. He looked so content, so complete.

Hurrying out to the number one tee box, both were zipping their wind-beakers when Jane observed, "It's really colder than it seems. The sunshine is deceiving, and if the wind gets up we might not be dressed warmly enough."

Jane pulled the driver from her bag and stepped up onto the men's tee box. Distance had never been a problem for her, and she had long ago started driving from the men's regular tee box, except when playing with the women's golf association. On lady's day they all had to tee off from the same tee box or be disqualified.

Her drive flew straight for almost two hundred yards, but when it landed the roll took it slightly off the fairway onto the nicely manicured rough on the right. "Guess I'll save my mulligan; I probably can't top that."

"It's just as well," Sharon said with a sly look. "I don't remember ever offering you a mulligan." And they both laughed. They were as competitive at golf as they were at bridge, even though Jane was the better athlete by several strokes. Sharon walked forward another thirty yards to the lady's tee and pulled out her prized newish metal wood. She felt good every time she addressed the ball with this beautiful club.

Her drive was shorter than Jane's by thirty or forty yards, but when it stopped rolling was conveniently located near the middle of the fairway. They hopped into the cart with good-natured taunts, threatening what they planned to do to each other for the rest of the game.

For some unexplained reason Sharon looked back toward the clubhouse and noticed that Charlie was standing on the terrace and had watched them tee-off. He raised his hand as he noticed her looking back. Sharon waved back and remarked, "Seems we had a gallery. Glad I didn't know it or I would have had stage fright." Jane looked back and waved, too.

The game was give and take, with Jane keeping a two- to three-stroke lead. There were bad lies with uneventful recoveries and much good-natured banter. Coming into the ninth green, they decided to get a go-cup of coffee to warm them up for the back nine.

Sharon remembered the back nine fondly, as a dear friend she had neglected to find time to visit. Number ten was a dog-leg to the left and down a steep slope. Number eleven was a long par five that reminded her of both good and bad times. Fourteen was the pretty par three with a pond wrapping around three sides of the green, and weeping willows along the back banks.

Before they holed out on the sixteenth green, Sharon could feel herself tensing up. She knew the time had come to think of Gloria. Was it six years now? No, she realized, it was closer to eight. Although Sharon had the honors, it was convenient for Jane to drive first since the men's tee was always several yards behind the ladies' tee. Jane made her drive, long and straight. Sharon climbed up onto the tee box, addressed the ball, and hooked a short drive into the rough.

Jane said nothing. They drove over to the rough on the left and easily found the yellow ball. Sharon pulled her four iron from her bag and swung at the ball with a vengeance. Jane chuckled at the size of divot Sharon had unearthed, and watched the sickly ball wobble drunkenly to the center of the fairway, only about fifty yards ahead. The divot had flown to the fairway, and since Jane was closer, she stepped out of the cart, picked up the clump and replaced it where it had been growing, tamping it down with her cleats.

"Why don't we pull over and let that foursome behind us play through?" she asked Sharon. Sharon nodded, looking back and noting that the foursome had not even gotten to the green of the previous hole and certainly were not rushing them. But she appreciated Jane's kindness and wanted to shrug off her feelings with some flippant joke. She couldn't think of a joke. She could only think of beautiful Gloria.

"You used to play a lot of golf with Gloria Spencer, didn't you?" Jane asked, not trying to be tactful. "I didn't know her well, just saw her around the club. She was one of those natural beauties, wasn't she? She didn't seem to know how pretty she really was." Jane said no more and they were both silent for awhile, thinking.

"Yes, she was beautiful. But more inwardly than outwardly, I think." Sharon sighed and began to speak quietly, and memories came flooding back. "What I like to remember is that she had such a cute quiet sense of humor. And she laughed at my jokes." She made a face resembling a smile. "She was a few years younger than I was. David had come along when she was in her thirties, and was the light of her life. And of mine. We both spoiled him rotten."

Sharon put a hand to her chest, unconscious of the pain she felt around her heart. "In some ways we didn't have much in common, but maybe we were drawn together because our husbands..." She paused. "Well, we traveled in the same circles, went to the same parties, members of the same study club. We both enjoyed golf and bridge." Pain showed on Sharon's face and she continued harshly. "And we never mentioned it aloud, not until now. But we were both expected to be show-pieces for ambitious husbands who wanted a well-dressed attractive woman on his arm to show off in public. And, of course, in private they wanted different attractive women to prove their manhood."

Her throat had tightened up with these words that had never been spoken, but had been eating away on her for so many years. Jane knew she had to press on with the subject, "Didn't you play golf together the day she died?"

"Yes, it was ladies' day and we were in the same foursome. I remember the day was gorgeous and my game was better than usual. Gloria was preoccupied with something and I didn't ask her about it. David had been giving them so much trouble, running with a bad crowd. She never mentioned it but I had heard that he was into drugs. Using and selling." Sharon was rubbing the brown spots on the back of her hands as Jane had seen her do several times when she was distressed. "I knew Bill was seeing that blond vamp with the boob job. You know, the one who was receptionist at his office at that time. Harvey had mentioned her several times. I think he was a little jealous of Bill, at least he certainly admired Bill's taste."

Sharon looked over at Jane, who was inscrutable. "Don't worry, I'm not going to cry. I've already cried. I've rehashed this whole thing so many times, and wondered whether I could have changed anything." She looked away into the distance and continued, "That day her game was not up to her usual, not real bad, just kind of blah. And then coming down the fairway here, on seventeen, she hit a great three-wood shot that rolled onto the green in two." She smiled again, loving a good shot, no matter who makes it.

"For just a little while she came out of her mood and was exhilarated. And then, you wouldn't believe her putt. You remember that jerk of a greens-keeper we had back then? He always watered on ladies' day, just as we teed off, and usually had the sprinklers on the whole time. He also put the cups in the most horrible places. We knew he hated women. But anyway, that day the cup was in the middle of that steep slope over on the back of the green, on the left. Almost any putt approaching the cup would just roll off onto the frog hair or into the sand trap. But Gloria's lie was clear across the green from the cup and it looked like she was going to lay up with a short putt. She must have had at least a thirty foot shot to the cup." Sharon had her right hand in the air, simulating the ball's travel across the green. "It was a very positive putt but looked like it was going to die short. And then it started down the slope a little, picking up speed and rolling right over and into the cup. She took a birdie on that hole, and the rest of us took at least a bogie. All she said was, 'I'd rather be lucky than good.'"

Sharon looked around at Jane who still said nothing. "I guess I thought I could block out some of the hurt if I just quit playing this back nine. Of course I was wrong. It just seems that I had so much pain then and for the next few years that it was all I could do to keep my sanity. I know about denial and all those psychology defense mechanisms. But let me ask you this. Don't you think it's better to use defense mechanisms and try to cope, or at least survive, than to just go to pieces? Look at Hillary, she's my role model. You'd think she was the happiest person in town if you didn't know how tough it is for her, with Pete and all. She's a real survivor. No, I don't think that's entirely accurate, either. I believe she really is happy because she's made up her mind to be. So that doesn't just make her a survivor, she's a winner." Sharon returned to her story. "Gloria died the same day of that golf game. We can't know exactly what happened. As I told you she was preoccupied all during the game. I didn't know whether it was trouble with David or with Bill and I didn't ask what was bothering her. There was nothing I could change and we both knew it.

"They say it looked like she hadn't been home from golf very long when perhaps the doorbell rang and when she answered the door she found David standing there, still alive, but his pants were soaked with blood. He had been castrated. The police said some drug deal had gone bad. Apparently he died in his mother's arms in the entry hall of their home. They found bloody tracks directly to the gun cabinet and back to the entry hall. She sat down and cradled David in her arms, put the gun in her mouth," Sharon paused and shuddered slightly, "and then was free of pain forever."

Sharon's throat was tight and painful with unshed tears. "And Bill didn't even get home to find them until nearly midnight." They both were silent with their own terrible thoughts. Crying would be a blessed relief, but neither could cry. "Bill was crazy with grief and guilt. He tried to see me several times and beg my forgiveness, I guess because I was Gloria's best friend. But I couldn't forgive him. I wouldn't give him that satisfaction. I said some pretty harsh things to him." She looked at Jane again, "So you see the guilt I'm carrying around. I haven't heard anything about him since he moved to Dallas. And besides all that I didn't know if I was grieving for Gloria or myself. I couldn't tell whether my anger was with Bill or with Harvey. And every waking hour I missed Gloria and I missed my sweet naughty David." Then she was silent again.

Jane asked, as if changing the subject, "How soon after that did you have your mastectomy?"

"Not quite a year. My anger with Harvey had turned into, well, I don't know, kind of a polite tolerance. He didn't even seem to mind or notice. He had his own interests. But after the mastectomy something happened to me. I became very introspective and it seemed like I woke up after a long hibernation. I decided I had to get out of my situation and take some control over my life. I'm not proud of the way I did it either. Harvey isn't really a bad man; he's just all wrapped up in himself. After all, he supported me very well. I have to thank him for that.

"But I was deceitful and played on his selfish nature. I asked him for a separation and later a divorce, convincing him that he deserved better now that I was only 'half a woman,' since I had been 'mutilated' by the surgery. It was almost amusing, if I hadn't been so angry, at how easy it was to convince him that he deserved better. The fact is, I never did feel any less a woman and certainly not mutilated." Sharon gave a bitter laugh. "But he still wanted to take me out to public functions, and I always accepted until the divorce was final. You remember the 'giant chrysanthemum' dress that covered my scar? That was during those times."

Sharon attempted to chose the right words. "You see, Jane, that was the deceitful part. I got a cash settlement that was generous enough, although it wasn't nearly 50% of the estate. He gave me the big house and transferred Major's papers over into my name. That's all I asked for. I already had some money of my own. Investments I made when my parents died. As soon as I could I sold that big house and bought my patio home. Then I quit being his fancy lady and started checking into breast reconstruction. I determined if I had it done it would be for me and not for some man."

Jane was not shocked. She had observed and suspected as much all along. What surprised her was the obvious guilt Sharon felt about the whole thing. Sharon had been brought up in a religious home and took the Biblical teachings very literally. She still believed that she should have made her marriage work regardless whether her husband had a new sweetie every few months and treated Sharon as his chattel, a beautiful ornament to be shown off. "But you've done so well the last few years. I would swear that you are actually happy now, maybe for the first time in years."

Sharon threw off her despondent mood and started talking of her favorite subject, Partners. "Do you know that Harvey didn't even know I had the MBA degree? He knew I took classes but probably presumed I was studying basket weaving or aerobics or something. I wanted to do something in business but didn't know what. I always wanted children but Harvey wouldn't hear of it. Then I started to think how badly working parents need someone reliable to care for their precious children. I did an in-depth feasibility study before opening the first one. It was successful immediately. I took out a reasonable salary and it made a profit. Then I started researching the possibility of opening another one on the north side of town. That was more of a problem. It was a high-crime area, but the rents were cheap. I had a big town-hall type meeting with the parents over there and I laid it out as plain as I could that I was no kind of welfare agency, offering free child care to them. I told them I couldn't stay in business unless all the fees were paid on time. And I expected them to see that there was no crime in the neighborhood that might endanger the children or staff." She looked sheepishly over at Jane and saw the smile on her face. "Would you listen to me rave on about Partners? We're sitting here freezing to death and I'm doing a commercial for child care."

"Sharon, I'm not your religious advisor or psychologist, but just let me say this, and I won't mind your business anymore. You've paid your dues, you tried to make a success of an impossible marriage. Now you're happy in your work and you're doing a service for the community. Don't be so hard on yourself. Just enjoy your success and don't worry about criticism. One more thing. If someone comes along that you can love, don't be afraid. It just might work." Jane wasn't accustomed to sermonizing and felt a little uncomfortable giving Sharon advice. Usually, she knew, she just popped off with her snap judgments and opinions and no one took her seriously when she did.

She added, "But you are right. We're going to freeze if we sit out here any longer. The sun is just about down. We did have a good game, though, all things considered."

Hillary was reading aloud to Pete. They both enjoyed Louis L'amour's western stories. He wove an interesting tale with a little history thrown in and the good guy was sure to win out after a fierce battle. They especially liked the Sackett family, a crusty bunch, most of whom were "so rough they wore out their clothes from the inside."

Pete displayed little interest in the story, and Hillary picked up another book that he was sure to like. It was a collection of vignettes of early Texas Rangers, a longtime passion of Pete's. In the early days of his illness, Hillary would take him to the Texas Rangers Museum down by the river, and they would spend hours reviewing the memorabilia and history of the Texas Rangers.

The day was dark and drizzling, threatening to sleet. Although Hillary was usually exhilarated on a rainy day, this cloudy cold front had stalled out and become very gloomy.

"Are you still awake, Dear? Do you like the story?" She was sitting on his bed propped up on the pillows and he was sprawled in the armchair, staring out the window. He didn't answer the question. "Why don't we go to the dining room and get some of that spiced tea? Doesn't that sound good?"

She took his hand and he got up without any resistance. She led him to the dining room where several families and residents were having their Sunday visit. Hillary sat Pete near the window and spoke to people she had met on other visits. She drew two cups from the big dispenser and took them back to the table she had chosen. "It's too hot to drink, but doesn't it smell good?" Pete did not respond.

Hillary kept up a difficult one-way conversation, occasionally coaxing Pete to take a drink of tea. She told him everything she could think of about their friends, civic happenings, if it was good news, news of his bank customers until she ran out. She didn't know if Pete heard or understood a single word she said. But what if his mind were receiving and his body just wouldn't respond? She knew she would keep on, just as she had talked and laughed with her babies when they were too little to comprehend. Maybe Pete didn't comprehend, and maybe he didn't even know who this woman was, she reasoned. But at least, if his mind was functioning at all, he would have to know the woman cared about him.

"Snow." Hillary looked up from her cup to see Pete smiling. "Snow," he repeated, seeming to be unable to elaborate.

"Yes, it is snowing. Oh, isn't that beautiful? Look at those giant fluffy flakes, they look like feathers falling." Everyone in the room began to notice the change in the weather and were coming over to the windows. Waco seldom had snowfalls and it was like a major holiday when a nice, sledding, snowman-building accumulation happened.

After watching the snow begin to build up into drifts, Hillary took the cups to the rack where the dirties were collected and went back to take Pete to his room. She held tightly to his hand, directing him where to walk. He seemed to change stride and caused Hillary to look down at his trousers, which were being soaked. He began walking with his feet apart to keep the wetness off his legs. She took him directly to his bathroom to change him and remembered to put adult diapers on him.

After settling Pete in front of a television set, where he seemed content, Hillary collected his dirty laundry, put on her warm coat, gloves, and hat, and kissed him goodbye with her usual short prayer for God's watchful care.

The snow was so beautiful that Hillary's mood was much improved. When she rounded the corner of her street, her house looked like a New England postcard. She noticed the powdery snow was sitting lightly on flowers that were still in bloom. She put away the car and went quickly to the backyard to see if Lady was suffering from the cold.

What she saw didn't look in the least like suffering, though. Lady was racing around the yard trying to catch snowflakes in her mouth. When Hillary began laughing, Lady showed off for her even more. Hillary scraped some snow together and packed it into a snowball, and then threw it across the yard. Lady raced after it, trying to catch it in her mouth. Hillary threw another and another until they were both tired and chilled.

After drying off and both having their supper, they settled down in front of a blazing fire, Lady to nap and Hillary to read the new book she had borrowed from the library. She had long since given up trying to buy every interesting-looking book that came along and felt very at home in the library. She had also discovered the video stores and enjoyed both the new and old films that she found on the shelves. A few times she had rented instructional tapes, but what she really liked was travel videos, and had seen every one they had at her neighborhood video rental store.

Hillary enjoyed mysteries and adventure stories, tales which would transport her away from the mundane and into that land of her fantasies. She knew she would never read the classics or anything very time-consuming. When she did sit down to read, she wanted to be entertained. What did she do with her time, that she had so little time to read? she wondered. Maybe she spent too much time on her home; she loved it so much. She didn't even consider the cleaning of it to be drudgery. Few of her friends shared this feeling. All her favorite memories were wrapped up in this house and the yard around it. These were memories of her children, their friends, the children's pets, and the parties they gave here. But the memories always included Pete. Her life and Pete's life, she determined, were distinct, but inseparable. Definitely inseparable. And now, what if she had to sell this house...

The phone rang before the anxiety attack became full-blown. It was Sunday night so the phone call must be from the Colorado Johnsons. "Hello," she answered in her cheerful, expectant voice.

"Hill, is that you?" a deep but unidentified voice answered back. "It's me, Sam. I haven't heard from you in ages. How's Pete?" He finally paused for an answer.

"Oh, Sam, what a great surprise! You're about the last person I'd expect to hear from." Sam knew Pete's condition and that it would not get better. "Pete's much the same. I was just thinking about you the other day. And Jesse, too. What do you hear from him?"

"Well, that's why I'm calling. He was in town recently and gave me a call. He asked a lot of questions about you that I couldn't answer and I was ashamed of myself that I didn't know how things are going with you." Their conversation was upbeat and spiced with many inside jokes from sharing their early lives together.

Sam had married a very pretty girl soon after he started his practice of pediatrics. She had enjoyed the affluence of being a doctor's wife, but over the years found that she couldn't compete with his calling. He was the junior member of the practice and got more than his share of the late-night duty. Debra had met and fallen for a very wealthy man who was a member of their country club and had more time for her. Sam had never blamed Debra but had also never remarried. He laughingly referred to medicine as his wife. Sam had many dates—he loved women and liked to dance—but when women tried to pin him down to a commitment he would tactfully and jokingly end the relationship.

Hillary found she was laughing at almost everything Sam said; he was always so funny. And he laughed at her remarks, too. When they hung up she rehashed the conversation over and over. *How nice it would be to have a man to talk with regularly*, she thought, but immediately felt a tinge of guilt that it was a betrayal to Pete to feel that way. Pete had never felt any jealousy of Sam she knew, but anyway maybe it wouldn't be proper to enjoy another man's company.

Later in the evening the Colorado Johnsons did call. They were all well and had been skiing. "How is Dad?" they asked, and Hillary told them things that had happened during the week, omitting anything that would have distressed them. They would be coming down after Christmas while the children were out of school, and they were all looking forward to the trip.

"Guess who else is going skiing!" Hillary excitedly told them of the ski trip she was planning with Jane and Sharon the following weekend and, just as she had anticipated, they were happy that she would go on a trip.

CHAPTER 7

Friday morning finally came, and Hillary was waiting in the driveway with her luggage before the sun was up. She had brought her skis and boots down from the attic and cleaned them up, wondering just how many years it had been since she had used them. It must have been just before Pete got really sick, during one of their visits to the kids in Colorado. She knew technology had changed a great deal in ski equipment and wondered whether anyone would notice her outdated gear. No matter, she thought, it had worked beautifully for her and she didn't place too much strain on it, like racing down steep moguls, as the young people did. She had taken her equipment to the ski shop to see if she needed any repairs and found that with a little adjustment to the bindings, everything was in working order. The clerk had, of course, tried to interest her in the latest models of skis and boots.

Hillary was pleased that her ski outfit still fit her comfortably and had packed several colors of cotton turtlenecks, the only variation she would have for the three days of skiing. She knew that Sharon would have a different elegant outfit for each day and was looking forward to seeing them. Hillary and Jane both took pleasure in Sharon's exotic dress but enjoyed teasing her anyway.

The only car on the streets this early in the morning was rounding the corner and Hillary could recognize it as Sharon's Suburban. They had agreed it was the only one that could carry all the luggage comfortably.

At the airport there were several other commuters sleepily drinking their coffee and waiting for the Dallas flight to be called. A couple of young businessmen stared at the three graying women and their ski equipment. This attention did not go unnoticed by the trio, and they passed knowing smiles to each other. Exhilaration was high among them.

In Dallas they re-checked their luggage onto the plane that would take them to Roswell, New Mexico, and just had time for a light breakfast before boarding. The weather was clear and all flights were running on time.

The west Texas and New Mexico skies were a brilliant blue. Hillary recognized the wisps of high clouds as signs of a high pressure system, or good and clear weather. That would be great skiing if there were already enough snow, she was thinking.

In Roswell Sharon picked up the rent car she had ordered, a four-wheel drive, not quite as large as her Suburban but adequate for the three of them and all their gear. She had insisted on snow tires as well, knowing the steep and sometimes icy road leading up to Sierra Blanca, which she knew they were now calling Ski Apache.

"Well, so much for the tour of Roswell. Didn't take long to show you New Mexico Military Institute, the main drag and the house where we lived." They turned onto the highway heading west. Off to the northwest, Mount Capitan was looming tall and blue violet. Straight ahead Sharon pointed out the snow-covered peaks of Sierra Blanca, but explained that it was really much farther than it appeared.

Hillary had such a feeling of well-being that she wondered whether this were one of her fantasies. *If it is,* she thought, *it sure is one of my better ones.*

"Hillary, why are you smiling so big?" Jane asked, laughing. "I'll bet I know how you must feel. Would you look at those rolling hills and the mountains in the background? And that sky! Doesn't it seem like there's more sky here in New Mexico?" Then they were all quiet, drinking in the arid beauty of the winter foothills to the southern Rocky Mountains.

"We'll be coming into the Hondo Valley soon. I always thought it was the most wonderful place on earth, the grass is lush and green in the summer and in the arroyos are giant cottonwood trees, just perfect for a high swing. The trouble is that the cottonwoods didn't have many low branches and it was hard to get up high enough to tie a swing."

Sharon was happily reminiscing about her childhood. "The best swing we ever had was the summer my cousins came from Virginia. My cousin, Tom, was several years older than I was and he climbed a really big cottonwood and tied our rope in it. Then we made a trapeze handle for it and climbed up in a smaller tree, a Chinese elm, I think, and swung out so wide that it took our breath away. We played on it every day until his little brother, Austin, fell off and knocked the breath out of him. He went home crying and tattled on us so the grownups made us take down our swing." Jane and Hillary could visualize the little blonde tomboy swinging from the trees.

"See this stone gate coming up? I won't drive in, I don't know who lives there now." Sharon stopped on the gravel road that seemed to lead right up a valley between two towering hills, with a branch leading up to a big white frame house nestled in a grove of trees at the foot of one of the hills. "That was my grandmother's house and we lived about five miles farther up the canyon. Most of the time I was the only child around and I spent lots of time by myself, not lonely exactly; I had some make-believe friends who would do anything I wanted. Sometimes I would blame them when I got into trouble, but it never worked."

"Does it snow a lot here, too? I see some snow in the shady places," Hillary asked.

"Yes, sometimes we were snowed in for days up in the canyon. And another thing is that we had floods. Anytime we had a big thaw or a flash flood in the high country, we couldn't get across the creeks to get down to Gram's. That's the main reason we moved to town, for me to go to school. Actually my mother, being a Virginia southern belle, wanted me to go back east to become a real lady. Daddy and I outvoted her, though, so I went to school in Roswell."

Sharon pointed to a towering windmill beside a big red barn. "I wasn't allowed to climb the windmill but that's where I remember spending most of my free time. I could see forever, I thought, over the tops of the trees. Probably not more than four or five miles, actually."

"How could you spend so much time up there? Weren't you scared?" Jane wondered.

"Sometimes I was kind of scared, like when the wind was strong. I knew to stay away from the blades because we had a friend who only had a thumb and index finger on his right hand because he lost it to a windmill. But danger was part of the attraction, I think. And since I was in a forbidden hideout, sometimes I would think about forbidden subjects," Sharon leered, "like sex. But since I knew so little about the subject, that didn't take very long. And then sometimes I would think about God, and the mysteries of religion." Sharon shrugged. "But I didn't know any more about God than I did about sex, so that didn't last very long either. Mainly I just planned what I was going to do 'someday,' who I would marry and how many horses he would have, that kind of thing."

The view brought hundreds of memories flooding back to Sharon of her parents and grandmother and being loved and adored. "I had a horse, Patches, a paint that my dad bought and trained when I was just a toddler. He was half shetland pony and just right for me till I was about eleven or twelve and wanted a 'real' horse. We had a neighbor on an adjoining ranch that rode the most beautiful horse I had ever seen. He was a tall, skinny cowboy and rode a gorgeous black with an arched neck and flowing tail. They said the horse was gaited. I'm thinking he must have been a Tennessee Walker. I was so in love with that horse. If Major were black they'd be twins.

"I got my real horse about then and spent part of every day horseback. The other thing I did was rope." She looked around to see how this was received. Both Hillary and Jane looked surprised but said nothing. "I had some bad experiences at first. I've been dragged by some of the smallest calves you've ever seen. But I'm a quick study. I didn't have to be dragged through the mud but a few times before I learned that you need a post or tree to snub to once you've caught your animal." They all laughed imagining the blond moppet being pulled through the dust by a frightened calf. "Well, I knew my dad would kill me if I lost the rope, so I just hung on as long as I could. But I got pretty good, finally." And to herself Sharon admitted, *Actually I got pretty DARNED good*, and smiled faintly.

Sharon put the car in gear and pulled out onto the highway. "I can see why you loved it so," Hillary said. "But you've said that your mother never adjusted to the solitude, and was never happy here?"

"Yes, that's right. But she was a lot happier when we moved into town. Daddy and I were the ones who enjoyed gathering the cattle and riding the fences."

"Riding the fences? Why would you ride a fence and how do you do it?" a laughing Jane wondered. Sharon grimaced, knowing Jane knew the answer and the question didn't deserve discussion.

The highway was curving around hills and following a stream, climbing gradually but steadily until coming into the village of Hollywood, where thoroughbreds and quarter horses were raced. "Harvey used to have two or three colts in training here every year. That's how I came to adopt Major as my riding horse. He had a slight injury that ended his racing, and since he was already gelded, Harvey wanted to just put him down. I wouldn't hear of it, and I shipped him back to Waco and took care of him till he was back in shape. He was so high-strung there for about a year that I didn't know if I had made a giant mistake, but we finally got comfortable with each other and now he's just perfect for me."

In the village of Ruidoso Sharon found her landmarks and made her way down winding streets until she found the one she sought. She drove steadily upward along a pine-covered mountainside, noticing more and more snow on the ground the higher they climbed. Finally she slowed on the side of the road above several rooftops. "This is it, if I remember right. I'll turn down this driveway, and there should be a sign that says 'The Howards,' and then one with a cartoon character and then the third one will be ours. The garages are in the front on the drive and all the houses have big porches on the other side with a town view."

The cottage was small but elegant. Downstairs was a large living room, or greatroom as Sharon called it, with a giant fireplace that was soon blazing and warming the entire room. Sharon knew how to turn on the water and electricity, and within the hour the three had made a cozy nest. Upstairs were two bedrooms which shared a bath and were furnished with two sets of bunkbeds each. On the kitchen cabinet was a note for Sharon inviting them to use any of the canned goods in the pantry and not to worry about the dirty linens when they left because someone locally came by to pick them up and return them before the next weekend.

Darkness fell quickly once the sun had set behind the mountain. Lights of the city of Ruidoso began to glow in the crisp night air like thousands of twinkling stars below them in the village. The three of them stood out on the porch to watch the view until they were chilled to the bone and had to go back into the warmth of the fireplace.

"How about a friendly game of bridge before we go to bed?" Jane suggested. "Remember, this is Mountain Standard Time and we will get to sleep an hour later. But we've got to allow plenty of time to get up the mountain to the ski slope." She grinned. "I'm so wired that I probably couldn't sleep anyway. What I'm wondering is, why haven't we done this before?"

"Well, I get up here several times each winter." Sharon added, "Usually when someone nice invites me. But I feel like kind of a fifth wheel since my friends all have husbands, and even though they include me in everything, it's just not the same as having you two up here with me. I'm so glad you both decided to come. And let's do make every effort to do this at least once a year, okay?"

Sharon's skillful driving got them to the ski slope as the lifts were starting to run. While doing their stretching exercises, they noticed several interested glances from passersby, mostly young people. Sharon directed her group to a nearby chair lift. "Let's do a couple of runs on the bunny slope before we go all the way to the top. And if you don't want to go up there, please don't think I'll feel bad about it. I can go alone or with one of you, or both, or whatever you're comfortable with. And remember we have three glorious days so we don't have to kill ourselves trying to get it all in today."

Jane and Hillary shared a chair lift. and even though they were very tense the chair picked them up without a bobble, lifting them up and away over the tops of the trees and giving them a magnificent vista of blue sky, dark green pines, and beautiful white landscape.

"Oh, Jane, this is so wonderful I feel like I might cry. Or at least I feel like I should sing the doxology," Hillary said, laughing.

"Well, I feel the same way, only I was thinking more in terms of just wetting my pants. As usual you have phrased the feeling more appropriately. 'Praise God from whom all blessings flow.. .'" Jane began in her beautiful contralto voice, and Hillary immediately started to sing along with her, not knowing or caring whether nearby skiers could hear them. When they finished the short chorus, a man in the chair ahead of them looked back and gave them a thumbs up, which Hillary and Jane returned with big smiles.

"My voice isn't too great this early and at this temperature, but how about another one?" Jane asked. "Oh, Lord, my God. When I, in awesome wonder, consider all the worlds thy hands have made." Jane began "How Great Thou Art" and Hillary was so moved she could hardly sing with her. The song was so very appropriate for the feelings she was experiencing, and she would be forever grateful to Jane for voicing them so well.

After two runs down the gentle slope, the trio was ready for a cup of cocoa and then, having no injuries or major misgivings about going to the top, each picked up her skis and poles and walked over to the gondola shed. The Mescalero Apaches operate Sierra Blanca on their reservation and a young Indian handed them carefully but quickly into the gondola.

"Good looking young Indian, isn't he? Or maybe you're supposed to say Native American, I'm not sure. These things change and I have a hard time keeping up." Another young Apache took them briskly from the gondola at the top. "I want to show you something special inside," Sharon said to Hillary and Jane as they climbed up into the building that was both restaurant and warming hut on the top of the mountain. They looked westward out onto the desert floor below the mountain range and saw that there was no snow down there but the equally snowy white of the White Sands. The White Sands stretched out of sight in their vastness, a sight that neither Jane nor Hillary had ever before seen.

"Oh, my soul!" Hillary exclaimed. "I've heard of this all my life but I never dreamed it was as white as they claimed. I can hardly wait to tell Pete about this."

* * *

Monday was their last day of skiing. They arose early in order to leave the cottage in good shape with the dirty linens in a bundle to be picked up later that day. The gray-haired trio were among the first on the chair lift, as they had decided a couple of runs down the gentle slopes was the best way to get warmed up. They continued to enjoy stares from young people as they donned their caps and goggles. As usual, the third day took some extra stretching exercises because the sore muscles had tightened up considerably. They took a quick early lunch in order to make two more runs from the top, which they did fairly fast but without taking chances.

They had already agreed that they would have to leave the slope by two o'clock in order to catch the last plane out of Roswell. And even at that they knew they'd miss the last shuttle in Dallas and have to rent a car to drive on to Waco.

The trip down the mountain highway was quiet, each woman having her own personal thoughts and nostalgia about leaving the mountains for the foothills, and the foothills for the desertland. El Capitan loomed off to the left now, tall and blue in the distance. Each claimed the mountain as her own personal landmark, the faithful sentinel over the surrounding desert.

The flight to Dallas was equally quiet as each woman nursed her sore muscles and bruises, experiencing again the euphoria of a perfect ski trip. At the end of the second day of skiing, a snow cloud had appeared over the crest of the mountain, depositing a steady but gentle new layer of fresh powdery snow. The next morning when they arrived at the slope they found a couple of inches of new snow at the lower levels and perhaps twice that on top.

After collecting their luggage in the Dallas airport, renting a station wagon, and starting toward home, the three women began to think about dinner. Jane suggested a great restaurant in Fort Worth; it would be on their way. At least it would only be a few blocks out of the way, off the expressway. The light meal revived them all and they chattered gaily all the way to Waco, arriving late Monday night and ready to tackle whatever was in store for them.

CHAPTER 8

The Christmas season was becoming more and more festive, with lights and outdoor decorations springing up in almost every yard. Hillary felt as though she should do more toward decorating but only put up her tree and the electric candles in each of the front windows. Without Pete at home it just didn't seem worth all the effort. Pedro and his family were not coming down until after Christmas and she wasn't having bridge until January. So far as she knew there may be no other person coming to her home until after Christmas. Everyone was so busy at this time. Everyone, that is, except herself.

"No self pity, old girl," she told herself in the mirror. "Let's just remember the true meaning of Christmas and count the blessings we still have." She knew how easily she could fall into the habit of counting losses instead. But even though she had made the decision long ago never to do that, sometimes in an unguarded moment she would feel overwhelmed with her grief and loneliness.

"Let's just pick ourselves up by our bootstraps and have a cup of spiced tea," she said to Lady. As she walked toward the kitchen, the telephone began to ring.

"Hill, something terrible has happened," Sharon said in a quavering voice. "Jane has fallen and they think she may have broken her hip." Sharon regained her composure and continued in her normal tone, "I'm on my way over to the hospital now. Do you want me to pick you up?"

"No, Sharon, you go on over, I'm completely out of the way. I'll come in my own car as soon as I feed Lady." Hillary felt her old nursing instincts coming to the surface. She knew that in a crisis her mind was clearer than ever, and rather than hysterics she remembered every little important detail. Except for one night, possibly, when she would have shot an intruder with a nail gun, she admitted. She would feed Lady and put her outside in case she was gone for many hours, perhaps all night. Who should she call? The pastor, of course, or maybe he already knew. And Martha Lodge, Jane's dear friend.

Hillary tried not to drive beyond the speed limit, and it seemed that every traffic light was red just because she needed to rush to the hospital. Martha had not been at home and Hillary had left her message on the recorder.

At the hospital information desk, Hillary inquired to learn the room number on the orthopedics floor. There was no one in the room when she arrived, and Hillary suspected that Jane might be in x-ray or even in surgery.

The floor nurses were very busy, and Hillary looked around till she found the charge nurse. "Oh, hi, Hillary. Are you looking for Mrs. Westerman? We sent her to the O.R. about an hour ago. The family is down in the surgery waiting room."

"Do you know what happened, Dorothy? How bad is the fracture, do you know?"

"I think it's pretty bad, Hillary. It's the neck of the femur and the leg is pretty badly internally rotated. They're doing an ORIF now." Dorothy looked very serious. "Maybe I heard wrong but someone said she broke it playing basketball. I didn't think that was possible, an elegant lady like Mrs. Westerman."

"Thanks, Dorothy. She does play basketball, though. In fact she was a coach. I'll go find the family." Hillary turned toward the surgical area where she knew the family would be and hoped she could be some comfort to the kids. Bruce and Chrissy were really good kids. It's just hard for two generations, any two generations, to live in the same house. And so what if they wanted all the trappings of wealth without having any wealth? Maybe we all would if we had the chance.

A very pale Bruce was sitting in the corner of the waiting room, talking quietly with Sharon. Several other people were in the waiting room, alone or in small groups, quietly waiting for their loved ones to return from the recovery room. Hillary joined Sharon and Bruce and was immediately bombarded with medical questions. What is an ORIF? What will she be able to do when she heals? And from a very scared Bruce, "Could she, maybe...die?"

"No, Bruce, there's not much chance that she would die." Hillary quickly tried to reassure Jane's son, noticing that he looked much younger than his thirty-four years. Bruce had taken the death of his father very hard, and now the realization that his mother's life may be in danger was almost more than he could bear to consider. "ORIF simply means open reduction and internal fixation. That means a surgical setting of the fracture. Sometimes certain fractures can be reduced without surgery and heal just fine. That would be a closed reduction."

Diversion, thought Hillary to herself. *This boy is about to faint he's so scared.* "Jane is a very healthy person, we all know. Thank goodness she stays active, especially with the basketball. She should heal nicely. I can't predict how long she might stay in the hospital. Once she's up in the wheelchair, just a couple of days from now probably, she'll start to feel much better." Hillary used her most optimistic tone of voice and relayed only a best-case scenario. "Soon she will be going to therapy and learn how to get around on a walker and then she could go home, not completely healed, but she could finish convalescing at home. Oh, dear," Hillary added purposely. "Her bedroom is upstairs; what will you do with her when she comes home?" She knew Bruce would have to start thinking ahead and get his mind off the dark thoughts he must be having.

"I know," said Bruce after a second of thought. "The maid's room. Well, we used to call it that, even though we've never had a live-in maid. We've always used it as a kind of office or hobby room. Junk room is more like it. But we can clean it out and repaint it while she's still here in the hospital. Chrissy would love to take charge of a project like that and she's real good at it, too." Bruce had regained his healthy color and was able to smile. Here was something he could do for his mother. They all knew how independent Jane was, and self-sufficient. She could take care of everyone and never ask a favor in return. Bruce had always accepted that his mother would take care of him—she always had—and even now he had his family living in her house. So, in a sense, his mother was still taking care of him.

"Why don't we go downstairs and get some hot tea or something? I think we'll still have a pretty long wait before anyone comes out to give us a report." Hillary wanted to keep moving, keep doing, in order to postpone her own fears for Jane. Even without inviting the dreary thoughts, they kept creeping into her consciousness. Jane on a walker, Jane unable to ever go skiing or play golf again, Jane unable to climb up onto a concert stage and share her remarkable talent. And, of course, the unspeakable dread—Jane an invalid in her own home and getting voted down on every decision. "Well, how about it?"

Bruce insisted on buying the ladies' drinks, and while he was waiting in line at the cashier's stand, Sharon and Hillary went ahead to find a quiet table. "Thank goodness you got here when you did, Hill." Hillary looked at Sharon with surprise, just now noticing her pallor as she had Bruce's. And she had not freshened her makeup, either, which was unusual for Sharon. "I kept trying to reassure him about all this, and the truth is, I don't know anything about a hip fracture. I thought only real old people broke their hip. And I certainly don't think of Jane as old." Sharon looked as though she might cry, begging for reassurance from Hillary. "Tell me the truth, will she get well?"

"Sharon, I really don't know. First of all I don't know the extent of the damage. And second, I don't know if this was just a traumatic fracture—that means she fell so hard on her hip that the bone broke. If so, it should heal okay, with a careful pinning."

"Or what? What's the other kind?"

"Or it could be a pathlogical fracture. Maybe, God forbid, a metastatic lesion. Or the more common thing is osteoporosis. You know, women our age are losing calcium and our bones tend to get brittle. Our doctors are always advising us to take in more calcium so we don't get a dowager's hump or porous bones. For now I don't even want to think of a pathological fracture. Well, here's Bruce with our drinks."

While the three were quietly sipping their drinks, Martha Lodge found them, and moments later, Chester McDonald, their pastor, joined the group. When they returned to the surgery waiting room, Chrissy had returned, after having found a sitter to stay with the children.

Another hour passed before the orthopedic surgeon came out to give the family a report. He was young and athletic looking and Hillary had never met him. She was appreciative of his apparent concern and the gentle way he explained the procedure, giving all his attention to Bruce. "I've moved her to the Intensive Care Unit just for the night. We gave her several units of packed red blood cells, kind of a standard precaution since she had lost quite a lot of blood before and during surgery. We'll get another CBC in the morning before we move her back to the orthopedic unit. I think she's doing fine now, but I have to tell you she's in for some pain before she gets well." The young doctor finally acknowledged the others of the group, and with a smile he said, "What I'd do, if I were you, is go home and get a good night's sleep. And by the time visiting hours start we should have Mrs. Westerman comfortably situated in her room on Orthopedics."

The solemn group walked out to the parking lot together and said goodnight, promising to remember Jane and each other in their prayers. "I had no idea it was so late," Martha remarked. "It's almost midnight."

Lady was happy to hear the car driving into the garage and began her "Please let me in" routine, half-bark and half-dance. Even after they had settled down for the night, Hillary had a hard time falling asleep. She started her prayer several times but couldn't seem to think of the right words. Of course Jane would get well with no complications, lots of people do. Maybe even most people. But Hillary knew what the complications might be and what if...

The salt spray was washing up over the bow each time the sloop nosed into a trough on the heavy seas. Hillary couldn't think of leaving the helm, even for a moment. Luckily she had found the slicker and sou'wester, but even so she was chilled through and through. She had to keep a firm hand on the wheel and keep her eye on the magnetic compass. She didn't even know where she was but decided that if she headed a little bit north of due west, she would have to sight land before too many hours. Her heading was 290 degrees, and she hoped this would land her on the Florida coast, hopefully around Fort Lauderdale.

If only she knew this boat better; there were probably navigation aids and auto pilot that would free her hands to check on Chuck and make sure the bleeding had stopped. At least she had known enough to reef the mainsail when it became so stormy, but the smoother sailing had only lasted a short time and the storm continued to rage ever stronger. The boat was a beauty, owned by a wealthy drug czar; also it was in top condition and well-stocked with food and first-aid equipment. These she had discovered before the storm hit. She had tried the radios but never knew whether her 'Maydays' were received, or by whom.

She refused to think negative thoughts, but little doubts kept sneaking into her mind, such as, "What if I miss Florida completely and sail clear across the Gulf of Mexico?" Well, it can't storm forever and we will at least make landfall eventually, that is, if the other boat doesn't catch us first. She knew Chuck had shot one and wounded another one or two of the smugglers, plus the henchman who was on this boat when they made their 'midnight requisition' of it. She didn't know Chuck was wounded during their frantic escape into the blackness of the night when the storm was still in the distance. But he finally had to ask her if she knew how to sail a boat, and she looked at him carefully for the first time, noticing how ashen pale he was and had his right hand over a bloody handkerchief covering his left upper arm.

Hillary had quickly grabbed a towel and torn a strip off the length of the towel, folded the rest of it into a small square pad which she tied tightly over the bullet wound for a pressure dressing. She then had to bully Chuck to get him to leave the helm and she led him, half dragging him down into the cabin. By this time they were almost an hour's sail sort of westerly from the island they had escaped.

The first aid box was well-stocked, and when Hillary felt the bleeding had slowed she took off the pressure dressing and looked at the bullet wound. She cleaned the jagged wound with peroxide and sterile water and used sterile gauze to make another slightly looser pressure dressing. She noticed that Chuck had fainted then, and she laid him down in the bunk and covered him over with the blankets she found in a locker. The boat was beginning to rock heavily, and she felt the first queasy symptoms of seasickness. She had to get back to the helm and check the sails. With no one tending them, they had drifted around, and the sails were slack and beating uselessly.

The wind was freshening, and Hillary found that the main was tied off too tightly. Even letting out the mainsail, the winds were battering the sail boat mercilessly. That was when she discovered the roller reefing of the mainsail and the furling jib. She hadn't known whether she could do this singlehandedly, but after the fourth try at different headings found that she could, indeed, reef the main.

She had been using a big beam flashlight and knew that their survival might depend on it. Finding a shockcord, she lashed the flashlight to the wheel in a position to be easily directed at the magnetic compass and settled down to a wet and windy night of sailing.

If only she can get some medical help for Chuck in time, before he bleeds too much, and before an unmanageable infection develops... He might even lose his arm. We might also lose our lives, she admitted. No, things could be a lot worse and I'll just do the best I can. We've uncovered the smuggling network and as soon as our reports are posted the streets of America will be much safer for the lack of drugs available to our youngsters.

The storm had abated somewhat, and Hillary had to keep moving to stay awake. She realized she could almost see the magnetic compass in the light— it was morning—and now if only she could sight land. Who knows how much the wind could blow the boat off course even though she had kept at her 290 degrees for most of the night?

The wheel spun and jolted Hillary awake. Her head had been resting against the ship's wheel and she felt the sun hot on her back. She looked behind her and noticed the sun was high above the watery horizon.

BLAAAAAAT!!! Hillary spun around only to see the monstrous black bow of the biggest ship she had ever seen in her life. Her reflexes jerked the wheel sharply to port, allowing the giant tanker to pass to starboard, churning the water around the diminutive sloop for the roughest ride of Hillary's life.

* * *

BLAAAAAAT!!! The telephone rang again as Hillary jumped off the barstool, spilling her coffee. Guiltily she glanced around, assuring herself that no one had witnessed her startled embarrassment. Who, indeed, would be watching her do dumb things, except for Lady, who at this time was observing Hillary with her head tilted in a questioning way. Once again she wondered whether she could get a phone that had a nice ring, rather than that irritating and demanding sound.

"Hello," she was finally able to answer on the third ring. "Yes, Sharon, I'm planning to go over there this morning." She listened while Sharon explained why she couldn't get to the hospital until evening. "Sure, I'll call you as soon as I've seen Jane and let you know. I won't stay long because she won't feel much like visiting. But I'll drop by again tonight for a quick visit to see if she needs anything. Okay, I know that number."

At the hospital Hillary greeted and was greeted by many friends on her way up to the orthopedic unit. Entering Jane's private room, Hillary almost gasped out loud at Jane's ashen appearance. A unit of packed cells was transfusing into Jane's right forearm while another peripheral IV of Isolyte was infusing slowly into her left wrist. Hillary noted a foley catheter bag hooked onto the side of the bed. *Good idea*, she thought, *bedpans are murder on a hip fracture*. In spite of her pallor Hillary noticed that Jane looked beautiful. Her dark hair was only lightly sprinkled with gray, but the streak growing from her right temple was completely white.

"Hi, Hill." Jane opened her eyes at Hillary's footsteps. "I'm not asleep, it just doesn't hurt as much if I lie here in a catatonic state with my eyes closed." She winced as she turned slightly to see Hillary. "I've really done it now, haven't I? Can't you just see me growing old in a wheelchair? Me? The jock?" A tear formed in the corner of each eye but did not spill down her cheek.

Hillary pulled the lounge chair close to the bed and reached for Jane's hand. She was careful not to disturb the intravenous lines attached to Jane's upper forearm where the blood was transfusing. "Jane, dear, it's not going to be like that. I know you're in a lot of pain right now. This is Day One, you couldn't feel too great right now. But there are certain things you've got to do each day. Remember that old saying, 'take one day at a time'? This is one of those situations where that's the only thing you can do. And today you need to take your pain injection whenever you need it. Don't try to be a martyr or think you'll get hooked. The shots you get will have two medicines in them, one to kill pain and the other is kind of a muscle relaxer that keeps you from being nauseated."

Hillary kept patting Jane's hand and talking quietly about the regimen that she could expect for the next few days. She reached for the blue plastic apparatus on the bedside table. "This is one of the most important things you'll do for the first few days. This is called an incentive spirometer. Did they show you how to use it?" Jane nodded slightly. Hillary continued in her gentle but professional manner, telling Jane what she could expect, encouraging her to breathe into her incentive spirometer to exercise her lungs, giving her no false hopes and bravado, but admitting to the pain and discomfort and the impatience she might feel with her progress.

"Jane, if you had your gallbladder out, you'd feel pretty rotten for a few days, right? But you'd heal and you'd get your strength back at some point. Well, bones heal, too, maybe not so fast as other tissue, but that hip will get better and much of your progress will depend on you. Your doctor and therapist are going to teach you just how to maximize your efforts, and you may be as strong as ever one day."

Hillary knew she was rambling but knew that Jane needed to hear some positive information at this point. She could not mention her own doubts about whether the fracture might be pathological, from some metastatic lesion, or severe osteoporosis. Whether Jane might not heal was a consideration that Hillary would not allow to form in her mind. Jane's eyes were closed again, and Hillary thought she might be dozing off, but kept her pale hand with the long, artistic fingers sandwiched tightly between her own small hands with the enlarged arthritic knuckles.

Jane chuckled, which startled Hillary and caused Jane to grab her hip in pain. She kept laughing and the tears that had puddled up in her eyes began to fall down her cheeks. "Dadgum it, Hillary, why don't you just say, 'Oh, poor baby,' and let me lie here and wallow in my self-pity? And become an invalid. And have people waiting on me for the rest of my life." She kept laughing. "Maybe I'll even get an electric wheelchair. And who knows what else?" Jane's eyes closed again but she kept smiling. "I just had a shot before you came in and I can't seem to keep my eyes open, but I'm not asleep. Keep telling me that sweet trash."

Hillary stood up and patted Jane's hand again. "I've stayed too long anyway. Why don't you go on to sleep? And when you wake up you reach for this little breathing toy, okay?" At the door Hillary turned back and said,

"I'll drop by tonight after I leave the Four Seasons, but, meantime, if you need anything just have your nurse leave a message on my machine."

Hillary ran her errands, which included the purchase of some nice body lotion and powder as a gift for Jane, bought her groceries, returned home to do a little light housecleaning, always thinking of Jane and what the next few months would hold. *How can we make this better for Jane? How will this affect Jane's personality? She's always been so vibrant, outgoing, so...well, physical. That's it, she just exudes vitality, whether on the basketball court, at the piano, or even at the bridge table. Nothing*, Hillary promised herself, *nothing is going to take that from her, if I can help it.*

How will Bruce and Chrissy react to the demands that will naturally be put on them with Jane incapacitated? Will they meet the challenge or just let the hired people take care of her needs? Hillary truly didn't know. But she knew of the mechanics of a dysfunctional family, where disabled members were sometimes mistreated and made to feel inferior or at least a nuisance. *That will not be the case with Jane. First of all, because Jane has such a strong personality herself. But still, when a person is handicapped and depressed over a period of time, even a strong person may be browbeaten into... No, no, no, not Jane*, she determined.

At the Four Seasons, Hillary's spirits were elevated by the beautiful Christmas decorations. The manger scene on the front lawn was nicely done, made of plyboard and painted, Hillary knew, by some of the residents under the watchful eye of the crafts director, who had been an art instructor at the university before she retired. The baby in the manger was lying on real hay. The wise men looked so intelligent and rich in their finery. Mary and Joseph had an expression of serene happiness. The shepherds, in their shabby clothes, had a look of awe and reverence. A young shepherd boy was looking up at an older shepherd, who Hillary thought must be his father, with a quizzical expression. She could imagine him asking, "Dad, what does all this mean? First, all those angels, and now this baby." But of course the daddy could not have imagined the significance of these events. *Even now*, Hillary thought, *maybe we still can't grasp the whole significance of those events.*

Hillary smiled and appreciated the work that went into the yard scene and knew that at sundown the flood lights would come on to give the scene a magical quality that would make the plywood people seem to come alive. Perhaps the lights would be on when she left. The days had grown short, and darkness fell early these days.

Pete greeted Hillary politely and made social small talk, which made her think he didn't know exactly who she was. She didn't make an issue of it and told him about her day and the accident that Jane had. In all her conversations with Pete, Hillary stressed the names of their friends and managed to include the day and the season and other information to orient him to time, place, and person. Sometimes he remembered these for hours and even days. At other times he was totally unresponsive or immediately forgot. But even when he was unresponsive, she couldn't help wondering whether his mind was still active and trapped in this uncooperative body, unable to verbalize his feelings and thoughts. Therefore she always spoke to him as if this were the case. Many times she was rewarded with an original conversation with Pete calling names of family and friends, or an opinion on some current event. These seemed to be getting fewer and farther apart she admitted.

Hillary stayed with Pete until he had eaten his supper and helped him into his coat to go outside and see the lights. He allowed her to take his hand and lead him around the building looking at all the decorations, but didn't make a comment. They were standing in front of the stable scene just as the photo-electric cell turned the spot lights on. Hillary was silent with emotion as the change brought the plywood people to apparent life. The lights picked up the moisture in the air, giving the scene an ethereal quality. Hillary stood silently with her own thoughts and realized that Pete was standing silently also, and she was wondering what his thoughts were. She turned and looked up into his face and noticed the smile on his lips. He looked down at Hillary and said simply, "The baby Jesus."

Pete was quietly watching the television when Hillary kissed him goodbye, telling him again that she was going by to see Jane and would see him tomorrow. It was completely dark when she came back to her car in the well-lighted parking lot. After several mild days it was turning very cold again. Hillary wouldn't be surprised if the temperature fell back down to the freezing level again tonght. She had already brought in all her plants from her patio when the early snowfall surprised them all. Wouldn't it be thrilling to have a white Christmas, she thought. An almost unheard-of event in Waco, or any place in central Texas. Smiling at the prospect, however slight, of a white Christmas, Hillary drove happily to the hospital.

CHAPTER 9

Her happy mood vanished immediately when Hillary walked into Jane's hospital room. Jane's color was still very pale and she was obviously in a lot of pain. Bruce and Chrissy were sitting awkwardly in the two guest chairs as if they didn't know what to say or what to do with their hands. All three brightened as Hillary walked into the room, a break in the tension, she determined.

"Well, what's new since this morning?" she asked on a positive note.

"What's new?" repeated Jane in a quarrelsome tone. "My hip is still broken, but of course that's not new. And now it's Laura Ashley prints. Honestly, Hillary, do I look like Laura Ashley prints?"

Hillary honestly did not think Jane was the floral print type, but yet she and Max had bought the colonial mansion and decorated it very appropriately in patterns of that period. Some of these might be akin to the Laura Ashley collection. She glanced at Bruce, who was squirming very uncomfortably, and at Chrissy, who looked as if she might cry, guessing that they had come here full of plans to re-do the maid's room and found that Jane was not yet receptive.

"I don't know about floral prints," she said neutrally, "but what I do know is that you're having so much pain right now that you wouldn't even like your favorite color or pattern, isn't that right?" Jane's eyes sparkled with tears as she nodded. "Let's call your nurse. Who's on tonight? Is it Nakesha?" She pressed the nurse call button and made the request.

The tall, handsome black nurse walked with a grace of motion that made one think of a ballerina. Actually she had been a terrific high school and college basketball player before entering nursing. Jane had been one of her first coaches, and it was obvious that Nakesha idolized her patient. "Mrs. Westerman, do you know you haven't had a shot since this morning? You shouldn't go that long. You need some relief, sweet angel. Isn't that true, Mrs. Johnson?" She injected the medicine into Jane's deltoid muscle as she continued her gentle scolding. "This old pain will just sneak up on you and make you grumpy or teary until you're so miserable you don't know what to do. You can have this shot every four hours if you need it, but you have to ask for it. Now don't you think you've got to be some kind of hero and go without your pain shots."

Nakesha gently rubbed the injection site with the alcohol pad and told Jane that she would be back in a little while to change her position and give her a backrub. Then she would tuck her in for the night. Hillary stayed for only a few more minutes, until she could see that Jane was beginning to relax. Bruce and Chrissy sat silently waiting for Jane to doze off before slipping out.

Hillary was going to see Jane anyway, even though she had secretly been dreading the visit all morning. Last night had been hard on all those involved and she wasn't relishing a repeat of that performance. The elevator door opened and Hillary didn't see anyone in the halls that she knew. She walked down the long hospital corridor toward Jane's room, and even before she reached the room she could hear the commotion, apparently coming from that room. Her step quickened and her pulse began to speed up.

Opening the door to Jane's room, Hillary could not believe what was going on inside. Jane and Sharon were laughing at something the orthopedic surgeon had been telling them. The color was back in Jane's face and her hair had been combed and braided. A little makeup was noticeable on her lips and around her eyes. Hillary let out her breath, not realizing that she had been holding it, as if preparing for some tragedy.

Jane was animated. "Hill, let me tell you what we've just learned, it's just wonderful news. No, doctor, you tell her. I didn't really understand it all and she knows about those things. Then if I have questions later, she can explain it to me again."

"Mrs. Johnson," the young doctor began, "nice to see you again. Your son-in-law, Tom, is one of my best friends. Or worst enemies, maybe. He beats my socks off at racquetball at least once a week."

The surgeon waited till Hillary settled herself into the other guest chair before he started. Hillary once again appreciated his relaxed bedside manner and willingness to explain procedures so that everyone more or less understood.

"When we took the initial x-rays of Mrs. Westerman's hip fracture, I couldn't see any apparent pathology that might have caused the fracture or made the neck of the femur so weak that it would break. I felt that we should check her bone density to be sure there was no pathlogical reason for the fracture. You're familiar with that procedure, aren't you, Mrs. Johnson?"

"Yes, sort of," Hillary answered.

"We got really good pictures and I saw no evidence of bone disease, very slight osteoporosis. I believe Mrs. Westerman has very good bone density. In fact, few women her age are so fortunate. This hip should heal just fine, barring any unforeseen complications. We always have to add our disclaimer, you know." He grinned at Jane. "We'll try to get you back on the basketball court one of these days."

No one said anything for a few moments, each thinking her own thoughts. Even after the doctor had gone, the three women had little to say and just sat with a smile on their faces. "I don't know whether to laugh or cry," said Sharon, wiping her nose and eyes with a tissue.

"Oh, dear." Jane suddenly remembered the previous night. "I was such a witch with the kids last night. Hillary, would you go over and make peace for me? You do that so well and I'm such a klutz. Tell them that I'll be fine and that I'm real excited about their plans for my new bedroom. I don't want to know any more about it. I'd just like to be surprised, okay? That will give them carte blanche and they need that." Jane was looking at Hillary with all the humility and pleading she could muster.

"Hey, I forgot to give you my gift," Sharon interrupted. "Just look what I have here. I'd better try it out myself first." She reached into her paper bag and brought out a basketball ring which fastened onto the closet door by suction cups and half a dozen bright pink basketballs which were almost lighter than air. Sharon stepped back to an imaginary free throw line and expertly imitated the professionals, lobbing each of the six pink basketballs at the ring, sinking not a single one.

Jane laughed harder with each missed throw and begged for her own turn. Her distance was slightly farther but she did manage to sink two of the six. "My nurses are going to hate me if I put on my call light just to have them pick up my basketballs." They each chuckled at the prospect, knowing Jane would not do that to her nurses.

Driving home, Hillary was much happier than she had been when approaching the hospital earlier. Jane was remarkable, and her first concern was that she had hurt the feelings of her son and his wife while she was in so much pain the night before. Hillary appreciated that.

When she pulled into the circular drive in front of the colonial home, Hillary realized that she would be going to the front door and ringing the bell, something she had never done. All Jane's good friends drove to the back of the house and came into the kitchen calling for Jane. Usually Maria was in the kitchen with wonderful aromas emanating from various pots on the stove. A kitchen that made memories, Hillary realized. In fact, the whole house had lots of happy memories attached to it.

Chrissy answered the doorbell promptly and was obviously surprised to see Hillary standing there. Her face showed that she feared bad news, so Hillary quickly said, "I've brought a message from Jane and some good news. Her tests looked very good and she should heal fine."

Chrissy recovered visibly and invited Hillary to come into the living room, which was strewn with fabric and wallpaper sample books. "Excuse my mess, Mrs. Johnson. I've been through these books over and over and I thought I had a plan developing, you know, a color scheme and some coordinating patterns." She warmed to her subject and began to describe certain florals, stripes, or plaids in the same color family that were called companion patterns. "For instance, look at this collection, see, the wallpaper is a subtle stripe, almost tailored-looking except for that soft string of flowers running between the stripes. Now here is the companion border with the same colors, only the flowers are a little more prominent. And over here are some solid fabrics and paint chips that will pick up the colors in the paper. Someplace under here..." She began moving books and fabrics until she found the carpet samples.

Chrissy was more animated than Hillary had ever seen her. "Now look, Mrs. Johnson, see what happens when I take one color out of the pattern and emphasize it? Here is the teal blue, or we could emphasize the forest green because there is a lot of it in the foliage." Chrissy was shuffling samples as fast and skillfully as a domino player might shuffle his dominoes. "Now look what happens when we pick up the lighter colors; see this maize? It's not really yellow it's so soft, almost a golden beige." The results brought an entirely different look.

"I'm astonished. These are simply beautiful. I had no idea you were this talented." Hillary applauded. "Where in the world did you learn to do this?"

Chrissy glowed with this praise coming from one whom she had always admired and had felt slightly intimidated by. "Well, I was an art major, but I'm not terribly good at oils or conventional types of art. But I've always loved colors. I respond to colors and patterns. They give me a good feelng or make me very uncomfortable. Maybe everyone feels that way, but I don't think so. Some people don't even seem to notice their surroundings. I see some pretty horrible colors and patterns thrown together sometimes. But here in this house, everything is so perfect, the colors, the furniture. I just know we won't be able to please Mother Westerman," she added sadly. "Maybe we should just call a decorator and turn the whole thing over to her."

Hillary had been surprised at the spirited conversation from Crissy, who had aways been so reserved. She didn't want to dampen her enthusiasm. "What exactly had you planned?"

"Well," Chrissy began, "what we want to do is give her a gift from *us*. We'll do the painting and pay for all the materials with our own money. I know she could have the best designers in town, but then it wouldn't be from us," she finished sadly. "We owe her so much."

"It seems to me, Chrissy, that you have an excellent eye for color and pattern." Hillary still had several samples in her hand. "Yes, it's true that Jane could have the best designers if she wanted them. She did use some very famous names when she and Max re-did this beautiful old house." She remembered the labor of love that transformed a neglected old mansion into the beauty it now is. "Bruce was just a little guy and always into everything." Hillary smiled at the memories. "Now let's get back to the point. You're right, it would be a lovely present for you and Bruce, and the children too, if you can include them somehow. Let me suggest one thing. Make your plan and when you go to the drapery or carpet supplier, you'll find that many of them have a decorator on staff and they can give you some suggestions without any extra cost. They might even save you money or suggest something that hadn't occurred to you that you might really like."

Chrissy thought it over quickly and jumped to her feet. "Oh, Mrs. Johnson, that's a great idea. You're right, I've seen them at the stores but I wasn't quite sure what they did and I was really scared that they would cost a lot of money. I didn't know they worked free."

On Hillary's next visit with Jane, she planted the idea that Jane was in for a good surprise and her daughter-in-law was an amazing woman. She wouldn't elaborate on the subject and left Jane pondering happy thoughts.

CHAPTER 10

Christmas Day came with little fanfare. Hillary dressed early and went across town to Elizabeth's home. She knew to be early because a couple of her favorite boys would be awake and agitating to open gifts. She kept trying to shed her feeling of... sadness? despair? anti-climax? Whatever the feeling was, it usually went away with counting her blessings, making a plan, doing a kind deed. And today of all days she couldn't be sad. She must remember that this was the birthday of the Savior and all the ramifications of that wonderful thought.

Hillary was singing along with the radio rendition of "The Little Drummer Boy" when she drove up in the driveway of Tom and Elizabeth's lovely home. "Pa rum pa pom pom," she sang happily at the top of her voice, feeling the familiar Christmas spirit washing over her. Before she could tap on the horn, her usual code meaning, "Boys, come out and help me with my things," the door flew open and both Greg and Damion rushed to her car, talking at the same time. They carefully picked up the packages and the tray of hot cinnamon rolls she had prepared for the brunch that she would share with her daughter's family before going on to the nursing home to have a big Christmas dinner with Pete.

The gifts were tasteful but not lavish. Elizabeth, or was it Tom, perhaps, had an uncanny knack for fitting a gift to the recipient. Most of the family gifts were ski gear, and the boys were full of their plans to burn up the slopes.

After brunch was finished and washed up, Hillary gathered her gifts and those for Pete. The boys again helped her pack the car. She hugged them all, thanking them for all the nice things. Being the mother she was, she also had to warn them not to get injured, do their warming-up exercises, and not tackle a slope too challenging the first couple of days.

Tom and the boys nodded and smiled, as she expected. Elizabeth, as she expected, just couldn't let it go and said, "Really, Mother, this isn't exactly our first ski trip. Don't you think we've learned anything?"

Hillary grinned her impish smile and said, "Just doing my job." Tom laughed out loud as he opened the car door for her and gave her a kiss on the cheek.

"Tell Dad we love him."

What a great son-in-law, Hillary reminded herself for about the millionth time. *And those boys are so considerate. Elizabeth is a very lucky woman. No, that's not fair. Elizabeth is a very special person, too. Are we in competition?* she wondered. *She always takes offense at anything I say. But then maybe I do bait her and cause her to overreact. Yes, maybe I do. Wonder what she would do if I quit, and maybe agreed with her. Especially when she's on her high horse and saying outlandish things.* She knew that Elizabeth was only defensive with her and not with her friends and family. *Dear God, maybe it is me*, Hillary admitted.

Christmas dinner at the Four Seasons was the expected turkey, dressing, and cranberry sauce. As usual Hillary led the conversation with Pete, not expecting him to carry his end. She exclaimed over his gifts of robe and a Texas Rangers book. She told him what a nice morning she had had with the kids, stressing their names and certain things about each one. Pete had tried to be attentive to the conversation, nodding and sometimes smiling when he thought it appropriate. But mid-afternoon he left the sunny dayroom, walked back to his bedroom as if Hillary were not there and stretched out on his bed for a nap. She didn't know what to do. If she followed him back to his room he might feel uncomfortable with that stranger watching him while he tried to sleep. If she went home, Lady would be happy to see her but it would be a long, melancholy day and she felt a great need to be around people.

Pedro's family was coming in a couple of days, but the house was clean and she didn't feel like starting the baking this early. She wouldn't go back to Elizabeth's because she knew they were busy with their packing for the ski trip. She might go see Jane at the hospital, but if her family were there she'd feel like an interloper. She began to wonder what Sharon was doing.

Hillary left the nursing home, walked out to take another look at the nativity scene for a few minutes and climbed into her car. It wasn't quite three o'clock and she felt genuinely lonely but not wanting to impose her company on anyone. The truth, she admitted, she didn't want just anyone's company either. *Maybe Sharon is at home alone and would welcome a kindred spirit.*

The drive along the bluff overlooking the lake was always thrilling to Hillary. How nice it would be to live up here and have this fabulous view. Sharon's home was narrow with a high profile and every detail from the landscaping to the brass hardware were beautiful and tasteful.

Just as Hillary rang the doorbell, the automatic garage door opened and she walked around to the side hallooing so that Sharon would hear her. At first Sharon didn't hear, as she was busy backing toward the street, looking each way for traffic along the quiet street. Just as she came even with Hillary, she slammed on the brake, all smiles, and rolled down her window.

"Well, Hillary," she said, "what brings you out this way? I thought you'd be with your kids or Pete today."

Hillary explained that she had been with her kids and with Pete until he fell asleep and now she just felt restless. "I guess that's how I was feeling. Hank and Marianne had me over for Christmas dinner and it was great. All their kids and grandchildren were there. They're all so goodlooking and always so sweet to me. I really do enjoy them, but after we ate and visited some more I started feeling kind of antsy. Wanta go out to the stables with me? I wasn't planning on riding, just talking to Major, maybe let him exercise in the big pen."

"Yes, I'd love it. I haven't seen Queen for days. Hope she isn't mad at me. Why don't I drive my own car and then I can just go on home afterward?"

"Oh, please don't. I'd really enjoy your company. When we get back we could have a glass of Christmas cheer or something. I bought this bottle of sparkling apple juice in case we had a reason to celebrate. However, I don't think I'll ever be hungry again in my life after that feast," Sharon laughed.

Hillary climbed into the Suburban, chatting gaily about the gifts, the children, the meal, and Sharon returned the chatter in like manner. When they got to the stables, their respective horses whinnied an unmistakable welcome.

The mare and gelding were happy to be out of their cramped stalls and knew they were headed for the big pen and relative freedom. Both were dancing an excited sidestep, heads high and tails flowing in the wind. When the lead ropes were released from their halters, the big gelding and the portly mare, both gentle and well-trained, became colts again, bucking and rearing and racing around the enclosure. Hillary and Sharon laughed at their antics, thanking their lucky stars that the horses didn't perform those same tricks under saddle, especially with them aboard.

"How are Hank and Marianne doing?" Hillary wanted to know. It seemed to her that it was awfully unfair after twenty years doing developments, not one of which was poorly planned or executed, that the banks called his loans and didn't even honor commitments they had given. She knew she hadn't understood the whole economy thing, but so many of her friends had been hurt through no wrong-doing on their part that she had wondered if that was the beginning of another Great Depression. She recalled these times and mentioned this to Sharon. "People who've been developing or running a bank or savings association successfully for twenty or thirty years can't, all of a sudden, become bad managers, can they? But they were discredited as if they were actual criminals it seems to me."

"I certainly agree with you and I'm thankful things have changed, somewhat, though some have been hurt so bad they'll never recoup. But as for Hank, I think he's doing pretty well, considering." She laughed remembering the animated conversation she had had with Hank just that morning. "He laughed when he told me how he had decided that he wasn't just going to sit around feeling sorry for himself, and had gone to the owner of his former chief competitor and asked for a job. He got hired right away and ever since then he's been managing some big development for the Walsham Company out of state, and when this one's done he's going down to Florida to do the next one. He says his salary is okay, but he's also going to get a bonus when the project is completed. Sounds like a happy man to me. Except that Marianne is here and not with him."

"Is Marianne going to stay on with the library?" Hillary asked.

"She says she is. When I asked her the same question, she actually lit up and admitted that she enjoys working more than she had ever imagined she would. She even said that if she works for a certain number of years, she would be entitled to a small retirement and mentioned some other benefits, especially insurance and savings. I think she's going to do it."

"Looks like there's a happy ending in the making for them. I sincerely hope that will be the case with the Williamsons. I took them one of my pumpkin bread loaves last night and they were all smiles and seemed to be optimistic. Now that Dan's become manager of the country club, he seems to like it very well. Still he couldn't help talking about the closing of the bank and that there was nothing he could have done about it. He still feels personally responsible for its failure and for the loss of so many people's investments. He even told me again that maybe Pete is the lucky one, not knowing what was happening. Also that I was wise when I sold my bank stock while it still had a good value." Hillary shrugged. "It didn't have anything to do with wisdom, though. I just needed the money."

The horses had stopped their playing and ambled back toward the two women to have their heads patted and get the attention they knew to expect. The breeze was picking up and the sun had gone behind a cloud, causing both Sharon and Hillary to shiver in spite of their warm coats.

Walking back toward the horses' stalls, both Major and Queen noticed that it was feeding time, and Roy had already started whistling and banging buckets, going from stall to stall calling each horse by his name. Sharon and Hillary knew that they were playing second fiddle to Roy at this hour of the day and happily took the halters off their horses and left them feeding on grain and alfalfa hay.

The cold wind and the outing with their horses left the women feeling exhilarated and very happy to return to the warmth of Sharon's living room. The fire in the fireplace had dwindled to a few red coals but was quickly brought back to life with some dry twigs and small logs.

Sharon glanced at the answering machine from habit and noticed the light was blinking. "Somebody called while we were out. Let me check this message and then I'll make us something hot to drink."

She pressed the button to replay the message and heard Jane's voice sounding very strained saying, "If you're not out too late, will you please give me a call or come by if you can. I'm feeling so lonely and so sick of these dadgummed Christmas specials on TV. The nurse said I could have company as late as I wanted since it's Christmas. I don't know where Hillary is, but I'm leaving the same message on her recorder."

They laughed when they heard Jane's call for help, and both understood completely. "Let's take our bottle of sparkling juice and a thermos of hot spiced cider," Sharon planned.

"And let's take the cards, too. I feel lucky," Hillary added.

Within half an hour the two were on their way up to the orthopedic floor with their party packed neatly in a carrying case. They found Jane up in her wheelchair and saw that she had tossed all her basketballs at the hoop and wasn't interested in retrieving them.

"Ho, ho, ho," Sharon said as she arranged her treats on the bedside table. "If you've been a very good girl we're going to ply you with juice and then beat your socks off at three-man bridge."

Hillary was giving Jane a big hug and then Sharon gave her a hug with a kiss on the cheek. "You can't imagine how glad I am to see you. I've been furious with myself for all this self-pity," she murmured. "The kids came by but then went over to Chrissy's parents for a late dinner, and after that it was so boring around this hospital that I felt like screaming or crying or something." Her brown eyes flashed their challenge. "You don't have a chance of beating me tonight. I've done nothing for days but plan my strategy. I'm going to be plenty tough," she bragged. "But first, how about that celebration? I've got some paper cups over there."

"No way are we going to use paper cups on Christmas," Sharon answered. She pulled out her plastic champagne stems and skillfully twisted the two pieces together and poured a glass for Jane and herself. "Hillary, what are you having? How about the spiced cider in a champagne flute?"

"Perfect," said Hillary, reaching for her glass. "How about a toast?" And they each offered a toast that they had heard given at one time or another. Then they made up their own version of toasts that should be given, trying to make them rhyme. Finally they had gotten so silly with their toasts and laughing that the charge nurse came in to see if everything was okay.

"My shift will be over soon and I'm not trying to pour cold water on your party, but I heard your laughing clear down at the other end of the unit and there may be patients who want to sleep tonight. Or join the party." She laughed at this preposterous idea.

"Knock, knock. Is this a private party, or can anyone join?"

"Hello, Dr. Fields, and Merry Christmas. Maybe you can control this rambunctious party. I'll be leaving here soon." The nurse smiled at the merry group as she gently shut the door.

"Julian, what brings you out on Christmas?" Jane was the first to ask. "Can you have a glass of sparkling apple juice with us?"

"Sure. I'm off duty. Actually I didn't even have the duty, but I was curious about some labs and came on over to check them." Sharon handed him a plastic flute filled with the bubbly juice.

"We've been toasting the season, the New Year, and everything else we could think of," Jane explained. "Do you have any good toasts you can offer? Or maybe some funny medical stories?"

Julian settled himself into a comfortable chair and leaned back, his long legs crossed at the ankle, his hands clasped together over his portly middle holding his glass. He put on his mock-serious expression they had all seen so many times. "Well, I will certainly wish you all your hearts' desire for this holiday season and for the coming year."

He lifted his glass and they each took a sip of drink as he continued. "But so far as funny medical stories, you see, I have a long-standing policy not to joke about such a serious profession." His eyes twinkled and the women knew they were in for a good story. He paused for the dramatic effect he needed and then proceeded in his deep James Earl Jones voice.

"Years ago, when I was doing my residency and pretty full of myself, way before I met Jasmine and before I became the modest person I now am..." He paused for this point to sink in. Jane rolled her eyes while Hillary and Sharon smiled expectantly. "I was doing a rotation in a public health clinic, delivering babies and taking care of young mothers with new babies, most of them young teenagers and unmarried. I delivered some twins, boy and girl, for a young mother and she wanted me to name them. She specifically wanted a very feminine name for the girl and a very masculine name for the boy."

Julian looked upward toward heaven in a contrite manner. "And now, because of my flippant approach to my calling, there are a couple of young adults out there saddled with the names Fallopia and Epididymus." The women howled with laughter and Julian could not keep a straight face. What a good Christmas the day had become.

Sometime after midnight Sharon and Hillary left Jane tucked in for a good night's sleep, all happy and tired. Hillary drove home to an expectant Lady wanting attention first and her supper next.

Pedro and his family drove into Waco late on the twenty-seventh, and Hillary's house became alive with activity and interesting aromas from the kitchen. His wife, Patty, was bouncy and pert, always fighting one diet or another with little success. She was an excellent cook and protective mother. Her family pretended to ignore all her admonishing but adored her in return. Patty clearly loved Hillary, and the two of them spent long periods talking in the kitchen, in the bedrooms, in the garden, exchanging ideas on their favorite subject, their home and family. Hillary was always amazed how alike they thought. She could not have had a daughter any more like herself than Patty. Once again she wondered how her daughter could be so different in every way. No, not every way, Elizabeth adored her family. That was the common thread that kept them all tied together.

Hillary was pleased that neither of the young women in family had needed to work outside their home, or do their own thing, to find themselves, or whatever the buzz words were today. They seemed to be happiest doing things that supported their loved ones as well as themselves. Team players. And look how those teams had flourished, she recounted. Patty's Jason and Patrice seemed to excel in all their school activities, both good students as well as athletes. And just look at them, she chided herself for being such a typical grandmother. There were never two more handsome teenagers. Patrice was becoming a real beauty, which might cause some anxiety. Funny how we wish our daughters to be beautiful and then worry that it will get them into trouble. But for now they were just wholesome kids. Of course they were loud, and did a lot of good-natured teasing. But never any whining or meanness.

The visit seemed to fly by with visiting Pete at the Four Seasons each day. They managed a couple of visits to Jane at the hospital, and Hillary took the kids to ride Queen one sunny afternoon while their parents went around town visiting old school friends.

And then they were gone. They begged Hillary once again to come and spend a week with them, or longer if she would. She agreed that it would be a real treat, knowing that it would never happen, at least in the near future.

For the next few days Hillary was busy catching up on news with Jane and Sharon. Jane was doing well in therapy and feeling pleased with herself. Sharon was immersed in Partners and her precious charges.

Hillary stopped by to see Chrissy and offer her any assistance with the conversion of the maid's room. The progress since her last visit was amazing. The walls were painted a deep shade of teal blue and Chrissy was busy painting the woodwork an off-white. "The carpet is going to be almost this shade of off-white," she explained to Hillary. "Only it's going to be just a little darker. You know how practical Mother Westerman is. She might not like a real white carpet." She was clearly enjoying this labor of love.

After complimenting and encouraging Chrissy, Hillary visited the hospital and gave Jane a report on the re-decorating activities without giving away any of Chrissy's secrets. Jane, finally, was beginning to look forward to her discharge and getting on with her life. She had never thought about going home while she was still in a lot of pain and so very incapacitated. But now her pain was subsiding and she could walk slowly but confidently on her walker. "Do you have any idea when the doctor will discharge you?" Hillary asked.

"He mentioned Monday but the kids said I'll have to wait till Wednesday for something-or-other to get installed and that's okay. I'll still have to come back for therapy several times a week." Jane looked wistful. "You know what I really miss?"

"Yes, I think so," Hillary answered immediately. "Playing your piano. First you're going to play it mellow and lovingly. Then you're going to play it fast and playfully, then you'll play it loud and boisterously. At least that's what I'd do if I were you," she added happily.

Jane laughed as though Hillary had read her mind. "You know, sometimes you're downright spooky. Especially when you say the things that I was about to say."

Their visit was pleasant and up-beat. Happy plans were being made and Jane's mood was expectant. Hillary duly noted the change in Jane's outlook as a professional would and was pleased that she had come along so well, with no apparent complications and set-backs. How nice it would be to have her back home and resume their bridge parties and listen to Jane play her concert grand piano.

CHAPTER 11

For the first time in television history the TV special would feature a major tap-dancing star sharing his billing with an aging matron. The two of them practiced several hours each morning preparing for the special coming up next month. Then it would be shown in the early spring. Hillary wondered what Pete would think if he saw it on his TV. Would he even recognize her? Would he wonder what she was doing with that multi-talented Gregory Hines? Would he even know Gregory Hines?

Rehearsals were very taxing and Hillary was learning more than she ever dreamed about tap-dancing. Mr. Hines was a perfect gentleman, even though he could dance circles around her, and frequently did. He was both teacher and supporter and Hillary admired him more each day.

The van ran the stop sign on Hillary's right, speeding past the front of her car, just barely swerving to avoid a collision and continued on at the same accelerating speed. Hillary jammed on the brakes, causing her car to stop suddenly, sliding sideways. She came to a stop in the wrong lane of the intersection.

For a few seconds she was totally disoriented and aware of her heart pounding violently. Cars were stopped at each stop sign of the four-way stop intersection and it looked as though the drivers were all staring right at her. What had happened and why was she out here on the wrong side of the street? A man she had never seen knocked on her window and said, "Lady, are you okay? I saw what that jerk did. You want me to call the police?"

Hillary shook her head, trying to get her bearings. Then she turned down the street toward which the car was heading and turned off into the parking lot of an office building until she quit shaking.

When Hillary's shaking had stopped, she remembered her interrupted fantasy and began to laugh. *Well, so much for my fame and fortune,* she told herself. She'd go right out to the Four Seasons and tell Pete about her day. Maybe he wouldn't understand a word of it, but then maybe he would. This was a question Hillary debated frequently and always concluded that Pete might actually understand more than he was able to acknowledge. And just as important was the fact that she needed to verbalize her thoughts to him. Besides, who would benefit from her sitting around silently waiting for him to show some sign of understanding or interest in her presence?

The day of Jane's homecoming was cold and clear. Hillary was in a state of excitement preparing one of her special cakes for the occasion. She knew Bruce and Chrissy had planned to pick her up at the hospital mid-morning and then she would need lunch. Then, of course, Hillary should allow a couple of hours for her to nap and rest or just spend time with her family. It was hard for her to wait till four o'clock in the afternoon to take her pretty strawberry cake over to the Westermans'.

Hillary knocked twice on the back door and went onto the utility porch and then into the kitchen. "Come on in," said a voice from inside the house. Laughter was coming from the former maid's room, which she realized would now have to be re-named. Hillary put down her cake on the kitchen counter and turned down the hall to the left.

"Hill, where have you been? I've been looking for you all day." Jane was flushed with the excitement of being home and having her friends around her. Martha Lodge and Sharon had already arrived and were equally excited to have Jane back home again. Martha got up out of the newly reupholstered Boston rocker and moved over to sit with Sharon on the newly slip-covered love seat.

Hillary gave Jane an affectionate hug and greeted Martha and Sharon. "Would you look at this room! How beautifully everything went together. Bruce and Chrissy did a very professional job on all this."

Jane glowed. "The children told me they helped, too. You should see the bathroom, Hillary. They thought of everything." While Hillary peeked into the bathroom, Jane continued, "They put a raised seat on the commode, a waterproof stool in the shower and a hand-held shower spray for me to use. How could they know about all those things?" When Hillary said nothing, Jane quizzed, "I'll bet they talked to some nurse about what I might need in my sickroom." Hillary still said nothing, just smiled and continued to look around the large bedroom for all the personal touches Chrissy had provided. There was a wooden bed tray that Chrissy had found in a re-sale store, sanded and repainted a pearl white, smooth as satin.

There were subtle patterns scattered around the room, all in harmonizing colors, yet no clashing of patterns because the large areas were decorated in solid colors, walls and bedspread. The coverlet was a white matelasse with a vivid plaid bedskirt that had matching pillows and bolsters, which were now behind Jane's back. "This is certainly no sissy bedroom," Jane declared. "Even though those are definitely Laura Ashley floral prints." She looked toward the rocker cushions. "I was really an ass that night, Hillary, and the kids have never even mentioned it again. They've been great." The women began to talk at once, asking and answering questions, laughing a lot. Hillary remembered the cake and, sniffing the air, realized that fresh coffee had already been brewed in the kitchen, and with Sharon close behind trailed off to the kitchen to bring coffee and cake for the four of them.

In less than an hour Hillary noticed that Jane had gotten quieter and recognized that her friend was beginning to tire. She gathered up her things and promised to come back by tomorrow after her stint at the hospital. Hillary promised to call first to see if Jane needed anything from the store. Backing out of the driveway, Hillary was once again surprised at the grandeur of the front porch, the columns so large that two people could barely reach around them, the grass so smooth, the evergreens neatly manicured, a perfect border for the winter-brown lawn. Martha and Sharon were coming out the front door to their cars. All waved and continued home to their silent houses—no children, no husband, just the pets and the lives they were each trying to carve out for themselves to fill the rest of their days.

It was late January before Jane felt up to a game of bridge at Hillary's house. Sharon drove by to pick up Jane and her walker. The day was not cold, merely cool, as if the calendar should show October rather than January. In fact, Sharon felt excitement much like late evenings before a football game, a feeling of happy expectation, as she picked up her special passenger and chauffeured her to the familiar neighborhood where the Johnsons had lived for over twenty years.

Lady was exuberant, as usual, to see her old friends. She was cautious with the walker, not quite sure what the strange metal contraption was that her dear person was attached to. Sharon walked nearby to balance Jane if she should need assistance, and she wasn't quite sure what Lady might do. Even a good-natured nudge might put Jane off balance, but Lady, as if she understood that things had changed somehow, waited until Jane was seated and then forced her black head under Jane's hand to get her deserved and expected attention.

The bridge game was short, just one party rubber, and then Hillary brought out a tasty dessert that she was famous for. Jane asked about all their friends, catching up on the news and gossip. She asked about Queen and Major and whether they had been ridden lately in the cold weather. Hillary didn't get the tap-dancing music out, sensing that Jane was not quite ready to play rock and roll. The three women were comfortable with one another and happy to have their bridge ritual resumed. The comfort of habit, routine, or ritual was very important to the older women who had had a large part of their lives taken away and left them trying very hard to fill the void.

CHAPTER 12

Sharon arrived at Partners on the north side mid-afternoon. The school children would already have been delivered, she realized, and knew that she would see her special young friend, Tony. It was collection day—actually the first of three collection days. She had set a policy of collecting fees on the first Monday of the month, whatever the date, and she would accept the fees through Wednesday. However, if the fees were not paid by the time the child was picked up on Wednesday, he would not be accepted on Thursday.

Sharon had been tested on this policy more than once by parents who had sent their child by a neighbor or older sibling who complained they didn't have the money to pay the monthly fee. Sharon had been firm even when the other person became loudly belligerent, shouting that they had to go to their job or to school and who was going to take care of the child? She was able to keep control of her temper, not arguing the point but stating clearly that she was not a welfare agency and much as she loved the children, she could not stay in business unless she operated Partners in a business-like manner. Before long the word got around and the parents were only too happy to pay their fees early in the month, especially when they became aware that the daycare center was full and could not accept more children unless someone dropped out.

Sharon locked up the Suburban and with her bank bag started up the sidewalk. She felt a surge of pride and thankfulness every time she drove up in front of the red barn with the western motif they had adopted. And this center was equally as well-staffed and furnished as the one on the affluent side of town. Fees were less here than over there simply because the real estate had cost so much less.

When she opened the front door Sharon immediately sensed that something was wrong. Several children were crying, not a hurt cry, more of a scared cry. What would they be afraid of? she wondered. Then she heard the tough voice say, "Shut up, you kids, or I'll just break your nannie's arm! You, over there, quit your squalling and get me that money. See this knife? Don't think

I won't use it, now hurry up!" Another child started crying loudly, causing the others to start up again.

Sharon felt the anger flare up inside her. She knew she could attack and overpower the man with this surge of adrenalin, but he had a knife and apparently was holding either Rosa or Mae Helen hostage, or maybe one of the high school girls who helped in the afternoons. She couldn't tell which he had, and he was badgering one of the others to get the money. Thank God that it was so noisy there in the large room; no one could have heard her come in, and her presence would not jeopardize the safety of those in the other room.

Looking around the room for a weapon, Sharon studied the western furniture, western coat rack, western regalia mounted on the wall, and quickly made her decision. She lifted the stiff lariat rope from a hook on the coat rack and quietly released the cattle prod, frequently called a hotshot, from its holder on the wall, knowing it had no batteries but hoping the young hoodlum would not know it had no batteries. Crying in the next room reached a new crescendo, and Sharon recognized that it was in part coming from Mae Helen, the older woman who had been so faithful to Sharon and the children. The little punk must be hurting her.

Sharon shook out a loop, thankful for the high ceilings in the great room and for the two pillars holding up the ceiling which she would need for snubbing quickly, as soon as the rope settled around the young man's shoulders. She prayed he would not be facing the door when she made her move, as she desperately needed the element of surprise. She listened for his voice, hoping she could determine which way he was facing.

Suddenly she knew she had her chance when he turned around to the back of the room and bellowed at a child. One of the pillars was between them, which helped hide her from view. Just as the boy turned back to the women, he was startled by a rope flying toward him and he tried to jump out of the way. But too late, he was caught, one arm pinned down to his side and with the free arm tried to cut through the rope with his switchblade. The lariat was too strong and before the blade slashed all the way through, Sharon jerked him off balance and had made her second wrap around the pillar, this time catching his free arm and forcing the blade from his grasp.

Panicky, he began to shout, "Let me go! Let me go! I was only joking!" Sharon tied a knot through the wraps so that she could let the rope go and check on injuries.

For the first time Sharon realized that her robber was only a boy, although he was tall and heavily muscled, late teens, maybe. He was still begging to be released, but the women ignored him, turning their attention to the children who were no longer crying but happily amused with the turn of events. This was a real adventure.

"Okay, boys and girls, this is what we must do. We have a robber here and we have to turn him over to the police." The boy yelled louder. The children began to cheer. "We're going to call the police. Rosa, I want you to call 911 and tell them what happened. Tell the police to meet us on Waco Drive."

"But, *Senora*, Waco Drive is many blocks away." She laughed. "Ah, *si*! Many blocks away."

"Now you big kids, Tony, you and your classmates, we need two signs to put on our robber, one for the front and one for the back. They need to say something like 'I'm a tough guy. I rob kids.'" Sharon found a jump rope and tied the boy's hands behind his back, then carefully unwound the lariat from the pillar, making several wraps around the boy's shoulders and all the way to his waist, leaving enough rope for Sharon to drive him from behind. When he started to pull away a quick jerk from Sharon put him on the floor. She stood over him with her foot on his chest, brandishing the hot shot. "See this," she said in almost a whisper. "It's called a hot shot because it is very, very hot. It might even burn a hole through your clothes and your skin."

"Miz Sharon, Miz Sharon, how many 'f's' in tough? One or two?" Tony wanted to know.

She thought quickly. "Two, yes, definitely two."

The signs, reading, "TUFF GUY. I ROB KIDS" were hung with cord and placed front and back of the squirming, yelling young criminal. "You can't do this to me. It's unusual cruelty. I want a lawyer," he continued to scream.

"Listen, punk. I'm not the police. We're your victims, see, and victims have rights, too, you know. Anything we do will be self-defense. The police will read you your rights and let you get a lawyer; that is, if there's anything left when we get through with you." He quit threatening and went back to pleading.

"Mae Helen, I want you and the big girls to stay here with all the smaller children." Protests were loud, begging to go with the group to turn in the robber. "I want the school kids to hold hands and follow Rosa behind me. Can you do that? Yes, that includes the kindergartners, if you're big enough to follow instructions. Mae Helen, I want you to call the TV stations and tell them where we're going to meet the police." She turned to the children who had already taken the hand of a smaller or older child. All were ready for the parade down the street to Waco Drive.

The group followed Sharon and her captive out the door and fell in line on the sidewalk. She had never felt so strong and in control, righteous indignation, she admitted. How close they were to an entirely different outcome she didn't know or even want to think about. She kept threatening the deadly hotshot, which, in fact, was harmless without its batteries.

The street was residential and children and parents came out of their houses to see what was happening. When they realized what had transpired they joined the parade, also taunting the "tough guy."

On the third block a woman sweeping her sidewalk looked up when she heard the noisy group approaching. "James!" She flew toward the prisoner with her broom in the air. "James, now what have you gotten into?" She began beating him on the shoulders with the broom. "Here I work at two jobs so you can go to school, and now look at you! Just look at you!"

"Mama, Mama, it was only a joke. I didn't mean any harm. Mama, don't whip me with the broom," the criminal begged, this time crying real tears.

The television truck had spotted the group coming down the street and rushed to get a scoop on the other station. Sharon was oblivious to the crowd but kept pushing and threatening her prisoner, driving him down the sidewalk toward the rendezvous with the police. Before they had reached Waco Drive, the police cars also spotted the television truck and the group they were filming. Sharon and her robber were acting as the Pied Piper, and what started out with Rosa and five schoolchildren along with four kindergartners had now turned into a crowd which included more than twenty neighborhood residents.

When Sharon had turned over her robber, promising to come by the police station to give her statement and press charges, she gathered up her children, and with Rosa made their way back to Partners in an orderly manner. She knew that she must act calm for the sake of the children but felt her insides turning to near hysteria. She took several deep breaths, and by the time she reached the red barn was more in control, knowing she would cry later.

Sharon stayed at Partners until the last child was picked up, explaining to the parents that a near tragedy was successfully turned around, that the staff and children were very brave, and that some of the children would be seen on television turning the robber over to the police.

After the last child had gone, Sharon examined Mae Helen's wounds again. The bruises had not been visible immediately but were now a vivid purple on both wrists. "My throat hurts, too, Miz Sharon. He choked me when I wouldn't give him the money. Then he put the knife under my chin and cut me a little bit. Said that's so I'd know he meant business."

"Mae Helen, we have to go to the police station to give our statement and report this. But first we need to go to the emergency room and have you examined." She held back the tears that were flooding her eyes. "If anything happened to you I don't know what I'd do."

After a thorough physical exam at the hospital and all the questions they answered at the police station, Sharon finally dropped Mae Helen back at her home near Partners and instructed her to stay at home the next day. "If Rosa's sister can't come in, then I'll just plan my day so that I can take your place." Mae Helen protested but Sharon was firm.

A light supper and a hot bath had revived Sharon's spirits, but she was still too keyed up to think of sleep. In her pajamas she watched TV and waited for the ten o'clock news to come on. Rosa had called back to say that her sister would love to work in Mae Helen's place the next day and longer, too, if she was needed.

Watching the news, Sharon sat up straight on her recliner and gasped. How clear the photography was. How vivid was her western outfit. What in the world would a stranger think seeing that older woman in a cowboy outfit driving a roped and protesting young man down the sidewalk brandishing a cattle prod, like a sword, always close but never touching him? *Oh, dear, and what will my friends think? Dear God, this looks so theatrical. At best I'll be the laughing stock of the city, maybe even ostracized from polite society. And Harvey, oh, no. Maybe Harvey won't see it. But they will probably play it again on the morning news and then he'll read me the riot act. What if they pick it up on network news?* she worried. *And maybe they'll want me on the talk shows. My life may be ruined and I will become a ridiculous caricature.*

But then Sharon remembered dear, gentle Mae Helen and the flood of righteous indignation returned, reassuring her that what she had done was the right thing, or maybe was too easy on the boy after what he had done.

Just as she had expected, the telephone began to ring. *Maybe I just won't answer,* she thought. *Why do I always get so defensive and feel that I have to justify everything with Harvey? After all, I am a grown woman. Boy, that's an understatement*, she told herself. "Hello," she finally said.

"Haw, haw, haw," a familiar deep voice came laughing through the telephone. She had been prepared to defend herself against Harvey's criticisms, but now she was caught off-guard by Charlie laughing at her. She felt her cheeks grow hot with embarrassment; of course Charlie would watch the evening news. So would everyone she knew. "Sharon, you were great," he managed to say between gales of laughter. "Really, Sharon. I loved it. Tell me, what did you say to that punk? I just caught the words, 'a two-thousand pound bull' and then the sound faded out."

Refusing to be ridiculed, Sharon answered evenly, "I think I said, 'Go ahead, make my day! This cattle prod can make a two-thousand pound bull jump a fence.'"

Trying hard to stifle his laughter, Charlie asked, "Tell me the truth, Sharon. Did the hot shot have any batteries in it?"

"Well, no," she admitted.

"Haw, haw, haw," he continued until Sharon was caught up in the infectious laughter and she began to laugh along with him.

When they finally quit laughing, Sharon said, "Oh, Charlie, I'm so embarrassed. What will people think? I want to just stay home till everyone has a chance to forget all this." She sat up straighter. "But I'm not going to. I don't want any more low-lifes terrorizing my staff and children." She continued in her righteous indignation anew.

"That's my girl," Charlie began, and then he was silent, embarrassed. She was not his girl. He wished she were. A woman like that...

Sharon was silent, too. No, she was not his girl. Anyway, how long had it been since anyone called her a "girl"? Charlie's girl. Charlie's girl. How many single women here in Waco would all but kill to be Charlie's girl?

She realized that no one had said anything in several moments and felt suddenly uncomfortable. She should break the silence and put him at his ease. "Well, thanks a lot for calling, Charlie. It really helps to know that at least one other person in the world thinks I did the right thing. I really appreciate your call." Awkwardly she chattered on and said, "Bye," before he could get in another word. Then she sat beside the phone wondering why he made her feel so inept, tongue-tied practically—and why did she hang up on him? Maybe he would have said something more—well, maybe something more personal—if she hadn't. *No, he's just big-hearted and would have called anyone and given them that kind of encouragement.*

Before she chastized herself any further, the phone rang again and it was Harvey. And he did scold her for taking such a chance, not only with the children's lives but with her own, and for pity's sake, why did she dress in such outlandish get-ups? Finally Sharon said, "Harvey, you wouldn't understand, and I'm very tired. It's been a hectic day. Thanks for worrying about me and goodnight." And again she hung up before he could say another word. She glanced at the clock and noticed it was past eleven o'clock and she was truly very tired. She turned her telephone bell to silent, knowing the answering machine would pick up her messages and she could listen to them in the morning when she was fresh. And more able to deal with them. Maybe she wouldn't answer the telephone at all for a few days and return only selected calls that she felt like answering. "I'll just think about this tomorrow," she said aloud in her most sugary Southern accent, thinking of Scarlett O'Hara.

Hillary called the next morning and was sympathetic and excited about Sharon's adventure and thankful that no one was seriously hurt. Jane also called and was incensed that a young punk would have the audacity to try and rob women. And the size of that kid! She wondered why Sharon didn't zing him with the cattle prod; after all, he certainly deserved it, a taste of his own medicine, so to speak.

"Well, if I had poked him with it, he would have known I didn't have any batteries in it, and there's no way I could have held a big guy like that. He might have really been mad, especially after we had made an example of him like we did." Sharon laughed, now comfortable with the events of the previous day.

And Jane laughed heartily, reminding Sharon of Charlie's call last night. Jane was volatile, changing from fury to a giggle to a belly laugh. "Sharon, I would never have believed all this if you hadn't told us how much time you spent throwing a rope when you were a kid. How long has it been since you've practiced this art form of yours, anyway?"

"Okay, Jane, almost a week. Now let's talk about something else. How is your hip? Have you been getting out any?"

"Yes, I have. I'm a regular social butterfly. And the nice part is that someone else has to come and get me and chauffeur me around. I never thought I'd like that, but I do. I may never drive again unless my friends get tired of me." She began to enumerate the places she had been this week already: to church, to a rehearsal of the symphony, and Martha was coming to take her to lunch at the Strawberry Patch tomorrow. The Strawberry Patch was a favorite with the women in town, and also with some businessmen who wanted a nourishing light lunch. Their specialties were crepes of many flavors, quiche, and other light meals.

The two friends said good-bye on the telephone, happily anticipating their bridge party next week at Sharon's house. Hillary would be coming by to pick up Jane and her walker for the outing.

CHAPTER 13

A stranger observing the two women having lunch together might wonder what they have in common, so different were they in their looks and bearing. The tall brunette, slightly gray but with a vivid white streak rising from her right temple, came into the restaurant on a walker, was regal and beautifully dressed in clothes that must have designer labels. She had an air of sophistication and self-assurance. One might think she would also be a formidable opponent. Or ally.

The other woman, whose hair was now totally gray, was dressed in a casual way, cardigan sweater and denim skirt. She was wearing canvas sneakers, but at least had on stockings. Her friends knew this to be her weekday uniform, although she dressed beautifully to teach on Sunday mornings, and they would have been surprised to see her in anything else. The casual observer might not even notice the kindness in her blue eyes or be aware of the strength of character that was manifest by the kindness. The thing she could do best for Jane was to make her laugh, silly little things, or self-effacing stories of bloopers she had made while pre-occupied or struck with what she called 'old-timers disease.'

Jane loved Martha and was completely at ease when they were together. After all, she told herself many times, she owed Martha her very life. How often had she thought her life was over after Max died. She had thought the old foreign tradition of throwing the widows on the funeral bier might be a good plan, a community service, so to speak. It would get the widow out of her misery and deliver the community from a whining, self-pitying old crone. She didn't actually say this in so many words.

What she actually said to Martha was her observation that God seemed to put the heaviest burdens on us when we are weak or old and the least able to deal with them.

She knew this might sound like self-pity.

Martha would never preach to Jane or suggest that she not be self-pitying. She would never say anything as thoughtless as, "Don't worry, time will take care of your grief." And maybe it would, Jane hoped, but perhaps she would go to her grave with the pain. When Max died it had only been two short years since Martha had lost her own precious husband through a slow and painful death of cancer. Because of this she knew much of what Jane felt after losing Max. She knew that many of Jane's feelings were secret and private and she would never mention them aloud.

What she said to Jane's observation about the heavy burdens caught Jane off-guard. Martha laughed and said, "Jane, that's right! Why didn't I think of that? After all I'm supposed to be something of a Bible scholar." Jane was perplexed; what had she said that would delight Martha so much? "You see, Jane, God does give us problems while we are at our weakest so that His strength will be appreciated. We get pretty cocky when we think we're solving our own problems. It even says as much in the Bible. Remember, God told Paul something like, 'My grace is sufficient for you, for my strength is made perfect in weakness.' Some versions say 'magnified' which is even more understandable." No, Jane didn't know that verse, but it was vaguely familiar. She always felt a little bit ashamed that she knew so little actual scripture.

Martha had spent a lifetime of searching the scriptures and then sharing them with her friends each Sunday in Bible Study.

Martha was no disapproving saint. She accepted her friends as they were, without judgment. How many times had Jane observed to herself that "here is a woman without guile?"

Sitting across from Martha, Jane realized she was monopolizing the conversation, telling about her therapy and explaining how she might participate in the string ensemble, even with her walker, when she heard above her own voice a string of profanity. She then realised that Martha had been squirming uncomfortably in her chair, a trait uncommon to Martha. In the interim between sentences she heard several more vile phrases, and knew that they had come from a young woman, late teens maybe, or early twenties. She turned around in her chair to see two pretty young women, probably college age, and a handsome young man with a university letter jacket sitting at the next table.

The boy and one of the girls were laughing quietly and seemed embarrassed, while the other girl kept up her string of filthy language, her volume increasing as she noticed the discomfort she was creating for diners at nearby tables. Two women at the next table stood up and left hurriedly with their meal only half-eaten.

Martha was not angry but was pale and looked terribly sad. Jane watched her carefully, fearing she was about to have a spell of some kind. Martha said quietly and firmly, "Young lady. Young lady," until she got the attention of the beautiful girl with long, silky blond hair. The girl looked surprised and turned to give Martha an insolent glare. The other girl and boy looked down at their hands in their laps. "My dear, please lower your voice. Many of us do not speak that way and are uncomfortable with such profanity."

The girl became louder than ever, hurling a new string of filthy phrases at Martha, asking her if she had never heard this was a free country. And in a free country there is freedom of speech. The beautiful girl's outburst became a crescendo, Jane felt, leading up to what? She would have spared Martha this abuse, but what could she do? The girl might be building up to some violent act. Her friends were quietly begging her to hush and asking her to leave with them. "I am not leaving here just because of some old lady. I was here first and I have freedom of speech," she emphasized again.

Jane looked away from the girl and back at Martha. Martha was sitting quietly and folded her hands together in front of her. She began, "Kind and gracious Heavenly Father, we do pray that you will touch the lips of this beautiful young woman..."

"Stop that, you old bitch!"

"Please cleanse her mouth, her heart..."

"You can't do that! You can't pray for me!" She was screaming so that the manager was coming to their side of the room.

"Young lady," Martha answered quietly, "I also have freedom of speech. Lord enfold her with your love and fill her heart with your tender mercies," she continued, not loudly but in a conversational tone. The girl was now standing, face red, yelling that Martha can't do that to her.

The manager was a large man. He towered above the girl and quietly said something that only she could hear. He handed her the check for her food and, still flushed, she left the restaurant, pausing at the cash register, throwing the check and some money toward the cashier.

People all around began to settle back to their meals, pretending nothing had happened. Jane reached for Martha's hand and patted it. "Bravo," she whispered.

The manager turned back to their table. "Ladies, I can only apologize for this unpleasantness. Your meal is on the house and we hope you come back again soon." The manager walked away and soon the house music system became slightly louder and the buzz of conversation resumed.

"Oh, Jane I hope I didn't embarrass you," she chuckled. "You know something, I didn't even know what some of those words meant. But since most of it was dirty, I have to assume they were bad, too." Jane was familiar with all the words, and yes, they were, indeed, bad.

Unnoticed now, the boy and girl who had been sitting with the foul-mouthed beauty stood up and walked over to the table where Martha and Jane were trying to finish their food. They stood for a minute not knowing what to say or how to say it. Finally the young man stammered, "Ladies, we're sure sorry. You see..." he began but didn't finish his sentence. "Well, damn! Oh, sorry again. But if my grandmother knew I was a party to this, she'd just kill me." He was still uncomfortable but growing more confident. "She'd like you. And she'd like what you did," he said to Martha. Unable to say more, they picked up their checks and wove their way through the tables to the cashier.

It was not raining when the posse started into the woods in search of the small girl reported missing when she didn't show up after school yesterday. Her friends said she got off at the bus stop with them, and instead of walking the half-mile down the gravel lane to her house, she decided to take the short cut through the woods, which she frequently did. This was all anyone knew and now it was almost twenty-four hours later.

They had started out at dawn combing the woods for the girl, and now, hours later, some of the men were suggesting she must have been abducted and they were wasting their time. Hillary, the only woman deputy the posse had ever had, disagreed and felt sure that they had overlooked something here in the woods. Lightning was flashing now, and the thunder had become an almost continuous roll. This would be a bad winter storm, and if the girl were out here they must find her before nightfall.

Hillary's duster was warm enough, but now she was glad she had thought to bring her slicker and had it rolled up behind her saddle. Rain was definitely on the way. She pulled up her collar and pulled down her hat to protect her face from the rain when it came. The wind was whipping the bushes nearby and several large branches caught at Hillary almost knocking her from the saddle. Queen's nostrils were flared and she snorted and side-stepped, showing Hillary that she was not at all comfortable in these dark woods. Hillary patted Queen's neck and spoke softly to settle her down.

When the rain started it seemed that the drops had been fired from a pellet gun, stinging Hillary's face, which she tried in vain to protect with her broad hat. Their trail began to descend to the creek. The trail was little more than a washout that game had used to get to the water. Although she never claimed to be a tracker, Hillary was confident that she had seen part of a shoe print. Now the rain would wash away every sign. She must hurry.

No, maybe she shouldn't hurry. Maybe she should stop and think like a nine-year-old child. Although the creek would not be on the short-cut to her home, it would certainly be enticing. The water was clear and fell over large granite boulders. Sometimes a fish would leave his cover and dart out into open waters. The cottonwoods along the bank soared high into the air and, although leafless, provided a shady arbor up and down the stream. It was a magical place, an enchanted forest. Hillary could envision a child wanting to come by here and play for awhile before going home to the poor rocky-soil farm that was her home. She probably had many chores awaiting her and simply wanted to delay them for a little while.

The rain was pelting harder and harder, coming from an up-stream direction. Hillary must be careful not to get trapped by rising waters. And above all, she must not allow herself to become lost or disoriented, which, she guessed, had happened to the child. The stream made a wide turn and Hillary could see a ledge above the bank that was protected from the north-westerly wind and rain. She kicked Queen into a trot and made for the ledge. Perhaps they could wait out the storm there. It would be safer than snuggling down under a tree that might be a good target for the lightning. It would be much more comfortable, too, than standing out in the open with the wind and rain striking them so hard.

The water in the creek was rising, Hillary noticed. Stones that she had used for markers were now under water and invisible. The water was no longer clear, but a muddy brown, and still the rain continued with increasing force. Hillary cuddled herself close to the ledge, squatting underneath Queen's long, muscular neck. No, she didn't think Queen would step on her, and she was ever so appreciative of the protection the massive mare provided. Queen's head was bowed away from the rain and her eyes were closed. She was no longer skittish but patiently waiting for the storm to pass. She must have been through many such storms when she was pastured, Hillary reasoned.

She could have easily dozed off, sitting here warm and relatively safe, since she had been up very early, in time to get out here by daylight. Hillary glanced upstream and downstream, hardly able to see in the pouring rain. Looking upstream again, Hillary thought she saw a small patch of bright color in the water. Staring again as it washed swiftly by, she was surprised that the color seemed to be on a badly soaked Barbie doll. Am I seeing things? she wondered. Grabbing the reins up in her right hand, Hillary led Queen to a wider spot on the ledge, pulled the reins over Queen's head and transferring them to her left hand, quickly vaulted into the saddle urging Queen along the river bank upstream.

If it were, indeed, a Barbie Doll, and if it belonged to the little girl, maybe it had been a Christmas present of only a few weeks ago. The child must have been near the stream with it, and would not have let it go, except for some tragic event that Hillary would not even contemplate. Queen plodded slowly on with Hillary's encouragement. Sometimes the underbrush was so thick that they had to detour away from the stream to make their way upriver. More than once Hillary had to dismount and lead Queen through the tight undergrowth.

The animal track they were following brought them out into a small opening surrounded by thick bushes. Queen's ears went forward and she began her snorting and dancing again. "What is it, baby? What do you smell, or feel? Are you scared? Are you trying to tell me something?" Cougars were not unheard of in these parts and there were lots of wolves, she knew. The hair on the back of Hillary's neck prickled under her skin. Still she kept talking quietly to Queen. They had spent lots of years together. Was this her frightened act or just an excited act? Hillary's hand was loose on the rein, and Queen was not backing away from any perceived danger but cautiously approaching a thick clump of bushes that was definitely too thick to penetrate. Queen nickered softly. Hillary stepped out of the saddle and on hands and knees disappeared into the bush. The water was now lapping the ground ever nearer the shrub. The clearing they had come into was already partially submerged, and the water was advancing steadily. Hillary could see that around the base of a cedar tree deep within the tangle of undergrowth there was a smaller clearing, just big enough for a child's "hideout," and curled up at the trunk of the tree was a brown coat with little girl shoes sticking out from under it.

Just let me be in time, she prayed, and the mass of coat moved slightly as she gently called the girl's name. Her name was Dawn but her family called her "Punkin," and Hillary began to use that nickname. She didn't move again, and Hillary reached farther under the limbs until she could grasp the coat. She pulled slowly until the coat was moving steadily toward her. Still the child did not respond more than an occasional soft moan. When she was close enough for Hillary to get both hands on the coat, she quickly pulled her out from under the brush and began to examine the child for injuries.

She could find none but was confident the child was suffering from exposure, having spent the winter night in the woods, and now the cold rain had been falling for the past couple of hours.

Queen was standing quietly nearby and didn't flinch when Hillary lifted the child into the saddle. The rain was a thick mist in the clearing, filtered through the trees above and Hillary knew that it would wet them good when they left the shelter of the trees. She took off her slicker and wrapped the child carefully so that her head was protected from the falling rain.

The trail along the creek was gone now, covered by several inches of water, and it was still rising steadily. Hillary stepped into the stirrup and settled herself behind the saddle so that she could have both arms wrapped around her precious cargo while urging Queen through the trees at right angles to the creek, toward (she hoped) the highway. Queen had no trouble finding the best trails through the thick woods. Only a couple of times did she find a dead-end and have to backtrack a short distance. Finally Hillary could see a grass slope through breaks in the trees. But when they emerged from the trees and could see the highway in the distance Hillary didn't know whether to turn upstream or downstream. She didn't see anything she recognized and just gave Queen her head. With loose reins they turned to the left, downstream, and still saw no landmarks. Maybe she should just go straight to the highway without trying to find the rescuers camp.

She kept up a steady conversation with Dawn and occasionally felt the child stir. The rain was cold on Hillary's back; she knew her duster was soaked through, but reasoned that she could take a little bit of discomfort better than the child who had been out in the weather for twenty-four hours. Suddenly Queen lifted her head and whinnied. Then she picked up her pace from a tired mud-dragging slog to a brisk, fast walk. If it hadn't been so slippery, Hillary would have let her trot. She knew now that the camp was just ahead, with the emergency vehicles and all that hot coffee.

"Ahchoo!" Hillary realized that she was soaking wet. How long had she been sitting in the porch swing in the rain? Her mail was beside her where she had put it down. Bills and more bills. She could pay them this month with what she had and maybe next month, too, but after that... "Oh, God, forgive me for being afraid. I know you took care of me in the past, are caring for me now, and will take care of my needs in the future." This was the prayer Hillary had forced herself to say aloud everytime the anxiety attacked her. Maybe someone would buy the lake house, but sales on the lake were slow during the winter months. How she hated to sell the lake house—so many memories of Pete and the children, of friends, and so many fish fries. Oh, well, it would not be the same without Pete. She had to once more remind herself that those days were then and this is now, and that somehow she was going to do whatever it took to take care of Pete in a nice nursing home. After all, he had taken very good care of her and the children all these years, and by golly, she was going to find a way to take care of him, for however long was necessary. As usual the anxiety attack was warded off by anger, by determination, and by resolve as Hillary squared her shoulders, drawing herself up to her full height and marching into the house for a hot shower and coffee.

CHAPTER 14

Hillary was awake several times each night. She just couldn't sleep as soundly as she did all those years when Pete was beside her. She re-fluffed her head pillow and kept another pillow between her knees that had to be re-positioned every time she turned. The light on the digital clock showed 1:16 and the alarm was set for 7:00, although Hillary knew she'd wake up long before that. She turned and replaced her pillows. If she kept her eyes closed she might go right back to sleep, but she didn't. She became aware of a low growl coming from the floor where Lady liked to sleep. Hillary lay very still wondering why Lady was growling; was she dreaming as she sometimes did? They used to watch her sleeping beside the fireplace and she would twitch and kick and sometimes a little bark or whine would escape while she was dreaming. Pete was always amused and speculated on the kind of dreams a black Lab would have.

But Lady was not asleep, nor even lying down. Hillary opened her eyes, and in the dim light of the bedside clock could see that Lady was standing up, and the hair on her back was also standing up. Someone was in the house. Someone had broken into her house with all the doors and windows locked and she didn't even have a gun. Maybe she had just heard a squirrel or a cat on the patio. No, she was not facing the French doors that led onto the patio. In the dim light Hillary could very plainly see that Lady was looking toward the bedroom door that led into the hall. The door was a large black rectangle, and somewhere behind the blackness was someone who should not have been there. Maybe Pete had left the nursing home again and... No, Lady would have been overjoyed with Pete coming home. The only times Lady had been this upset, the boy next door had been up to some of his antics, which Hillary wanted to believe were simple teenage pranks. But someone was in her house and Hillary was angry to have her privacy violated.

She reached for the telephone and dragged the whole instrument into the bed with her and under the covers. She reached out and pulled the pillows over her head to muffle her voice. In the dark it was hard to remember which buttons were 911. She attempted once and only heard silence. Why hadn't she memorized the position of the numbers? Maybe she was confusing the number sequence with her calculator, which were the reverse of the telephone digits. On the third try a human voice answered and Hillary realized that she was shivering so hard she could hardly hold the telephone. "Someone is in my house," she whispered. "My name is Hillary Johnson." She had never stuttered in her life that she remembered and now she could hardly speak. Hillary gave her address and added, "P-p-please send someone to help me."

When she hung up the telephone, she cautiously peered out from under her covers. Lady was standing as still as a statue looking toward the blackness that was the door, but not growling. Hillary could hear no sound. Maybe the intruder had gone. She didn't dare move. Yet. She would watch Lady and know when it was safe. Finally Lady walked to the door and disappeared down the hall and Hillary reached for her lamp. With the light on in the bedroom, nothing was changed and it made Hillary feel as though nothing had happened. But it had. Lady was proof of it.

Hillary reached for her robe and stepped into her slippers. At the bedroom door she reached around the corner and turned on the hall light. She walked to the end of the hall and reached into the den and turned on the two ceiling lights and turned the dimmer up to full bright. She went into each room turning on lights as she went, reassured that no one was now in the house. She had quit trembling, and with all the lights on in the house and yard, everything looked so normal she thought the police would think her a very foolish old lady.

The patrolman who came to her front door was named Robinson, looked hardly old enough to be a policeman, but was dead serious about the investigation. They went from room to room assuring that nothing had been stolen or vandalized. Hillary was surprised when the young patrolman asked what things had happened before that were out of the ordinary, had scared her, or had made her uncomfortable. The surprise was the way he phrased the question, not "if" other things had happened, just what were those other things. Hillary remembered someone or something on the patio that had upset Lady, then she remembered the blasts of loud music coming from the house next door, obviously aimed at her bedroom. The more she talked the more she remembered little things that were not quite right, like her poor little flowering quince and the motorcycle ruts through her yard.

"Mrs. Johnson," the patrolman began with all seriousness, "you aren't the only one in this neighborhood who's had this sort of problem. I don't want you to think someone's singled you out to harrass. We've had numerous complaints but, like yours, they're sometimes hard to prove and sometimes people don't complain to the police until something more drastic happens. We've had reports of pets being injured, and one killed, in their own yards." He patted Lady's head since she had taken a position next to his chair so that her head was very close to his knee. "You'd do well to keep your dog inside at night."

They had determined that the intruder had come in through the window in the utility room, which Hillary had been sure was locked earlier. Outside the window was a concrete sidewalk so no footprints could be identified. It looked as though someone had come into her house just to look around, possibly for a future theft or possibly just to scare her. Or do her harm. Was this a simple boyish prank or did she read something more in Officer Robinson's questions?

After the police had left, Hillary could not sleep. She made herself a cup of tea and took Lady outside briefly. What was really going on here? she wondered. She knew that all these things could have been done by Patrick, the young terrorist from next door. And were they harmless pranks? Or were they symptoms of a very sick mind? Maybe it wasn't him afterall, but some adult psychopath, knowing she lived alone and... She knew she needed to talk with Greg about their plan and get his opinion of Patrick.

Meanwhile Hillary determined, once again, not to be held captive in her own home, frightened into cowering under her covers like a child afraid of the shadows the nightlight makes. A nightlight would be a good idea, she admitted. Maybe several nightlights throughout the house. And a gun? Hillary had shot a gun so few times in her life that she was more scared of the gun than the possibility of an intruder. Maybe mace or something like that. Patrolman Robinson seemed to think that Lady was her best protection, and that was probably true. She wondered what other widows did for peace of mind. They didn't seem to discuss it. Maybe she should ask around.

Hillary hadn't seen Jane in several days and made a quick decision to stop by on her way home from visiting Jim. She should have called first and she might find Jane had gone out, but anyway it was worth a try since she was sort of in the neighborhood.

Hillary drove to the back parking area and knocked on the back door before sticking her head in and yoo-hooing, as she always did. No one was in the kitchen, but she heard Jane answer, "Hill is that you? Come on back here." No one but Jane seemed to be at home this afternoon, so Hillary was glad she had chanced the visit.

Jane was sitting up in her bed with the telephone, typewriter, TV guides, and various pieces of scrap paper on the rolling bedside table someone had found for her. "Hillary, I'm so glad you've come. I need a cool head, I'm so mad." Jane didn't appear to be mad but something had certainly roused her to action.

"You can't believe what I've seen on television the past few weeks. Some of these soaps and talk shows are not fit for anyone to watch. I won't even tell you what I just heard being discussed on a talk show this morning. Where do they get those awful people? They must get together in some kind of perverse committee and discuss what could be the most shocking subject they could present and then where do they get those amoral people that appear on their shows?" Jane had written several letters and now picked them up to show Hillary. "I've written the local stations, the networks, and the individual programs. I know these are just the tip of the iceberg. I can't possibly write to every base and vulgar show that comes on, but dadgummit, I'm going to let them know what one woman thinks of that filth."

Jane didn't really expect Hillary to comment and kept on with her tirade. "We are SO modern, and SO liberal-minded," she fumed. "We must hate our children. Yes, this will be known as the generation that hated our children."

"Well, but..." Hillary began, but didn't get to present her view.

"What can we expect from our precious children when they've grown up with this kind of filth in their own living rooms? Where are their mothers? Surely their mothers would not allow this trash on television if they knew their children were watching. And you know they are. Not just children, how about teenagers, or impressionable adults. Your mind is only as good as what you put into it, you know. If you fill it with filth, you've got a damaged mind. What if you dumped your trash into the swimming pool instead of going on out to the alley to the trash cans? It wouldn't take long to have a sewer instead of a nice clean swimming pool. Now why can't people see that it's also true of our minds? How can a mind filled with that garbage also be capable of lofty thoughts? Or do people still have lofty thoughts?" Jane pondered her question. "Another thing about those talk shows: aren't good people or intelligent people interesting anymore? People who accomplish things. People who suffer bitter losses, and come back to win a victory, maybe. How about someone who demonstrates a great amount of love, or bravery, or anything that would motivate us to try to be better people? Wouldn't you rather hear what they have to say instead of the degrading things that people do that make you wonder if we really are a higher level of animal, and not just animals?"

"Jane, you are certainly right," Hillary agreed. "But I've wondered what can be done about it. At the hospital I see parts of those programs you're talking about, and sometimes my patients will change channels when I walk into the room, or at least turn down the volume." Hillary paused, sure that Jane would continue her thesis, but she was silent. "I guess I'm not a crusader, maybe I'm just a coward," she admitted. "But, by golly, you're right. Just give me some addresses and I'll write a few letters myself. We may not be able to change a single person's mind or affect a single program but at least we'll know we did the right thing."

Hillary finally got around to asking Jane how she had been and got a brief answer. Her broken hip had taken up as much of her time as she would allow and now there were other, more interesting things on her mind. She could walk with cane or walker and the pain was subsiding, so she didn't want to think of that any longer. Other things, mainly basketball, were occupying her attention. "How about those Rockets?" she asked. "Did you see that game last night? I've never seen them play together so well. We've got a few super stars that sometimes monopolize the game, and they're great, but last night their teamwork was just textbook perfect." Jane was still the basketball coach at heart and thoroughly enjoyed watching a team do what it was supposed to do. Hillary didn't answer, knowing Jane didn't expect her to.

The visit turned to catching up to date on their friends, who was doing what. How was Pete, Jane wanted to know. Hillary answered briefly, mentioning all the hopeful things and failing to mention her own fear that Pete had taken a downturn that just might be permanent. Among friends the unsaid thoughts were sometimes louder than the ones verbalized, and Jane understood. Just as Hillary understood very well when Jane was missing Max with a physical painful longing, although Jane would never have said as much. There was also that unstated understanding that Sharon was also missing—not so much Harvey as missing that feeling of marriedness, belonging to someone. And someone belonging to you, if only part-time. They understood that marriage is much more than just the two people involved. Marriage is the true definition of synergy, when the whole is greater than the sum of the parts. Even if they never said it in so many words, they knew it to be true, especially now that they had lost it.

139

Jane picked herself clumsily off her bed and reached for her walker. "Let's have some tea and cookies. I've got some really good ones." They went into the kitchen and sat at the bar talking, and talking, and talking. Finally Hillary looked at her watch and apologized for taking up so much of Jane's afternoon.

The telephone was ringing when Hillary put her key into the back door lock. Hurrying made her fumble and drop her key. Oh, well, the answering machine would pick up the message, she knew. When she walked into the kitchen, the message was just starting and Hillary recognized the voice of Dianne Perkins-Holder, who was the real estate broker that had the listing on the lake house.

Hillary picked up the phone. "Dianne, I was just unlocking the back door when I heard the phone ringing. Please start over. I hope you have some good news for me."

"Mrs. Johnson," Dianne began. She was very reserved and professional. Hillary appreciated her business-like poise and her knowledge of the real estate industry. She valued Dianne's advice on marketing, and although the house had been on the market for several months, Hillary felt that Dianne would get her a good price eventually. "Will you be at home this evening? I need to present a contract to you. I won't go into detail, but it looks pretty good. Of course, you know that you can always make a counter-offer if some of the details are not acceptable. But as I told you before, a counter-offer is the same as a refusal, and it's possible you may not get another offer from the people."

There were so many technicalities about the real estate field that Hillary had not known, and Dianne had patiently taught her some of these at the time she took the listing. Dianne had been good to stay in touch and describe the people and their remarks each time she had taken potential buyers out for a showing. Sometimes Hillary would be very depressed and wonder whether she should lower the price, remodel the property, or spend money just redecorating. Dianne, knowing something of Hillary's situation, assured her that the house was in good condition, decorated nicely, and had no latent defects. The buyers would probably want to redecorate anyway. Many of the people looking just could not afford this fine a second home, but the right people would come along in time. Hillary always felt better after an encouraging talk with Dianne, but then later another anxiety attack would destroy her hope and optimism for a time.

"Yes, Dianne, I'll be home for the rest of the evening. Just say when and

I'll have some snacks out."

"Thanks, Mrs. Johnson, a cup of decaf will be fine. I'll come over about eight o'clock so that I won't rush you with dinner."

Hillary had the decaf perked and fat-free cookies on the table, knowing that Dianne would not touch them. She was very slim and stylish, and Hillary had never known her to eat the snacks she had offered.

Dianne brought her briefcase to the kitchen table and spread the contract out for Hillary to examine. They had been over the forms before so that they would not look unfamiliar when the time came to accept a contract. They had also looked at closing statements so that Hillary would have no surprises when various charges appeared at the closing. Sometimes sellers were disappointed that they netted less than expected, and Dianne didn't want this to happen to Hillary.

"You see right here that it's a full-price contract. However, here is what they're offering in the way of financing. They want you to do an owner-finance and they would pay 20% down and pay the balance over the next ten years. Here's the interest rate they're offering, which is about a point and a half above the market rate and your incentive to owner-finance. But I'll remind you that it's several points above your CD rate." Dianne answered several questions for Hillary and then pointed out the addendum which stated that the buyers would pay an extra amount for the furnishings at closing. They loved the colors and the furniture, even the dishes. Hillary was both pleased and sad—pleased that someone else had thought the place as pretty as she did, but sad to think of giving up those things that had meant so much to Pete and her.

"Mrs. Johnson, I'm not asking you to make any decision tonight. Think about these things over night, or even longer if you need to. You have my pager number and you can reach me anytime if you have anymore questions."

Dianne said goodnight without attempting to influence Hillary's decision. Hillary was very appreciative. So many times since Pete had been in the nursing home, various people had tried to coerce her into buying things or making decisions against her better judgment. She became very uncomfortable and sometimes came to doubt her own judgment, wondering if she really was capable of ordering her own affairs.

After Dianne left, Hillary pondered the various alterations to the contract that she might make. But did she really want to keep any of the lake furniture or dishes? The monthly payment for ten years would give her a measure of comfort that she had not had since Pete's salary had stopped. Dianne had prepared an amortization schedule for Hillary to consider. Ah, for ten years she would not have to rack her brains to come up with extra money or try to cut back even more on expenditures. There could, of course, be some unforeseen disaster that might befall her, but she would deal with each disaster as it came. Maybe her anxiety attacks would stop.

Hillary tried to read for awhile before going to sleep, but her thoughts kept coming back to the contract. To the lake house and all those weekends on the boat, swimming, fishing, skiing. What wonderful times they had, how tired and blistered they all were after a day in the sun and water.

What great wintry days they had enjoyed—weathered in, as they called it in pilot terms—with a good book and tasty snacks. She and Pete had spent so many dreary days on the lake, enjoying every minute of it. They were good company, even when they didn't speak for hours, wrapped up in their books. *Nevertheless, that was then, and this is now*, Hillary reminded herself. Nothing could ever return to the way it was then.

But there are still wonderful things going on now, she scolded herself. *Such as this contract and a new freedom from worry. Thank you, God*, she said silently.

It was well after midnight when her mind began to slow down from all the thoughts that came racing through, and she fell asleep thinking how happy the new family would be in her lake house, hoping they had children who would have lots of fun in the cottage and that once again there would be laughter ringing throughout the house and alongside the lake.

CHAPTER 15

Sunday morning Hillary awoke early, looking forward to seeing her friends in Sunday School and at the preaching service. Then afterward, as usual, she would have lunch with Tom, Elizabeth, and the boys. She hadn't seen any of them all week and she was really missing them. They'll be so surprised when she tells them the news about the lake cottage and she hoped they would be as happy as she was. And she needed to talk with Greg privately. Maybe she would have the opportunity to invite him over for cookies or something. She certainly didn't want to appear to have a clandestine meeting with Greg to the exclusion of Damion. He was a precious and tender-hearted child, and she loved them both for their distinct and wonderful personalities.

Hillary looked around her Sunday School class as she often did, marvelling at the different colors of gray that her friends' hair had become. And, of course, there were a few reds, blacks, and dark browns that could not be blamed on God or nature. And strangely enough many of them were still beautiful, slender, and not showing their mature years. These were dear, sweet friends, most of whom Hillary had known since they were young mothers together. They had shared both happiness and grief, triumph and defeat, for all these years. If anyone was hurting, they were all hurting. If there was a loss or illness in a family, cakes and casseroles started showing up for the evening meal.

As usual Martha started out the class by asking, "Well, girls, have you claimed your Joy this week?" Hillary loved that question. To her it meant that if she hadn't claimed her joy, it was her own fault. Then Martha asked for prayer requests and finally, "Does anyone have any Praise?"

Hillary lifted her hand and told the class about her contract on some real estate and that it had certainly come at the right time. She laughingly admitted that it was definitely an answer to prayer. There were smiles and chuckles around the room from mature women who had experienced various answers to various prayers. How many times had they shared with each other their needs, their heart's desires, and then later, almost surprised, marvelled that the answer to the prayer came from such an unexpected source.

In the following service, a visiting preacher delivered a mediocre message, laced with numerous statistics that Hillary found boring, and she wished for their pastor back from his trip. *Shame on me*, she thought. *There may be many people here who are receiving a blessing from this message. Not likely though*, she admitted. Then again she shamed herself, which made her chuckle out loud. The friends on either side of Hillary turned to frown at her with a questioning look. For some unknown reason this also struck Hillary as funny, and she couldn't suppress another giggle. *Oh, how awful*, she thought. *What will people think?* Trying very hard to hold her mouth shut with her hand over her face, she heard another chuckle, first from her friend to her right and then from the friend on her left. Her own shoulders were heaving with laughter, and she knew that any minute she might burst out with a loud guffaw. Why was it she couldn't quit laughing at this terribly inopportune time? And now she had her friends giggling too, and they apparently were unable to stop.

Hillary reached into her purse quickly and pulled out the embroidered linen handkerchief that she almost never used, held it up to her mouth, and then she began to dab at the tears spilling over from her eyes. Perhaps the people around her would just think she was terribly moved with emotion by this dry speaker. It would certainly be more acceptable. And that ridiculous thought made her laugh even harder.

The three gray-haired women definitely had the giggles, and those around them were at first surprised and then amused. Not knowing what was so funny, it just looked so preposterous that people of all ages within several pews began to chuckle and then try to suppress their laughter.

Hillary sensed, rather than saw, that the visiting preacher had become confused and quickly ended his message. The choir director, who had a perfect view of the disruption, jumped up and led the choir in an invitational hymn. The congregation couldn't remember a time when they only sang one verse of "Just As I Am," and then the Associate Pastor led a brief benediction. Suddenly the service was over and Hillary tried to just disappear before anyone could ask her about the outburst. Perhaps there were some who wouldn't know how it got started. Anyway, she hoped this would be the case.

"Grandmother, can I ride with you to the cafeteria? I already told Mother I was, so it's alright."

"Yes, Damion, I'd love to have you." She gave her handsome, intense grandson a hug and again thought how much he looked like Pete must have at that age.

At the cafeteria Elizabeth remarked that there was apparently some kind of commotion during the message and she wondered what it might have been. She couldn't see anything from where she sat. "It looked as though it came from down front near where you always sit, Mother. Do you know what happened?"

"I really couldn't say," Hillary answered evasively, wide-eyed with innocence. She then broke the news that she had accepted a contract on the lake house and the terms were very good.

"Mother, what a selfish thing to do! You know we like to go out there. Why didn't you ask what we thought about it?"

Hillary, surprised and hurt, tried to explain. "I'm sorry, I didn't think you'd have an opinion either way. You don't go out there twice a year. I just couldn't afford to keep it."

Tom frowned at his wife, wondering why she invariably cut down her mother when they got together. Sometimes it seemed as if Hillary invited it, but today it was unexpected as Tom had a jolt of understanding. He had never discussed finances with Hillary and assumed they had plenty of retirement funds for her to go on living as usual and keep Pete in the finest nursing home in the area. He knew she had sold the bank stock a few years back, but it didn't occur to him that she needed the money. He just thought she was shrewd, predicting the bank's stock to go down. And it certainly had gone down; in fact, the regulators had closed the bank, and none of the owners had gotten a dime from their investment.

From the hurt expression on Hillary's face, Tom knew without a doubt that she had needed the sale in order to keep the bills paid. Why had he never thought of that? She had never asked for any money; maybe her pride would not allow it. Yes, he thought, she would probably sell her house and car rather than ask for any help. It would not occur to her that she had two children living very comfortably who could help with their father's care. He'd talk with Pedro tomorrow and then present the idea to Hillary when they had decided how much they could contribute. He knew she still might refuse the offer.

Tom gently steered the conversation in other directions. Greg was doing well in basketball. Like his father he was becoming tall and lean, and with practice was also becoming very fast and agile. Greg was embarrassed at the praise, but once the topic of basketball came up he had many things to say about the team and who they would be playing against this week.

"Grandmother, will you be home this afternoon? And do you have any of those brownies left?" Greg wanted to know. Hillary was relieved that she didn't have to finagle the secret meeting now.

Hillary kept several small brownie mixes on hand just in case Greg or Damion might drop by. She seldom ate them herself—too high in fat and calories. Maybe it was like a little bribe to keep her grandsons wanting to come by regularly. *So what,* she told herself, *it's a lot better than just sitting at home being hurt that they don't come by, like some grandmothers I know.*

Greg arrived out of breath and boasting that he had made it all the way from his house on his 10-speed in less than 22 minutes. "I could have done better except for the traffic."

They took their brownies and milk to the den in the comfortable chairs where they always had their serious conversations, a habit Hillary started years ago. She used to say, "Let's visit. I haven't seen you in awhile and I want to know what's going on in your life." She had started early, when the boys were hardly more than toddlers, saying, "Let's go to the den and have a tea party, okay?" The children always fell into the mood and would carefully drink their milk or Kool-Aid, usually without any spills. No one ever wondered why they didn't drink tea at a tea party.

Then, taking their cue from their grandmother, they would say, "And how are you today, Grandmother?" And moving on to, "What do you think about this weather? It's been pretty warm (cold, rainy) lately." Making conversation was a serious undertaking to each of the children, and then, after the rather artificial beginnings, Hillary would realize that they began talking about real things that were happening in their lives. Over the years conversation with Hillary became very natural to them and she loved it. She remembered that once Damion had said, "Scott punched me in the eye on the playground, and I got this HORRIBLE black eye, only it was gone before we went in so the teacher didn't believe me."

Through a mouthful of brownie Greg began, "Grandmother, I've spent a lot of time with Patrick, like we planned, and I don't think it's going to work." He paused, not knowing just how to describe his feelings about Patrick. "He's spooky," he finally said. "Sometimes we'll be talking or shooting baskets and he just, sort of drifts away, you know?" Greg leaned forward with his elbows on his knees, conspiratorially. "One day we were talking and his eyes kind of glazed over, you know, like that alien, when his eyes were all white and everything? Well, I don't guess his eyes were really white but he sure looked like an alien, and didn't hear a word I said. I even grabbed his arm to shake him out of it, like if it were some kind of trance or something. And he just looked right through me and walked off. It gave me goosebumps." Greg shook his head remembering.

"Well, Greg, I appreciate your trying. I do feel sorry for the boy, but this is obviously a deeper problem than we can handle. He probably needs professional help, and I don't know whether his parents are aware of it. On the other hand I may just be exaggerating the whole thing." Hillary did not mention the break-in to Greg, knowing how protective he might feel, as though it were his problem and he would need to solve it. "I don't suppose you have the time to take Lady over to the park for a little Frisbee?"

"Sure, where's the leash?" When Lady saw the leash she began to dance around with joy, knowing her favorite boy was going to take her out for some fun. With the leash in one hand and the Frisbee in the other, Greg trotted down the sidewalk toward the little neighborhood park where he and Lady spent the next forty-five minutes playing and romping in the brown winter grass. They returned very tired. Greg refused another snack in order to get back home before sundown, and Lady, exhausted, lay down on her rug in front of the fireplace for a long nap.

It was hard for Hillary to throw off the sad feeling and prepare her snacks for the bridge party tonight. She ought to have lots of quarters to contribute to the gritch kitty. When Dan Williamson called this afternoon, Hillary knew by the sound of his voice that he was still grieving over the bank closure. He said the big bank who had bought the deposits and opened in another name had refused to even let him apply for a job there. He didn't think he knew how to do anything else, but seemed to be happy with his position at the country club. And he was surrounded by his friends so that he didn't have time for self-pity. Once again he mentioned how lucky Pete was that he hadn't been here to see the bank go down. The bank they had both invested their business careers and their savings in. Hillary felt both guilty and relieved that she had sold her stock before she had any idea that the bank would fail. She knew from her conversations with both Pete and Dan that they had tried everything possible to keep the bank sound and profitable. But there were so many regulations that kept tripping them up—regulations and the continual need for new capital and juggling liquidity requirements. Now it was over, completely and forever over.

Poor Dan, she thought. *He has the added guilt of imagining his father and grandfather, from the grave shaming him for the poor management of the family bank.* Hillary wished that she could say something, anything, to give Dan some comfort. What was there to say? It was very like a death in the family, and the grief continues even years later. She wished she knew a comforting thing to say. Then she remembered something.

"Dan, do you remember those years after you came back from Wharton, and your dad was grooming you for management?" He mumbled that he remembered, and wondered what she might say. "Well, Pete had always assumed that he would be appointed Executive Vice-President and then someday CEO, even though it was a family-owned bank. But then you came along so fast and your promotions so frequent that Pete accepted the fact that you would eventually pass him by."

"Gosh, Hillary, I didn't know how he felt about that. I was young and ambitious and just thinking of myself, I guess."

"No, Dan, let me finish. One day, I think when you had just received some promotion or other, Pete told me that you were one of the finest young bankers he had ever worked with. And that some day you would be CEO and not just because you were family. He said you were bright and energetic and had more innovative ideas than all the rest of the staff combined. Dan, he believed in you and I know that you did everything possible for the bank."

There was silence on the line and Hillary wondered for a moment if he had hung up. No, there would be a dial tone if he had. When he spoke, his voice was hoarse, "Hillary, thanks for that. Pete was a fine banker, too. And not just that, he was a fine man and my role model."

Afterward, Hillary relived those painful months when Pete's tirades became so frequent. Everyone around him felt that he was just angry with the bank regulators. And then he began to bring his anger home, yelling at Hillary, which was so unlike Pete. Even though he would forget many things, she attributed it to the stress he was under at the bank. Later she was surprised at herself, a nurse, for not recognizing the symptoms in her own husband. If she had heard their story played back as a case history, she knew she would have been the first to suspect Alzheimer's disease, or at least she might have labeled the behavior as *senile dementia*, which Hillary knew to be kind of a broad term encompassing many conditions.

And then Hillary let herself remember the terrible night that she woke up with Pete standing over her with the knife, demanding to know who she was and what she was doing in his house. Luckily she talked her way out of the situation, as she had talked to many agitated and violent patients, and soothed him until she could go to the phone and call Tom and Elizabeth. How sweet they had been in helping her to get Pete to the hospital that night, and then weeks later the psychiatrist had told them all that Pete would need long term care. What a hard time in their lives. But they had lived through it and they would continue to live, day after day, doing the best they knew how to do.

Well, back to the real world, she reminded herself. The girls will be here in an hour and I've still got to shower. With that she quickly put away the negative thoughts in a mental closet where she could deal with them later.

Jane and Sharon arrived together, and Lady was, as usual, ecstatic, but still a little leery of the walker. Sharon had changed into casual clothes, a warm-up suit with running shoes, and Jane had almost the same uniform on. Hillary looked down at her own casual get-up and smiled. It was almost as if they had gotten together and decided to dress alike. Her own navy outfit had stripes of red and white down one sleeve and the opposite pants leg, and underneath the lightweight jacket Hillary always wore a short sleeve cotton shell. Except on the really cold days she would wear a long-sleeve turtleneck undershirt.

"Hank's back in town for a few days," Sharon informed the other two women. "I had dinner with them last night." She let this sink in while she sorted out her own thoughts. "You know, I really admire them. They are certainly heroes in my book. I don't know anyone who has lost so much and they're still optimistic and laugh about some of the things they've done to get by. I'm sure I've told you that once they rented a stall at the flea market and sold a lot of their things just to get their household utilities paid?" They smiled at the thought of Hank and Marianne, one of the community's wealthiest couples just a short time ago, hawking their wares. But they also felt the sadness the two must have felt disposing of their nice things. "I don't know if worry really causes gray hair or if it's genetic—you hear conflicting opinions—but they've both gotten very gray and their faces are lined from worry. However, to hear them talk, everything is going just great." Sharon frowned, wondering how they could have the outlook they did, when obviously everything had cratered around them.

"Marianne is still happy at the library and has gotten a couple of raises. She says it's been a real blessing in disguise because now that the kids are grown she had way too much time on her hands." They could each identify with that feeling; after so many years of rushing to get everything done for their family, it seemed that suddenly there was way too much time, and they had to look for meaningful ways to occupy their days.

"Hank seems to be having a blast except that Marianne's here and he's in Florida. He says they're tied to that big house of theirs until they can get free of the Internal Revenue Service. He laughs and says they were mad at him for going broke and he's in a big dispute over losses and the IRS has a lien on their house so they can't sell it. But even though they're doing so well right now, Hank has developed high blood pressure and has to take medication for it every day. When they settle with the IRS they plan to sell their house, and Marianne will move out to Florida or wherever he's working and they'll just rent a condo or something so they won't be tied down for the years he has left to work."

"I would have been happy enough to do that with Max," Jane volunteered. "A big house is nice, and I've loved mine, but when you put all your priorities side-by-side, then a house isn't even in the top rating. But now I'm worried that my kids are thinking too much about the house." She didn't elaborate on the subject because she never liked to air her private life in public, even among her close friends. Bruce and Chrissy had wanted all the trappings of affluence ever since their engagement and fashionable marriage. But the facts were that Bruce was only a junior member of an accounting firm and Chrissy had given up her job when she became pregnant the first time, and their income was far from impressive. They did, however, have a nice and cheap place to live, Jane admitted. *But is it good for them?* she wondered. *Am I doing the right thing? Will it make them better people?* She asked herself these things regularly and still didn't know the answer.

Hillary put the pastry in the oven and set the timer. "Let's deal the cards and play while this cooks." It looked as though they were all preoccupied with their concerns, and Hillary's instinct was always to try to elevate the mood if possible. Worries were such a heavy burden to her, it felt like a physical weight bearing down on her chest and she had to get it off by some means. She wondered if other people felt this same way. No, she didn't think so. She knew women who seemed to treasure their problems and tell them to anyone who would listen. There were some at the Four Seasons who dumped on anyone, and Hillary had learned to give them the briefest of greetings and get rid of them. It wasn't that she was unsympathetic, she knew. It was just that she couldn't bear to dwell on hurtful things. She had to use every means she could to feel good. And she had learned that by not talking about her problems—keeping them just below the surface of her consciousness—made them more bearable.

Sharon had won the deal and shuffled the cards with a special flare before passing them to Jane to cut. "I don't suppose I should mention this again, but wouldn't it be great to play real bridge for a change?"

Hillary said nothing. Jane said, "Hmmph," while they sorted their hands. But she couldn't keep silent on the subject. "Can you imagine how boring it would be if we had a fourth person who was a motormouth and just had to tell us the cute things her grandchildren did? Or how about some Susie Homemaker who had to tell about this wonderful new recipe she had discovered?" Both Sharon and Hillary were smiling at the thought, amused at Jane's dramatic gestures. "Or how about the woman I played with at the club meeting the other day? She switched to Blackwood and had to tell her partner she was asking for aces, and then she counted on her fingers to determine how many she had answered. My partner was rolling her eyes and I thought she was about to throw down her cards. It just struck me funny, somehow." Jane laughed, remembering. "But believe me, that's what we'd get if we went out looking for a fourth."

Bridge hands were not exceptional, and they were happy to hear the timer going off on the oven. They ate the pastry in near silence and drank coffee and tea. Several times one of them would make an effort at conversation, but after a couple of half-hearted answers they would let it drop. They were each far away in their thoughts. Finally Jane said, "You know the Williamson bank has been reopened under the new name."

"Yes, it's so awful!" Sharon said, surprised. "I always thought it was the best bank in town, especially when Pete was there."

Hillary smiled sadly at the compliment to Pete. "Dan called me, kind of nostalgic, and we talked awhile about better days. He says he's enjoying his job with the country club. And he's really good at what he does."

Silence and gloom hung heavily around the table. Several more attempts at conversation failed. Jane reached for her walker and walked over to the bookshelf where the gritch kitty was and carefully balanced it so that she had control of the walker while holding the little pot upright. "Okay, girls, pay up. We've done nothing but complain tonight." She sat down and reached for her purse to contribute, too. No one disagreed.

"I've been doing a lot of reading the last few weeks. I read everything I can get my hands on, and especially books that someone brings me or recommends. I like to know that someone has enjoyed the book before I waste my time on it. It's not a guarantee, but it's usually a good indication.

"Now if we were the heroines in a book and sitting here in this gloom and doom, someone would come up with the idea of a party. In fact it would probably be a ball." Sharon and Hillary stared at Jane as if she had suddenly become senile and out of touch with reality.

"No, I'm serious," Jane declared. "Now that I've adopted my new motto I have to put it in practice." Hillary and Sharon didn't know Jane had a new motto and looked from one to another questioning. "I found it in the 2nd book of Timothy. Well, anyway, Martha found it for me. It goes something like this: 'God didn't give us a spirit of fear and timidity, but of power, and love, and a sound mind.' Isn't that good?" Sharon and Hillary didn't know how to respond; this was not the usual blustery Jane. "Now, listen. It's been a cold and dark winter and if we're sitting here bored and depressed, I'll bet you there's a bunch more of our best friends just as bored and depressed. We could do something foolish and unexpected and make everyone laugh." Jane paused. "How about this? I'll play the piano and both of you can dance."

"Oh, no," Hillary put in. "I'm not going to do that in front of anybody. I'm not even any good. I'd just die of embarrassment."

"No, Hillary, it would be great," Sharon agreed. "Remember when you said that we missed the point when we apologized for laughing at you? It would be the same for them. If they laughed then they'd feel good, not bad. And I can be a side-show barker and introduce you. Maybe I can dance a little bit, but you'd be the star."

"Well, maybe I could practice up a little, and just do a couple of routines." Then Hillary began to have some plans. "Jane, can we have it at your house? Maybe we really could have a ball, of sorts. Your place would be perfect."

"If it were Halloween we could have a masked ball." Sharon was thinking aloud. "But it will soon be springtime and that's not very appropriate."

They were silent again but not glumly. Each of them were thinking of fun things to do. "I've got it." Jane asked, "What do people call my house?"

"Yes, that's it!" Sharon agreed. "They call it 'Tara on the Brazos' and not always in kindness, either. So we'll make it a 'Gone With the Wind' formal ball and invite all of our favorite people. Or at least as many as you think we can entertain, Jane. What do you think?"

"I think it would be super." Jane's thoughts were racing. "We could put together a buffet between us three and hire a D.J. A band would be prohibitive and besides a D.J. could play a bigger variety of music. I know one who is very well-liked and has lots of bookings. And then at midnight, when the D.J. leaves, we can have our buffet. But we'll get lots of help in the kitchen so we can spend all our time with our guests. And we'll get new dresses and have our hair done so gorgeous no one will believe it's really us."

"Oh, wait a minute, I just thought of something." Hillary looked worried. "A Civil War theme might be offensive to Julian and Jasmine, you know, the slavery issue and all."

Jane was not to be discouraged. "Well, we'll just see about it." She again pulled up to her walker and briskly pushed it over to the telephone. She dialed and waited. "Julian, this is Jane. Tell me, would you be offended if you were invited to a 'Gone With the Wind' formal ball?" Sharon and Hillary winced at Jane's straightforward approach but watched her face as she listened to his reply. He must have said something funny because Jane laughed heartily. She put her hand over the phone and said, "He's gone to ask Jasmine if she'd be offended." A minute later Jane burst out laughing again and then explained to Jasmine that the three of them were sitting here twiddling their thumbs and decided to have a party. A few more pleasantries and Jane hung up. "No, they won't be offened," she concluded. "Julian said he wouldn't be at all offended. He could wear livery and stand outside with a big iron ring in his hand to hitch the horses to." And then what did Jasmine say that was so funny, they wanted to know. "And then Jasmine said she's always wanted a chance to get to say, 'Lands sake, Miss Scahlett, Ah don't know nuthin' 'bout birthin' babies.' She can be so funny when she gets into a mood." They all laughed at Julian and Jasmine's response and were relieved that they had not taken offense but had found the prospects highly humorous.

"Okay," Jane continued, ever the organizer. "Let's meet day after tomorrow, at my house, if that's alright. We'll have had a chance to do some planning and thinking of what might be fun, but not too expensive or complex." She was still thinking aloud. "We can get together and brainstorm and write it all down. Then we can choose the best parts and start planning. We can decide who to invite, how many, choose music, maybe decorate the house. Also we'll need to check the church calendar and civic calendars so that we don't conflict with anything important."

Each of them had started planning silently and were exhilarated with the prospects. No longer were they gloomy and negative. Life was suddenly full of possibilities, the best of which was entertaining their friends, making them laugh, giving them something to plan for and look forward to.

"We've just got to invite Sue-Sue and Ed." Sharon laughed, and Jane and Hillary shared the laughter. Sue-Sue and Ed were the oldest of their group of friends and probably the most colorful. Everyone loved them. They were short and looked as if they could have been brother and sister. Ed was losing his vision, and Sue-Sue had lost most of her hearing, but they were as vibrant as ever, good dancers, and interested in everything that was going on in Waco and the world. They could be seen walking hand-in-hand at church or on the street, with one of them explaining to the other what they were missing in sight or sound.

"But remember, Sue-Sue is getting old. She told me again the other day, very confidentially, that, after all, she was nearly seventy." They all laughed again, knowing that Sue-Sue had been saying the exact same thing for twelve or fifteen years. In fact, they would be very disappointed if she quit saying it.

It was hard for the trio to tear themselves away, so engrossed were they in party plans. But the time had flown by, and they were all surprised how late it had gotten. After the others had gone, Hillary rinsed the dishes and put them into the dishwasher to run later when she had a full load. She went to bed with a happy feeling and fell asleep immediately.

"Mrs. Johnson," the deep voice of officer Robinson said on the telephone. "I'm just following up on the incident that happened last week. Any new developments?" His sentences were brisk and to the point, but Hillary was impressed that he was a very good listener.

"Well, no, I guess not."

"Any new thoughts, or have you remembered anything that we didn't discuss? Maybe something that didn't seem important to you that I should know?"

"It's probably not important, and it may not even be fair. I just hate to judge someone on my own circumstantial evidence." Hillary hesitated and then started at the beginning, repeating the events that she knew Patrick was responsible for: blasting her bedroom window with his amplifiers and tearing up her lawn with his motorcycle. From then on it was natural for her to think that everything that happened was his doing. She admitted that she felt sorry for him as a lonely kid and the plot she and Greg had devised of befriending him to see if he might be socialized into a good citizen. She then felt a little foolish for practicing this amateur psychology on her neighbor and confessed as much to the patrolman, who didn't offer any comment. And through his very silence was encouraging her to remember and divulge anything else that occurred to her. At his encouragement she told again of the times that Lady had warned of someone on the patio and again inside the house. Of Lady barking and yelping in the backyard when there was apparently no one around.

"I do feel badly about judging the boy on those few occasions. But, Officer

Robinson, I have the utmost confidence in the judgment of my grandson, Greg." Hillary tried to tell the patrolman everything that Greg had said and in his own words. "There is one more thing. And it may not be important. But one day I was in the back of the garden where we have a bench and I noticed several cigarette butts. As if someone sat there for some time, waiting maybe, for someone to come home." Hillary sensed that the officer had taken a fresh interest in the conversation. "There may be some simple explanation, of course, but at the time I felt very frightened." When she finished, she wanted to know what he concluded from this information, but again he made no comment, just thanked her for her time and asked her to give him a call if she remembered anything else, or if something else unpleasant happened.

Hillary sat beside the telephone long after Officer Robinson had hung up. She had the uneasy feeling that there was something more he wanted to say. Maybe something she was reading between the lines that he would not or could not say.

CHAPTER 16

Hillary put away her worries and threw herself completely into the planning of the party. She would excitedly tell Pete about their progress. "I'm in charge of ordering and mailing the invitations," she told him as he watched the television and gave no hint whether he was listening to her. "We got together for the invitation list, each of us had our own list and there were lots of duplications, naturally, since we have many of the same friends." Sometimes she talked to Pete as if he were a child and had difficulty understanding. Other times she realized that she was speaking as if to a complete stranger, explaining everything down to the smallest detail. She told Pete who some of the guests would be and what fun it was going to be to dress up in Civil War vintage formal dress. She didn't know yet what she would wear and discussed her thoughts with Pete as if he could help her decide. She admitted that he did help her decide many things, even in his silence. Problems seemed much clearer after discussing them out loud to him, and she then wondered why they had ever given her any difficulty. She continued to inform Pete that Jane wanted to be in charge of the house and yard and that Sharon wanted to plan the food and drinks. They would, of course, all assist each other as needed. She would have the invitations printed up and mailed a full month in advance so that everyone would have plenty of time to plan and prepare, which she considered to be half the fun of a party or vacation or whatever.

Jane also was enjoying the increased activity of party preparations. She had to gently tell Chrissy that it was not going to be a general social event and that no young people would be invited. It was to be a group of old friends. They were not all rich and influential, but some were. They were friends who had lived, suffered, triumphed, shared, survived, and most of all who loved and accepted one another in spite of the tricks of time and fate. Chrissy did not understand, but quietly withdrew her offer to help.

Her yard would be in full bloom with all the bulbs bursting forth, Jane knew. But it was kind of iffy whether the grass would be fully green that early in the season, so she would make sure her lawn service gave it a good feeding and maybe that would force it. She planned to order a few large and strategic floral arrangements to help set the mood inside. One large oriental rug could be taken up, leaving a fairly adequate dance floor on the shiny hardwood. Each thought that occurred to her got written down in her steno pad and later transcribed into a list that had to be dealt with in a chronological order.

Many times as she planned a small detail Jane would feel a shiver of excitement that she had not felt since... well, she couldn't remember when she had been this happy and excited. Not since Max had become ill, anyway. What fun this would be if Max were here for the party. He had always loved parties, and they had given several every year—dinners, cocktail parties, and open houses on holidays. Any excuse was a good excuse for a party, and she had gotten the preparations down to a routine that varied just slightly for the occasion and made it very easy to put together a nice party with a minimum of effort. This party may be her last, Jane knew, or perhaps the first of many. *Maybe we will have so much fun that we'll want to have more*, she told herself more than once. She hoped this would be the case.

What shall we do about parking? she worried. *I can't have valet parking; it seems that the liability would be more than I want to tackle*, Jane pondered. *Maybe they can all park in the church parking lot and we can rent a couple of vans to shuttle them over and back.*

After many deliberations, the invitation list had settled around thirty-seven. Twenty nine of these were couples and there were eight single, who were invited to bring a guest. No one had been black-balled. Any name that had been recommended was put on the list. Almost daily the list grew because one of the three remembered friends they wanted to add. Several friends from out of town were invited and were sure to show up. Jane could hardly wait till the RSVPs started coming in.

"Jane," Sharon said when the phone was answered, "what if we make up a lot of this food in advance? Will you have room in your freezer? And some of the other things we could stock up in your pantry if you have room. I have a little space myself and so will Hillary, but not like yours."

Sharon was planning the food and drinks. They would all help with the expense of it and the cooking that had to be done in advance. Luckily Jane had a vast pantry and freezer, and she hoped they could do almost all the cooking in advance to have time for finishing touches on the last day. The most comfortable way to serve, Sharon felt, would be hors d'ouerves and a tangy punch during the dancing. Most of their friends had given up alcohol for religious or health reasons. Then at midnight, when the music was over, they would have an elegant buffet breakfast. Each of them had already planned some of her favorite offerings, and among the three of them they had exquisite serving pieces, mostly silver and crystal, but some copper and brass as well. The plates, however, would have to come from the rental agency. Nobody had dishes alike to serve seventy people. *There may not be seventy people*, Sharon admitted realistically, *but if even fifty show up it can be a great party.*

This party would be her gift to her dearest friends, she thought. She had no idea that Jane and Hillary were thinking of the party in the same way, their gift to make their friends happy. To have something to plan for, if only for a little while. And then to have some memories to reflect on, perhaps for a little longer. Some of these friends had serious health problems and needed to have a little reprieve from the cares associated with them. Others may have fallen into a humdrum existence as they have retired from public life and employment, but Sharon knew they all needed this little shot in the arm to make their lives more fun.

Sharon was enjoying planning her dress, as well as the food. Without Harvey to dictate the color and style, she felt very undecided at first. This time she would not wear a vibrant red, yellow, or electric blue. She would have a pretty style but truly did not want to be the center of attention. She examined herself in her bathroom mirrors, front and back. Her hair had been blonde and now was more than half gray. The color mixture was actually sort of gray-beige she decided, and they call that color taupe. Yes, she had taupe hair and so did many other people, but she had never heard anyone say as much. When she took the yards of taupe-colored georgette to the dressmaker she had used so many times in the past, Sharon was braced to have to justify herself, but Ramona picked up the fabric almost reverently and held it up to Sharon's face and shoulder to check the colors.

"Oh, *senora*, it is so lovely. But you need something to break the, how do you say, monotony? You need some white lace, I think." She draped the fabric across Sharon's shoulders and kept on smiling. "You will be the most beautiful one as always." Sharon and Ramona chatted for almost an hour, about the pattern, about the way she should wear her hair. Then they talked about her jewelry and her shoes. Ramona had always enjoyed sewing something beautiful for Sharon when she got the chance. For too many years Harvey had insisted that Sharon buy an expensive designer label in order to be well-dressed. But she had always been more comfortable in the creations that Ramona had made for her. For one reason, she didn't think she was a true size for ready-made clothes. Hardly anyone is, in fact, and once the alterations were made and added to the price Sharon felt a heavy sense of guilt. Ramona's finish work was always excellent, and Sharon left feeling very good about her party dress. She could hardly wait to see Harvey's reaction to it. Harvey would probably think it dowdy, but it seemed to Sharon to be understated elegance. Subtlety was something Harvey would never understand.

Gloria would have enjoyed the party preparations, Sharon thought. How many times had they planned for a special occasion like this, wondering what to wear, how to style their hair, all the little things they knew were merely affectations but had been extremely successful when they were both young and pretty. For a few minutes she let her mind dwell on those occasions, trying to face up to the fact that Gloria was gone. Trying to console herself that Gloria was not hurting. Maybe she and David were together in some heavenly place and having a happy life. *Yes, that's a great idea. That's how I'm always going to remember them*, she promised herself.

Sharon wondered if Charlie would like her dress. *Maybe he won't even notice. Maybe he won't even come. There won't be any young single women invited.* Suddenly Sharon became afraid that he might decline the invitation and the whole party would seem a little less exciting, hardly worth all this trouble. And there was the possibility that he might actually bring a date. How would she feel about that?

Across town Hillary was having her own doubts. She wanted to invite Sam. Most of the guests would have escorts, and Hillary's best friend was Sam, outside of Pete, of course. He was always cheerful and interesting. It would be fun to get him together with Julian. She had always thought they were alike in many ways. Maybe the seriousness of their profession required that they have a frivolous relief in their lives. Would people think her too bold? Inviting a "date" before poor Pete was even dead. On the other hand, Sam might be hurt if he found out they had this party without inviting him. This was a problem she couldn't discuss with anyone; she had to make the decision on her own. How she would love to see Sam again, and he did enjoy parties. Also he knew many of her friends and would feel right at home with them. Actually, he seemed to feel at home with any group, however humble, however affluent. She decided to invite him. Then the next time she thought about it, she wondered whether he might feel that she was being forward. She even began to doubt her own feelings and ask herself, *Am I trying to start something between Sam and me? Shoot*, she finally decided, *I'll invite him and let him accept or decline.*

How long had it been since she was forced to summon an escape fantasy? It had been a long time. Not since they had decided to have the party, she realized. *How about my intruder*, she wondered. *How about my impending poverty and debtors' prison*, she asked herself. She stood up straight and squared her shoulders in an act of bravado that she was very familiar with and dismissed all negative thoughts.

April in central Texas flows in with color and good smells in the blooming trees and shrubbery. By the end of March the bulbs have heralded the season and died back to make way for the next series of leafy and flowering plants. Lawns were green and had been mowed once or twice already. The sky was bright and clear most days but was occasionally punctuated by a short but violent thunderstorm. Jane spent much time out of doors with her yard crew, planning ways to make certain existing plants bloom or green up to be at their peak for her party weekend, and she was having good success. The gardener suggested buying some pots of blooming flowers and sinking them in front of hedges and other borders of evergreens.

Jane parked her walker in a closet and was walking with a cane. She would deny any accusation of vanity, preferring to have a reputation for sports and the arts; nevertheless, she spent hours each day planning her dress and accessories. She would look in the mirror as if for the first time, wondering what she really looked like to a stranger, or even her friends. Her looks had never taken much of her time and effort, but now it seemed important to look and dress her finest for the ball. She had spent hours in department stores trying colors and finally felt that a dusty rose, almost mauve, was very flattering to her dark complexion and dark hair with the gray streak rising from her right forehead. She had also planned to use a little more makeup than usual for this special occasion, then felt a stab of guilt to be acting so vain. But then she would smile to herself and imagine that her friends across town and some in nearby cities were doing the same thing in preparation for this important occasion. The day of the ball finally arrived. Everyone had started referring to the gala as *the ball*, not "the party," or even "the dance." The three hostesses had agreed that the most important thing was to have everything and everyone in place well beforehand so that they could be free to enjoy the festivities with their guests. Checklists had been completed and new ones started.

The vans and drivers were obtained by Jane. The drivers had driven for the Westerman Trucking Company and had years of experience and safe-driving commendations. The grounds were so carefully manicured that hardly a square foot of the yard was without something growing and blooming. Jane could not remember a time when it was more beautiful and again wished she could share this moment with Max. Maria had enlisted several relatives for the final preparations in the kitchen and would become a tyrant in her domain so that all would be perfect. Jane would be careful to stay out of her way in the kitchen, and yet she knew that whenever she came into the dining room with the guests, Maria would be the epitome of grace and hospitality.

The day was long for Hillary. She had everything laid out in order to dress early and go to the Four Seasons to show herself off to Pete. She didn't expect him to do or say anything—he had practically been ignoring her lately—but it was something she felt she must do for herself. If he were conscious of her conversations, he would know this was the day of the ball. And if he were not aware of anything, then it would still make her feel better.

Hillary was disappointed that Sam had declined the invitation; she would love to have seen him. And she admitted to herself that she would like to have been seen by him, too, looking so pretty in her party dress. The dress was a shade of blue that she knew was becoming to her—darker than sky blue and not quite as deep as royal blue. She had laid out her aquamarine set that Pete had surprised her with one anniversary long ago, necklace and earrings. The surprise was both that it was so elegant for her own simple tastes and that Pete, who never seemed to notice women's jewelry, had chosen it for her. Much as she loved the jewelry, she seldom wore it, feeling a little bit conspicuous in such beautiful stones. Years later she herself had found a bracelet of aquamarines set in a similar silver pattern and had asked the jeweler to let her pay it out over time. Somehow it seemed a little less extravagant if she paid it out over time.

Lady was lying on the carpet, lazily watching Hillary as she dressed up in her finery. She cocked her head to one side as Hillary put on her satin shoes, dyed to the shade of blue that matched the dress. And then completely dressed, Hillary stood in front of the full-length mirror, threw back her head with arms outstretched, and danced around the bedroom. Hillary began to laugh at Lady's puzzled actions and kept dancing. Lady, sensing a playful moment jumped up, barking, and followed Hillary's steps around the bedroom. *Oh, if only Pete could see us dance.*

At the Four Seasons Hillary parked and got out of her car with care. She was aware of stares from many residents and graciously accepted the compliments given her. Pete was sitting in his room, prepared to go into dinner when the attendant came for him. *He's so handsome*, Hillary thought. *I certainly played my cards right.* This was an inside joke to Pete and Hillary. When they had announced their engagement, a classmate of Hillary's, who made no secret of trying to attract Pete's attention, congratulated Hillary with that pronouncement.

He was staring silently ahead as if he could not turn to look at her as she walked into the room. Hillary walked over to Pete and stood in front of him. Taking his face gently in her hands she said, "Pete, tonight is the night of the ball at Jane's house. Do you like my dress?" She waited for a sign of recognition. He looked squarely at her for a few seconds and then resumed his stare into space. "See the jewelry? Remember when you gave me these beautiful things on our anniversary?" She fingered the necklace and earrings and held out the bracelet for him to see. She picked up his hand and let him feel of the stones. His fingers moved back and forth over the large stones in the necklace and then stopped.

Maybe Pete didn't remember, she admitted. On the other hand, it was possible that he could hear her and understand her, so by golly, that's the way she was going to behave. She stood up in Pete's line of vision and twirled around so that her skirt with the many petticoats stood right out. She had considered wearing a hoop but knew she would be miserable all evening. She laughed and told Pete how excited Lady had become when she was dancing around the bedroom. While she was still talking in her animated way, the attendant came to get Pete for supper. "Well, Darling, you go and eat a good supper. I'm going over to Jane's to help her with last-minute preparations. I'll come over tomorrow and give you a blow-by-blow description of who was there and what they wore."

The attendant helped Pete to stand and held him by the left elbow and hand with his own muscular right arm. Hillary reached up to give Pete a goodbye kiss. As she stepped back he said, "Pretty, so... pretty." Hillary beamed and gave Pete another kiss.

CHAPTER 17

There was parking for several cars at the back of Jane's house. Sharon's Suburban was already parked, but the other cars were unfamiliar to Hillary. The garage and parking area took up about half of Jane's backyard and the rest was a beautifully landscaped formal garden, complete with an arbor and flowing fountain. Hillary was compelled to peek into the back yard and enjoy the sights and smells of the spring garden. Picking up her skirts, she made her way around the brick sidewalk that formed borders for the carpet grass and flower beds.

She wished once again that Sam had been able to come for the ball. She really did understand that he was the guest speaker for a medical meeting in Austin. And even though he promised to try to work something out she knew he wouldn't be able to come. Maybe he thought she was being too forward in asking him to come as if for her "date" and was uncomfortable with the idea.

Hillary glanced up into the giant live oak which was the focal point of Jane's backyard and happily envisioned three skinny adolescents building a treehouse, each with a homemade sword in his belt. Giving orders to the two willing boys was the spunky little girl with coarse black hair cut in bangs and a pageboy. One of the boys was dashingly handsome already, with Hispanic coloring, and the other was medium height, had medium brown hair, might have been totally nondescript except for the quick, crooked smile that lit up his features so often. *Ah, those were good memories. But that was then. And this is now.*

Hillary was still smiling as she opened the French doors into Jane's dining room. "Well, what's so funny, Hillary?" Jane had caught the slight smile as Hillary walked in. "You look like you just ate the canary, all those feathers on your face." Jane was happy to see Hillary smiling. She had feared that the party might be painful without Pete.

"I was just thinking about climbing your big live oak, but I guess I won't try it tonight," she evaded.

"Well, come on in and see what we've got here." They walked out into the broad hall that was the predominate feature of the house and that separated open areas for sitting, music, dining, and another set up for a library. Hillary gasped at the number of floral arrangements sitting along the hall near the entry. "It seems that nearly everyone we invited has sent a big gorgeous arrangement. Sharon has already started placing them around on tables and in boring corners. So just grab some and put them anywhere you think they'd look good." She added, "Just don't go into the kitchen if you value your life. The dictator has taken over and we don't dare interrupt her."

Jane had bought several large bouquets herself for the serving tables and her entry hall but now there were flowers everywhere. Hillary glanced into the powder room and found a place for two of the smaller bouquets. Still there were so many flowers along the floor that they wondered what to do with them. "Jane, where is that baker's rack you used to have in your breakfast area? It would hold a lot of these and look like a wall of flowers."

"It's out in the sun room with some stuff on it, ivies and African violets and just nicknacks. Let's take a look at it." They walked to the back of the house, carefully avoiding the kitchen, and found that the bakers rack had few things on it and would, indeed, make a suitable wall of flowers. "Let's see if we can borrow Albert from the kitchen to help us with it."

Albert was delighted to be out of the kitchen and helping the ladies. He was to double as bartender serving punch after he finished with preparations in the kitchen. He grabbed a towel and washed down the rack after its treasures had been redistributed and carefully carried it to the great hall. The rack was white enamel and had large shiny knobs of brass. Placed in the hall, the rack made a lovely room divider for the sitting area. The three women went to work arranging and re-arranging the flowers on the shelves.

At eight-thirty the hostesses had completed all the preparations they had on their many lists. They walked to the front driveway to look at the grounds. Jane turned on the lights that lit up the trees and the lower lights that lit up the shrubbery. The effect was a fantasy land and they all were pleased. Then they walked into the entry hall and down the great hall once again, glancing each way to see if anything was out of order—nothing was. The kitchen captives were now busy setting up the hors d'oeuvres table, and Albert had his punch bowl set up with ice and plenty of glasses and napkins. Jane had ordered special swizzle sticks and napkins just for the occasion from a specialty advertising company. Perhaps a frivolous expense but one that she felt good about. They had "Tara" and the date printed on them. She hoped her friends would take them home as a memento of the occasion.

The dining table was crowned with an elegant floral arrangement but was bare otherwise, waiting for the feast to be placed there at the specified time. Nearby was the matching sideboard laden with beautiful silver and the cut glass plates that had been supplied by the rental service. The hostesses opened the french doors to the garden and breathed in the crisp spring air. "I hope people will want to come out into the garden and enjoy this," Jane said as she switched on the lights that turned her garden into a fairyland. "Max would love this." They stood on the terrace, quiet, each with her own thoughts, enjoying the beauty around them and almost simultaneously looked at their watch. "It's show time, girls," Jane said as she turned back to the house. "If I forgot to tell you, you both look gorgeous."

"Well, so do you, Jane. Even your cane has a festive look to it." Hillary had noticed the rhinestones and beads on the cane that was painted in a color that matched Jane's dress. "I'll bet your talented daughter-in-law had something to do with that."

"Yes, Chrissy made it for me. She seemed miffed at first that she and her friends were not going to be invited. But then finally, when I got my dress and shoes and showed them to her, I complained that I couldn't really look elegant on that stupid cane. So she secretly bought this one and painted it to match my dress and then put the rhinestones on it to match the ones on my bodice and shoes. She's good to come through when the chips are down. She really is a great person."

The first van load of guests brought Sue-Sue and Ed along with several other couples who were laughing and joking, generally having a wonderful time, although the evening was just beginning. It was not quite nine o'clock, the actual time for the ball to start, but these couples, as well as their hostesses, could hardly wait for the party to begin. Everyone was talking and laughing at the same time, complimenting each other on their innovative Scarlett or Rhett costume. Some were definitely Melanie or Ashley, but others didn't claim to be a character, just a Confederate soldier or grand dame of the era.

The guests took a cup of punch from Albert, and Sharon led some into the back garden while the disc jockey set up his equipment in the music room. Jane had soft music already playing through the intercom, and she turned the dimmer down on all the lights in the great hall, eagerly waiting for the second van to arrive.

When the second van arrived, the first was close behind with another load of Civil War vintage party-goers. The aging Scarletts and Rhetts were very handsome in their finery, all in high spirits. Jane was complimented on her lovely Tara and her dress, and then the guests went on into the house to find a drink and make their way out to the terrace.

Martha Lodge, beautifully groomed as always, arrived on the arm of a tall gray gentleman in Confederate uniform, not handsome exactly, but Jane quickly summed him up as *interesting*. *Good for Martha*, she silently congratulated.

Hank and Marianne Caldwell came in as a goodlooking Ashley and Melanie. Watching their smiles and laughter, one was reminded of earlier times when they gave and attended so many pleasant galas.

The early guests wandered back into the hall as the dance music began, soft and undemanding, but yet with a rhythm that invited them to dance. Harvey had arrived in a finely tailored suit with white lace cuffs and a large gemstone tie tack. He found Sharon immediately and monopolized her attention so that she became uncomfortable. They danced a waltz as they had many times before, as skillfully as ballroom dancers. And then they danced a second number, each anticipating the other's movements. Over Harvey's shoulder Sharon spied another tall Rhett Butler watching them solemnly, and she suddenly felt very self-conscious.

"You look very nice," Harvey said into Sharon's ear. "I wouldn't have chosen those colors for you. I always associate gray with middle-aged frumps," he said as Sharon had predicted.

He is not going to rattle me tonight, Sharon promised herself. "But, Harvey," she said sweetly, "I am NOT a middle-aged frump." She kept laughing. "I'm an OLD frump." She was enjoying her joke and seeing Harvey's discomfort. When the dance ended, she suggested he go and freshen up his drink while she greeted her guests.

Sharon made small talk with several of her friends while making her way to the corner where Charlie was chatting with another man. She could hear that the conversation was about livestock, not surprisingly. She kept glancing around to see whether he had brought a "guest" as the singles had been invited to do in the invitation. Sharon greeted the two men, as is appropriate for a hostess, and started to move on through the crowd when the new group coming in the door caused people around her to push back, pressing her up against Charlie's thick chest. She glanced up at him and saw the amused smile on his face. *He knows*, she accused herself, *he knows that I have this teenage crush on him and he's just standing there laughing at me*. "Well," she tried to tease in an offhand manner, "that worked out just like I planned." Then she got away from Charlie as fast as she could, and feeling very warm, wondered whether she was blushing. Ripples of laughter were floating through the crowd starting near the entry hall. Sharon's embarrassment was covered by this welcomed diversion, and she strained to see where everyone was looking and what was so amusing. The crowd parted to allow the newcomers an entrance. There in the entry hall and entering the grand hall in their grand manner were Julian and Jasmine. Sharon began to laugh along with the others, for Julian was dressed as a carpet-bagger, indeed, with a carpet bag in one hand and the other arm around his fancy lady who was wearing a very low-cut gown that showed a great deal of her ample bosom. Jasmine, looking every inch the part she was playing, was more beautiful than Sharon had ever seen her. "Offended, my eye," she said aloud, and felt very good.

Dancing was spirited, mellow, and hearty, and many couples danced almost every dance, although there were some who did not dance. Jane was pleased with the variety of music the D.J. had chosen. These couples had favorites from several decades and enjoyed "Sentimental Journey" and "Cotton-Eyed Joe" equally. Jane put away her cane to dance with Martha's friend. He was a smooth dancer although it seemed strange to Jane to be in the arms of a man several inches taller than herself. Even after all these years Jane was used to being the same height as Max when she was wearing dress shoes and they had danced well together. The man's name was Preston something-or-other, she didn't quite hear his last name over the noise of the crowd. Someone said he was a doctor from over in Temple, the big medical center. But as the saying goes, there are as many doctors in Temple as there are Baptists in Waco. Anyway he was a good dancer and Jane was pleased that he suggested they stay on the dance floor for the next number as well.

Several men asked Hillary to dance, and Sharon was chosen frequently, usually by Harvey. Jane noticed that Charlie watched Sharon every dance but did not invite her to dance with him; she wondered why not. It seemed to her that they might even have an attraction for each other, but their conversations were always brief, if not curt.

Harvey was holding Sharon tightly and their bodies and steps were in sync. "We're a terrific pair, Sharon. We never should have broken up." He felt Sharon tense and continued talking softly into her ear. "I've missed you so much I can't even begin to tell you. And I've never needed you so much as I do now that my health is failing. Let's start over, okay? On your terms, whatever you want. I'll court you like we just met..."

Sharon stopped dancing and pulled away, aware that she might be causing a small scene, although she wasn't talking loudly. "Harvey, we are divorced for only one reason. You are incapable of being true to one woman. I've tried hard to forgive you and I honestly don't know whether I can or not. What I choose to do is forget about you completely. You'd be surprised how seldom you even cross my mind. And besides that..."

"Excuse me, may I cut in?" Before either Harvey or Sharon could collect their thoughts, Charlie took Sharon into his big arms and twirled her across the dance floor to the opposite side of the room.

Sharon felt dizzy and was grateful for the strong arms holding her up. She might not have been able to stand otherwise. "Thank you, Charlie. I needed rescuing."

Charlie held her close. "Heck, it looked to me like Harvey needed the rescuing," and he chuckled that infectious laugh of his. Sharon didn't want to think, just to enjoy this dance. For a big man, Charlie was very light on his feet. They danced the next two dances together, and when the D.J. chose a polka decided to get a cold drink. They stood with their drinks for a few minutes at the edge of the dance floor watching Sue-Sue and Ed execute a flawless polka.

Sharon felt that she was about to get tongue-tied again in the presence of this big man who was the secret infatuation of her life. They took their drinks out the french doors to the terrace. Sharon wanted to be witty or interesting or at least say something special to make Charlie want to stay out here a little longer and visit with her. But what in the world could she say that would be of the slightest interest to him?

"So, Charlie," she babbled, "do you like to ride horses or just doctor them?" *What a stupid thing to say. Maybe he'll just turn around and leave me out here*, she worried.

"I guess I'd rather ride a good horse than just about anything I know of." He seemed surprised at her question but soon warmed to the subject. "I used to do a little calf roping, but I'm too old and stiff now so that it's not much fun." Charlie's eyes twinkled. "I used to think I was pretty good, but actually, I'm probably a pretty mediocre roper compared to present company." He looked down to see Sharon smile at this. "What I really like to do is take Old Red up the Bosque to a place we have in the hills. We've got a few head of cattle there too, but mainly I just like the beauty of the place." He was quiet a few minutes, then, "Why do you ask?"

"Oh, I don't know. I just wondered if you would start to take them for granted since you're around them all the time. Hillary and I really love our horses and try to ride them as often as we can. Every time we ride we talk about 'someday' and 'maybe.' Someday we're going to go on a real trail ride in some pretty place, maybe along a river. And maybe in the mountains. Maybe we'll even camp out and sleep under the stars." Sharon sounded wistful. "I guess that's about the dumbest thing you've ever heard from a couple of gray-haired women. But Queen and Major are sound and they act like they really enjoy our outings." She glanced over at Charlie to determine his reaction but he seemed to be giving her his sincere attention. "Do you think horses enjoy outings, or is that our imagination?"

"Sure they do. You should see Red when I drive up with the trailer on the pickup. He acts like a colt. And some days he dances around so much that I can hardly settle him down."

Charlie looked out into the darkness with a frown on his face. "I don't know if it would be proper or not. And I don't know if you'd even enjoy it, but maybe we could take a little trail ride up the Bosque River and end up at my place. You wouldn't get to sleep out under the stars, though, and we even have hot water." He looked at her squarely. "Do you think Hillary would enjoy that? Would you? I've always wanted to do something like that myself, but it wouldn't be much fun alone and I haven't had a riding buddy since Jenny got married."

Charlie became serious with his planning. "Think about this and talk to Hillary about it. I can pick up the horses in the long stock trailer and haul them to this spot I know of just beyond Valley Mills. Then we can pack from there to the cabin and have lunch over a campfire along the way. Does that sound like any fun to you?"

Sharon could hardly believe the conversation. It occurred to her that she might be dreaming and could wake up at any moment.

"Anyone out here want to dance the last dance?" someone shouted from the French doors.

"We'd better go and dance the last one," Charlie said as he possessively tucked Sharon's hand into the bend of his elbow with his other hand tightly on top. "And from the good smells coming from the kitchen, I think we're in for a feast after the dancing. Anything else planned for this evening?"

Sharon had to laugh out loud as she told him, "Yes, you just can't imagine the other entertainment that's been planned for your pleasure." Somehow she didn't feel any stage fright, remembering that making a fool of herself, along with Hillary and her tap dancing, was, in a way, their gift to their friends. She hoped, no, she KNEW that they would all laugh and enjoy the spectacle tremendously.

171

The "last dance" was actually a medley of three romantic good night songs, and almost all the guests were on the dance floor at the same time. It was very crowded, but no one was taking any big dance steps, just more or less swaying in time to the music with the partner of their choice. Charlie and Sharon were no longer talking, just enjoying the moment that each had been sure would never happen.

The guests lined up for the buffet in the dining room and were pleased with the beauty of the serving table. Jane had planned beforehand that Julian ask the blessing. His deep, booming voice led the group to acknowledge the giver of all good and perfect gifts. And this cheerful gathering was certainly a perfect gift.

Jane and Sharon were visiting with guests in the serving line, not wanting to be served until last, when the doorbell rang. Hillary was nearer to the door and went to see who could be there. Most of the guests had come in the vans and had not rung the bell. When she opened the big door she gasped and whooped with delight as she reached out and pulled the two men into the entry hall of Jane's house.

Hillary gave Sam and Jesse an enthusiastic hug and then stepped back to admire their outfits. "Sorry we couldn't arrange to be in Civil War costumes. Our old tuxedos will have to do at this late hour. We were more than a little bit overdressed for the medical meeting, though," Sam laughed.

"And I had to sit through the longest evening of my life," Jesse complained. "I understand English and Spanish, but I didn't understand a word they said all night in that medical language. Besides that, dressed up in this monkey suit most of them thought I was the waiter." They all laughed as he lied about fetching drinks for the doctors and all the tips he made.

Hillary beamed. She couldn't quit smiling as she introduced her two old friends to other old friends. Sam had met many of them on other occasions. Jesse was happy to meet all the new people and loved to be the center of attention. He exuded a Latin charm and gallantry that fit the house and festivities perfectly.

No one seemed to notice that the hostesses disappeared toward the end of the meal until they heard a blasting, "Ladies and gentlemen!" from the sound system that the disc jockey had set up, followed by an equally loud fanfare from Jane's piano. Everyone turned to see the music room off the great hall which had been dark, suddenly light up with spotlights over the piano and one over an area of bare floor into which stepped Sharon, acting as sideshow barker. With a microphone in her hand and a straw hat at a jaunty angle,

Sharon shouted again, not quite so loudly, "Ladies and gentlemen of Waco, for your entertainment, for your amazement, the establishment presents, straight from her engagement at the Four Seasons, the new dancing sensation, Hillary Johnson!"

The crowd laughed and applauded loudly as Hillary stepped into the spotlight, with a cane and straw hat that matched Sharon's. The Four Seasons irony was not lost on a one. Both Sharon and Hillary had drapery tapes sewn into the front of their gowns so that, when the time came, they could pull up the tapes and with a neat shirred effect, shorten their skirts by several inches. Hillary began by dancing a very simple "Tea For Two" routine that everyone would expect from a beginning tap dancer, then without a break in the music, Jane picked up the tempo with Hillary's first favorite, "She Used to be Somebody's Baby." The combinations became more difficult and the guests were surprised that Hillary could execute them. Several times during the number, applause broke out. She was so glad that Sam and Jesse were here. There was something about having them present that made her want to show off a little bit. She couldn't analyze this feeling. *Maybe it's just knowing someone is here*, she reasoned, *who will give me unconditional acceptance, even if I fall on my face.* She continued to dance with abandon as if she were only in front of her bedroom mirror.

Sharon had also gotten into the swing of things with her Jazzercize dance routines but not enough to take any attention from Hillary. When Jane picked up the tempo once again with "Born to Boogie," all the guests were swaying in time to the music and snapping their fingers. The entire routine was only a few minutes, but Hillary was warm and exhausted when she took her bows.

The guests were well-known to each other, and Jane guessed that if she played a lilting rendition of "Alabama Jubilee," one of the guests would not be able to contain himself. She had only played a few bars when they noticed the carpet bagger taking off his opulent jacket for his fancy lady to hold. They all laughed and clapped as Julian danced his Bo Jangles routine. As one the crowd aaahhhed as he went down on his knees, knowing the price he would pay in the morning, if he could walk at all. But tonight there was not a sign of stiffness as the agile dancer won the hearts of the crowd. A lusty soft shoe, turns and half-turns, down on his knees, leaps, and the grand finale was always the sliding splits. Loving the applause, Julian made deep humble bows to his appreciative audience.

While the crowd was still clapping, laughing, and talking at the same time, Jane began a medley of sing-a-long tunes that were welcomed heartily.

No one seemed in a hurry to leave, no one was thinking they had things to do tomorrow. It was as if they all were trying to make this night last forever. Everyone at one time or another checked on Sue-Sue and Ed to see how they were holding up under this activity and this late hour. They seemed to be having more fun than anyone. Sometimes one or the other would be seen explaining something the spouse had not heard or couldn't see well enough.

There was still another talent that had not yet come forward, and Jane gave her the opportunity by starting to play the introduction to "Just a Closer Walk With Thee." Everyone looked toward Jasmine, knowing she was Waco's finest gospel singer. Her voice was deep and mellow, and although she had enjoyed a formal classical education, her style was simplicity itself. Jane coaxed her further with "Do Lord." As she began singing "I've got a home in glory land," she started to clap and encourage the group to sing along with her.

As one song would end, someone would shout the name of another and another until finally Jane began playing "Good Night Ladies" which gave a very good hint to the guests that the hostess thought it was time to end the party. They laughed and some pretended to be hurt that she would be so obvious. But Jane said, "Oh, you don't have to leave, but I'm going to bed now."

Sharon didn't know when Harvey left. As Charlie was leaving, he said to her, "We need to get together and talk about our trail ride. See if Hillary would enjoy doing something like I described. If not, we can plan something different."

There was very little cleaning up that needed to be done after the guests had gone. The kitchen crew had done most of the washing up while the entertainment was going on and they were coming back in the morning, around nine o'clock, to put the house back in order. Jane went happily off to her room when the lights were out and the doors all locked.

Sharon went home to her small elegant patio home overlooking the lake but could not sleep. She put on a shawl and went out onto her deck to enjoy the night. The water was inky black with very few lights reflecting this late at night. She recalled over and over the events of the evening and several times felt shivers of excitement remembering things that Charlie had said, hoping that he was sincere. Perhaps he was just being a polite guest.

Her moral dilemma was the same as it ever was. She felt like a married lady. She had a public formal wedding and pledged, "For better or for worse." Her prayer, always on her lips with little variation, was, "Dear God, if you wish me to remain single, I will give you the glory and be happy. If you wish me to have a companion, I will wait for you to give me one. And I will give you the glory and be happy."

Hillary let herself in the back door, checking lights and locks as she made her way to her bedroom in the back of the house. Lady followed her into every room and sprawled out beside the bed in her usual place as Hillary put on her pajamas and prepared for bed. The end of a perfect day, she reminded herself. How many perfect days had prompted her to say that? she wondered. Many. Maybe hundreds. Could it be thousands?

Sam and Jesse had been the best surprise she had enjoyed since she couldn't remember when. They explained that Jesse had been in Dallas on business when he learned that Sam had been invited to Hillary's party. Together they plotted a way to attend the mandatory medical meeting and also make it to her party. Afterward they still had to drive to Dallas, and she smiled thinking how tired they'd be. And they did it all for her. Before she went to sleep she remembered taking the two men into the garden to see the big live oak tree. She told them how she had envisioned them making a treehouse in it that would be their fort. The two men argued about where they would put the treehouse until finally Jesse turned to her and said, "You tell us, Muñeca, where shall we put the treehouse? We always do your bidding, *¿verdad?*"

CHAPTER 18

Charlie came in from the stalls with his hands full of equipment that needed to be cleaned and sterilized. "What is it with you, Dad?" Jenny yelled from an examining room. "You've been whistling all morning. You're gonna spook the livestock," she teased.

"It sure is a pretty spring day, don't you think?" was all that Charlie would answer.

Hillary spent the afternoon with Pete telling him over and over about the ball and what the costumes were like. She specifically mentioned each of their friends by name and repeated them several times in her re-telling. Only last fall Pete would carry on a conversation with her, although at times she felt he spoke to her as a stranger, but now many times his answers to her direct questions were just single words or no answer at all. She asked the nurses whether he would converse with them and they had made the same assessment. He did, however, respond well in his modeling class. Not verbally but with his hands. His animals were excellent, especially his dogs, which always resembled a Labrador retriever. His birds could be identified: some dove, some quail, some ducks— all the birds that he had hunted and Lady had retrieved.

Her telephone began to ring as Hillary unlocked the back door. "Mrs. Johnson? This is Officer Robinson. I have a report to give you concerning your recent break-in and the other mischief you reported." Hillary realized that she was holding her breath. "Your young neighbor, Patrick, has been taken into custody for psychiatric evaluation. He's admitted to some of the things you and your neighbors have reported. Thank you for your cooperation and please call us again immediately if you have any further problems. And Mrs. Johnson, just to be on the safe side, keep your dog inside at night."

When he hung up Hillary felt an overwhelming sadness for her neighbors, professional people, often too busy in their own careers to spend time with Patrick, but nevertheless they obviously loved and cared for him. Many children in the same circumstances did just fine. What is the determining factor? Would Patrick have been any different if his mom had stayed home to bake cookies and be den mother? Maybe there is no answer to these questions. Once again she said a prayer of thanksgiving for her children and grandchildren.

Hillary had the feeling that there was something else Officer Robinson had started to say or ask. What could that be? Or did she imagine it?

The evening was quiet for Hillary. No one was coming over, but she was not lonely. She busied herself with routine chores, cleaning the house, bathing and brushing Lady, eating a small salad for her supper. After a shower she put on her pajamas to watch the evening television shows. Tomorrow she would volunteer at the hospital, and the day after she would have Jane and Sharon over for an evening of three-handed bridge.

Life was not bad, she admitted. Maybe it wasn't exactly the way she had thought her life might be at this stage, but all things considered, it wasn't that bad. She was eagerly looking forward to the bridge game. The three women had not had a real visit since the success of their "Gone With the Wind" ball but had shared by telephone their many thank you notes and letters from their friends who claimed to have had the best time of their life. Marianne had written to all three. She and Hank had enjoyed themselves thoroughly and appreciated the opportunity to get together with their friends during one of his infrequent trips back home. His next construction job was near Atlanta, and Marianne was planning to spend all of her vacation time with him in June.

Sharon had mentioned a surprise that she had. Hillary couldn't guess what it might be. She had mentioned the trail ride that Charlie had proposed and Hillary thought it would be great fun, so the trail ride wouldn't be the surprise. Jane also had hinted at some news she would be sharing on bridge night. Although Hillary was curious, she admitted to herself that it was good to have these little surprises to look forward to.

Hillary was startled to hear the phone ring at almost eleven o'clock. She didn't know who would call this late. Most of her friends would wait till morning. She answered the phone half-dreading to hear what the message would be that could not wait till tomorrow. "Mom, you weren't asleep, were you?" Hillary relaxed to hear Pedro's voice. There was an hour's time difference in Colorado, and many times he had awakened her just after falling asleep.

"No, I wasn't asleep. It's nice to hear your voice. Is everyone okay?"

"Sure, we're fine. I was just talking with Tom. Did you really sell the lake house?"

Maybe I should have consulted the children first; they're so upset. "Yes, dear. I'm sorry, I didn't think it would matter to you."

"Matter to me? Of course it doesn't *matter* to me. I live in Denver, remember? But why did you sell it, that's what I want you to tell me." She was right; he was anxious. His voice was very strained. She would have recognized that even in a bad connection half way around the world. *But he said it didn't matter to him; then what is it that does matter about the sale?* she wondered. Something was definitely mattering.

"The reason I sold it was to raise money, of course. I must pay my bills and keep Dad well cared for. Even though I sold the bank stock, I know that money won't last forever, and I'm trying to be very frugal." How did one discuss money with one's children? Tom and Pedro were very good businessmen, but she didn't want to bother them with her trivial problems. It was as plain as black and white: when you have expenses, you just pay them with the next income you get. She felt very guilty that the money was going so fast. She wanted her children to know that she was no spendthrift; she had done without so many things in order to stretch the savings as far as possible. "Why, Darling, what has you so worried? I got a good price and owner financed it so that I'll get a monthly check," she explained.

"Oh, Mother. I could just kick myself for not asking sooner. It never occurred to me that Dad's retirement wouldn't take care of the nursing home and let you live like you always have. Tom called me and said he suspected that you might have been doing without in order to keep Dad's bill paid. He was right, wasn't he?"

"Well, it's the only honorable thing to do. I have to pay my bills. There are lots of things I used to do that just aren't that important now. But with the sale of the lake house I should be fine."

"And when that runs out, I guess you'll sell your house, and then what will you do?"

"I'll just..." Hillary stammered.

"Mother, what I'm trying to say in my clumsy way is that you're not the only grown-up in this family. You're not the only one who cares about Dad, either. Tom and I have good incomes and we want to take over the nursing home expenses. Now don't tell me no."

Hillary's eyes had puddled up and were spilling over. "Oh, my. Oh, my." She couldn't think of anything appropriate to say.

"Mother, all my life you and Dad gave me everything I needed, including a good education. And you did the same for Elizabeth. This is just as much our problem as yours, can't you see that?"

Hillary tried not to choke up while on the phone with her precious son. She told him how much income she received from all sources and how much over and above that was due to the Four Seasons each month, but that she planned to use the payment from the lake house to pay that overage.

"Now, listen, Mom. Tom and I want to do this and we want you to take that payment and go shopping, or go to Europe. We also know that one day we'll inherit the whole estate so we'll get paid back. That's our ulterior motive." He tried to make light of the plan, but Hillary was more than a little overwhelmed still.

They visited a few more minutes before saying goodnight, and when Hillary hung up she had to shed her tears. How wonderful things were working out. She would never have guessed that this was one of the solutions to her problems. It just had not occurred to her that her children felt so much responsibility toward their father. She lay awake for a long time marveling at tonight's conversation.

CHAPTER 19

Sharon and Jane arrived vibrant and animated, both talking at the same time. Hillary was happy to see them, and she could hardly wait to hear all the news. Not visiting with her friends for almost three weeks, she knew they each had saved many stories to share. They absently took one of Hillary's hot hors d'ouevres, and when they took the first bite, said, "Mmmm." Hillary smiled.

"Now I want to know what all those secrets are that you two have been hinting about. Jane, you go first. I'm just dying to hear. But go ahead and have some coffee or hot tea and then get comfortable. I'm all ears." Hillary settled expectantly on the barstool to hear all the news.

"I don't know where to start," Jane began, trying to organize her thoughts. "Maybe I should mention first that Martha's beau is not a beau, but a cousin." Jane attempted to appear inscrutable but was definitely scrutable. "He and Martha met up and visited recently at a family funeral after being out of touch for a long time. He's a widower and about to retire from his medical practice. You know Martha, the great healer. She felt that he was a little off balance about retiring when he had planned his retirement with his wife and now he doesn't know exactly what he wants to do with the rest of his life. Martha didn't say that in so many words, I just read between the lines, so to speak. Anyway she brought him to the party and he says he had a marvelous time. He asked if he could call me sometime and of course I said yes. I forgot to ask if he was an orthopedic surgeon. Because why else would some man notice a woman on a cane?

"But that's not all my news. Where to begin? I guess at the party, thanks to you both my house was prettier than it had been in years. The day after the party Julian called me and asked if I would consider selling my home. It caught me by surprise and I couldn't tell him yes or no. But later I talked with Dianne Perkins-Holder and asked if she had any idea how much it might be worth. She did what she called a *Market Analysis*, that's kind of an informal appraisal. Then she gave me a broad range that the actual value would fall within. When Julian called back he told me what he planned to offer, if I would consider an offer, and it was in the high range of that Market Analysis. I had no idea that values had grown so much in the last twenty years. If I had been asked to name a price it would have been much lower. And I still would have made a profit."

"What did you tell him?" Sharon wanted to know.

"I told him yes."

"What about the kids? How did they take it?" Hillary suspected the decision had not been unanimous.

"Well, at first they couldn't believe that I would make a decision like that without consulting them. At best they were resentful and argumentative. You would have thought that I was throwing them out onto the street. I've always felt that they expected to put me in a nursing home at their earliest convenience so they could have the house to themselves. Maybe that's not entirely fair, but the truth is that I've had my feelings hurt lots of times for just trying to live in my own home."

Jane was a fair person, and both Sharon and Hillary knew she had not made any snap decisions without considering Bruce and Chrissy. "The first time I brought up the subject, I knew they were stunned and couldn't grasp any of the details, just like I had been the first time that Julian called."

Jane gestured with her beautiful artistic hands and continued, "So I let them think about it a whole day and then at supper the next night I told them what I would do. I told them to find a house that they like and CAN AFFORD. A house that they could qualify for with their own income, and I would give them the down payment. That's not exactly what they had hoped for, but I had anticipated their arguments, and I had definitely made up my mind not to be manipulated into giving them enough to live beyond their means. I reminded them that I would need a home, too, and needed to plan for my old age." She smiled then and relaxed. "It was pretty tense around my house for a few days but I didn't budge. And guess what, now I see smiles and hear about plans for touring subdivisions and they've been talking about the pros and cons of certain houses. The best thing I'm hearing is that they're talking among their old friends and planning to live near some of them. That's ever so much better than having them live in a house like mine."

Hillary and Sharon listened with an occasional nod and smile, surprised that Jane would ever part with her beautiful old house, but happy with the overall plan. "Jasmine told me that her daughter and grandchild would be moving back in 'for awhile,'" Sharon offered. "I know they hope that marriage will get put back together soon. Your house will be perfect for them, at least for the next few years while they have so many children at home."

"Yes, but even after they move out you know the children will all be coming back for holidays. Then they'll have their own families to bring home. Maybe the best part is that I'm not selling to strangers and I can visit whenever I feel the need." Jane was pleased with her decision.

"But where will you live?" Sharon wanted to know. "Oh please, come live near me out on the point."

"I've been thinking about it," Jane admitted. "I might have something designed, you know, barrier free. Since I had my accident it's made me think about things. I'd like to have some wide open spaces, like in the halls, and doors that would accommodate a wheelchair, if necessary. Also, I'd like to have at least one shower that you could wheel a chair into."

"You really have given it some thought," Hillary commented. "You have a natural treasure in your own family, you know. Chrissy has some of the best decorating ideas I have ever seen. I know she'd feel honored if you included her in the planning."

"Hillary, you always cut to the heart of things, don't you? You are right, as always, and I've been so wrapped up in playing defense that I hadn't even given it a thought. She'll be busy for awhile getting her own home straight, but then by the time I finish with the architect, get my bids and get ready for decorating, she should have time to help me." She pondered for a moment, thinking how this just might work and then they would all be involved in "Mother Westerman's" little house.

"I hate to change the subject, but I'm just about to burst with my own plans." Jane and Hillary looked at Sharon expectantly. "I've been working on a new business venture for almost a year and it's coming together better than I could have imagined. It's a perfect adjunct for Partners, and we've done an exhaustive feasibility study. Well, the bottom line is that I'm opening my new business the first of September. The name of it will be, are you ready for this?" She looked from one to another to heighten the suspense. "Senior Partners."

"I don't understand," Hillary admitted. Then it dawned on her. She remembered seeing Sharon's Suburban several times near the Four Seasons and had wondered who she might be visiting. "Are you opening a day care center for older adults?"

"Yes, and they're not all old, some are merely crippled up or incapacitated in some way, and can't take care of themselves while their families are away in school and at work. I already have a waiting list of more than I can accommodate at the beginning. But usually when it comes to opening day some of the people will not show. At least that's what I'm expecting. In many ways it will be similar to Partners. We'll offer a safe environment. A hot lunch. Something stimulating to do besides just watching soaps and talk shows. We'll have crafts, book reviews, guest speakers occasionally. It's going to have a western theme, too. Oh, it's so exciting I just can't list all the possibilities. There are so many people in nursing homes that don't really need twenty-four-hour care. And there are a lot of other people at home who could benefit from spending the day with others. I think I've talked with several hundreds of people, and almost everybody knows someone who needs this kind of care. Isn't it wonderful?"

"Yes, it certainly is wonderful. My goodness, the news around here just keeps getting better and better. And remember just a few weeks ago we were so down and bored. I don't have much to contribute. Well, there is one thing. My son and son-in-law have ganged up on me and insisted on taking care of Pete's expenses at the Four Seasons." Even now it was hard for Hillary to talk about the subject without getting choked up with emotion and gratitude for these two young men whom she loved so well. And their wives too, because they would not be offering if their wives weren't in agreement.

Conversation was spirited around the bridge table when Jane realized that she had shuffled the cards a dozen times or more. They laughed at themselves and agreed to get on with their brand of three-handed bridge, because, after all, it was bridge night.

"Do you know who plays bridge? And very well I'm told," Sharon ventured, knowing the old argument she was about to stir up.

"No, who plays bridge well?" Jane mocked disinterestedly, and with an exasperated sigh.

"Marianne."

"Marianne plays bridge?" Jane sat up straight.

"Yes, we used to play in the same club. And she told me at our party she hopes to join some group that plays at night so she can attend. She gets pretty lonely staying home every night while Hank is out of town on jobs." Sharon said no more and pretended to study her cards while watching Jane's reaction in her peripheral vision.

"Well, why didn't you ask her to join us?"

"Oh, I knew your objections. She might want to bring her recipes or pictures of her grandchildren." Sharon was still looking at her cards as if they were the most important thing in the room. Hillary could hardly suppress her laughter. Sharon could read Jane so well and even now was working her so beautifully that Hillary suspected the entire scene had been staged. "Besides all that, she may not even play the way we do."

Jane sat up straighter still. "I'll teach her!" Jane had not looked at her hand. "And if she brings pictures of her grandchildren, well, who cares. Those are about the cutest little muffins I've ever seen." Jane had both palms down on the table and looked first at Sharon and then at Hillary and said confidentially, "You know that Marianne is one of the best gourmet cooks in town or maybe in the state. And if she brings recipes to share with us then we should feel honored."

Hillary could not contain herself any longer and burst into gales of laughter, joined immediately by Sharon. "I've been set up. You two..." Jane pretended a huff and picked up her cards. "I hate it when people know me better than I do myself." Then she laughed at herself and continued the conversation, planning how they could include Marianne in their regular bridge nights.

The first rubber went by quickly. Sharon and Hillary discussed the trailride that Charlie had invited them on. Both were excited and could hardly wait till he had the time to take them. Were they up to it? How hard was trailriding? What if it stormed? And Hillary wondered what if her creaky old joints all seized up and she couldn't get off her horse? "Don't worry," Jane volunteered simplisticly, "you can always fall off."

When the telephone rang, Hillary automatically looked at the clock. Almost eleven. *Maybe it's Pedro again*, she hoped, but felt the familiar dread that came with all late-night calls.

"Hello. Yes, this is Mrs. Johnson." Both Jane and Sharon were wide-eyed in anticipation and felt a touch of dread themselves.

"He did?" Hillary's face said more than words. "Did he hurt her?" Her voice was beginning to crack. "Thank God. Did he hurt himself?" She waited for the lengthy answer. "Should I come out now and sit with him?"

Sharon had moved over to the counter and now had her arm around Hillary's shoulders. When she hung up the phone, Hillary was looking, unseeing, into space, and the words wouldn't form themselves. She finally said, "Soft protective devices." Soft protective devices, they said. Hillary had frequently used that term herself. A euphemism for a posey vest and wrist restraints. Or maybe it was four-point restraints, surely not leathers. She knew the Four Seasons had a strict policy against physical restraints, or even chemical restraints. What could have made Pete shove the nurse who was giving his bedtime medication? Was he really violent or could it have been an accident? At any rate they said he was sleeping quietly now and she mustn't come out.

Thoughts were racing through Hillary's head. She had never imagined Pete in a violent action. Even the events that precipitated his being admitted to the nursing home had faded in her memory. How many times had she wondered whether she had just over-reacted to those events and perhaps she could have kept him at home just as well? No, it had been Tom who had suggested custodial care. Tom would know. He would have good judgment. Pedro had been supportive but had also hated to take Pete out to the Four Seasons that first time. They all had hated it, and Pete had given them the silent treatment as if he didn't really care. What should she have done differently? What should she do now? Hillary was aware of her ears ringing— no, it was more like a buzzing. She was in a fog, and her ears were ringing so that she couldn't hear or see anything around her. She was not in control of herself, and she couldn't help Pete. They were both lost and sinking down, down, down.

Where is the fantasy that will save her? Hillary felt so tired. Maybe she didn't have anymore fight left in her. What happened to her bootstrap philosophy that had always before brought her back to the reality of the situation? She could give in and she could give up. How comfortable it would be to just close her eyes and give up. *I can't change anything*, she thought. *I'm just a leaf blown here and there and I'm just kidding myself if I believe anything different. But give up to what?* she asked herself pragmatically.

Sharon had her arm tightly around Hillary's shoulders and felt her tremble. Neither woman said anything. Sharon could almost see the thoughts racing around inside Hillary's head. She looked so tired, so sad. What pain she must be suffering. She was still staring into space, but Sharon noticed a relaxing of Hillary's shoulders and saw her chin lift slightly. Then she looked perplexed and wondering.

Hillary's thoughts began to pick up speed. *Well, I may not be able to make things better*, she chided herself. *But by golly, I'm not going to make them worse with my self-pity. There's really only one thing I can do, the same as I've always done once I've had a chance to think things over. I'll just FACE IT. Whatever happens, I'll just face it. And whatever happens will not destroy me. Yes, I do have control of one tiny little thing. I can control how I respond. My attitude. And if that's the only thing in this world that's within my control, then by golly...*

The fog lifted, and the ringing in her ears fell suddenly silent. Hillary realized that Sharon was holding her and Jane was at the piano. Jane was running some chords up and down the keyboard. Jane was starting to play a mellow bluesy bass. Sharon and Hillary began to rock back and forth in time to the bluesy sound they all loved.

Jane picked up the tempo with snatches of favorite tunes, and when she settled into one of Hillary's favorites, "She Used To Be Somebody's Baby," Sharon released Hillary and began to roll the carpet back off the hardwood floor. Automatically Hillary reached around the cabinet for her tap shoes. The first few steps were heavy and difficult, but Jane's rhythm was seductive. Sharon was swaying in time to the music, inviting Hillary to dance.

She hadn't had her tap shoes on since the night of the ball and was experimentally trying out her routine. It was coming back to her.

A verse from the Bible came to Hillary's mind: "...A time for everything, and a season for every activity under heaven...a time to mourn and a time to dance..." *Possibly this is the former*, she admitted, *but I can't deal with that yet, and I can deal with the latter.*

When Jane moved into her raucous rendition of "Born to Boogie," Hillary had to laugh out loud. "You two. You're crazy people! Certifiable!" she accused them affectionately.

"Well, it takes one to know one," Jane shouted over the joyful noise she was making on Hillary's piano.

Jane continued to play *allegro vivace* and more than a little bit *fortissimo*.

Sharon and Hillary laughed and danced.

CHAPTER 20

The three of them were making their way up the dry creek bed as quietly as possible. As quiet as three shod horses clinking against river pebbles could be. And the chorus of constantly creaking saddles.

They weren't talking, but then they didn't need to. Their hearts were heavy with grief and mad. Mad as they could be, and determined to do something about it.

Why McCaffrey was singled out for this vicious act was a mystery. Maybe he was just convenient, an easy target.

"Hillary," Sharon whispered. "What do you really think? Do you think the boy will live?"

"I just have to hope. What I noticed was the bruise on his forehead and it looked like one of those steers stepped right on his chest." Hillary paused to collect her thoughts. She whispered, "Although he was in shock, the EMT got some fluids started pretty fast. And, well, I just don't know."

Charlie was up ahead a few yards, watching the hoof prints along the trail and giving Red his head. Red seemed to know that they were following the cattle, his quarter horse instincts leading him on. His ears were forward and his step brisk. This is what he was bred to do and he seemed to love it.

"Sharon, what was McCaffrey saying to you when they put him on the stretcher?" Hillary asked quietly.

"He was kind of incoherent and raving, but what I got out of it was mostly a lot of profanity and he kept saying 'redneck white trash.' Makes me think he knows the person or persons who shot him and stole his herd." Poor McCaffrey, Sharon was thinking. Charlie has known him a long time. He knew his wife had died a few years back, and McCaffrey was trying to raise his three children on this poor rocky acreage. He did odd jobs for his neighbors and could support only about thirty head of mother cows and their calves on his small ranch.

And now some thief had shot McCaffrey and driven the herd over the boy who was trying to prevent the stampede up the creek.

What had started out as just an enjoyable outing on their horses had become much more. Charlie had promised Sharon and Hillary a nice trail ride up the Bosque in the beautiful spring weather.

When they heard the shots they, at first, thought someone was hunting nearby. Then they heard the children yelling and instantly touched their heels to their horses and galloped up the trail to the McCaffrey cabin.

"Jimmy, Jimmy!" one little girl had cried to her motionless brother. He was covered with dirt and a trickle of blood was dripping from his nose and coursing down his cheek.

"McCaffrey!" Charlie had shouted at the man stirring on the ground. "Don't move! We'll get some help. Hillary, check out the boy while I look at this shoulder." The girls were hovering together, whimpering quietly, not knowing what to do. Just knowing that their world had been turned upside-down.

Charlie had shouted, "Sharon, they have a phone, I think. Call for an ambulance. Get those little girls busy, too. We need soap and water. And lots of clean towels."

Sharon rushed to the front door before Charlie finished barking his orders. "Girls, get some clean towels, quickly. Draw up some warm water and get some soap. Yes, the dishwashing liquid soap should do fine."

When the ambulance arrived, the first aid had been accomplished very professionally. What good fortune to have a veterinarian and registered nurse to happen upon these injuries. The daddy was still mumbling rambling phrases, and the boy had not responded when the ambulance sped away, sirens blasting.

Charlie, obviously in charge, then called the sheriff's office only to learn that the whole force was on the other side of the county and no one available to give chase to the rustlers, possible murderers.

Deep in thought, Charlie walked over to Red, ground-hitched since Charlie barrelled off him to care for the hemorrhaging McCaffrey. Queen and Major were nearby and not likely to run off even though they had not been specifically trained to stay ground-hitched.

Charlie reached into the worn saddle holster and pulled out his Winchester 94, checked the shells, and reached for more in his saddlebag. The other saddlebag held a pistol with a long barrel, with its own cartridge belt and holster. Once again he checked to see that it was fully loaded, then Charlie strapped it around his waist and tied it down on his left thigh.

Hillary took note of Charlie's deliberate actions and watched out of the corner of her eye as Sharon caught up Major and reached into her saddlebag for a very businesslike revolver. Sheepishly she explained to Hillary, "I just thought we might see a snake." Knowing what she must do, Hillary then climbed the steps to the cabin and faced the two solemn big-eyed children. "Girls, does your daddy keep any guns?"

"Yes, ma'am, but we're not allowed to touch them," the big one answered, still snuffling from her long cry. "They're in that closet and it's locked." Hillary felt a moment of panic before the girl finished, "But Daddy usually keeps the key up there on the ledge over the door."

Hillary found the key and inside chose a .22 rifle and pistol that she would be comfortable with, knowing they were not as powerful as she might need. Emptying a box of .22 long rifle shells into her vest pocket, she strode out the door, advising the girls to go down to their neighbor's house until this business was over.

Red picked up his head a split second ahead of Queen and Major. They all quickened their pace, and Hillary hoped they would not feel the need to whinny and give away their location. She soon realized it would not matter, as the cattle were making such a racket.

"Sounds like they've got them penned already. Probably have a truck or trailer ready to ship them out of here." Charlie had turned in his saddle to talk to the two women and now reached for his rifle. At the edge of the trees and across a meadow, they could see the entire operation, holding pens, rickety loading chute, and cattle truck, ready to ship another man's cattle.

As the two women pulled out their weapons, Hillary made a mental note that they were an unlikely trio, two graying women and a burly veterinarian, chasing rustlers. No, not just rustlers— thieves and murderers.

Suddenly, the rustlers' two horses, tied beyond the makeshift corral, sensed the newcomers and began nickering. The scruffy, skinny young man dashed over to his horse to retrieve his shotgun while the pot-bellied older man ran to the truck to take down his weapon from the rack behind the seat.

Charlie was relieved to see that both weapons were shotguns and felt he had range in his favor.

The last thing Hillary remembered before they spurred their horses out into the meadow with guns blazing was Charlie's battle cry, "Well, ladies, let's show 'em TRUE GRIT!"

Hillary chuckled. Then she laughed out loud. The trail ride up the Bosque would be such fun. She hoped they didn't encounter any rustlers along the way, but squared her shoulders and with pretend bravado was sure that she, Charlie, and Sharon could handle anything that came along.

As she picked up the book she had been reading, she remembered the uneasy feeling that had precipitated her fantasy. She stood up and put the book back on the porch swing, drawn to the bench at the back of her garden. There were many places in her back yard where the bench was out of sight. For the first time she noticed that it was not visible from any window of the house.

Approaching the bench, Hillary looked around, half-expecting the see someone lurking behind a shrub watching her. She felt a tingling sensation on the back of her neck and wondered if the hair does, indeed, stand up when one is frightened. Where was Lady? She remembered that she had left her sleeping on the kitchen floor, and Hillary hadn't wanted to disturb her.

Seeing no dastardly villains, Hillary silently chided herself that she was worrying about nothing. However, how could she explain the cigarette butts that she had found near the bench? And more than once. Should she call Officer Robinson, who had been so kind when the boy next door was harrassing her?

The troubled boy was safely put away now, in a private school, or hospital perhaps. But Officer Robinson had insisted that she call him if anything else unusual happened. What had he meant? Did he expect something more?

Hillary sat down on the stone bench, pulling her cardigan closer, suddenly chilled. She looked around the lawn for any tell-tale signs of footprints or more cigarettes. The grass was thick, and there were stepping stones at convenient intervals, so a footprint would be hard to spot.

An object under the bench caught Hillary's eye. It looked like a small toy. She reached to pick it up. It was a small house, not much larger than Monopoly houses. To her knowledge there had been no children in her yard. Her own grandchildren were too big to play with tiny little toys. The neighbors' maybe? No, it didn't seem likely. A very small child, one who might choose such a tiny toy, could never get over her tall fence. And wouldn't this child be very well supervised, too, by a parent or grandparent, because he was so small?

The house was put there deliberately, Hillary conceded. Why?

Hillary was having trouble concentrating on the book she was reading aloud to Pete. Usually the Texas Rangers stories would bring about some reaction. But it seemed that he responded to her less and less. She couldn't tell whether he was listening or if his mind was just wandering. Did his mind wander? Was he ever able to concentrate on a subject? Here again was her permanent dilemma. Is an Alzheimer's patient thinking? But with a mind locked in an uncooperative body? Maybe he really didn't even know her and wished that strange woman would just get out of his room.

But, on the other hand, if she treated Pete like an old fool, but he really did know her, remembered their marriage and good times, how hurt he would be. He was always a gentle fellow, easily hurt, and careful not to offend. *Well, by golly*, Hillary told herself for the hundredth, maybe millionth time, *I'm just going to treat him as if he knows exactly what I'm saying and doing. As if we have a future together, even though I can't help but doubt it.*

"Pete, remember when we heard that story about the Texas Rangers that kept us laughing? Some little town out west was having a riot and sent for the Rangers. When only one Ranger showed up the city fathers asked, 'Why did they just send one Ranger? We're having a riot out here.' And the Ranger supposedly drawled, 'Well, it's only one riot, ain't it?'" Hillary peered over at Pete to see if he smiled or acknowledged her story at all. No, he didn't. He was still staring into space.

"Pete," Hillary said, standing over him forcing him to look into her eyes, "why don't we go walk outside? I'm feeling kind of restless, cooped up in this room. Aren't you?" Pete pulled himself out of the chair with some difficulty and held out his hand for Hillary to direct him out the door.

Several residents of the nursing home were sitting in wheelchairs and geriatric chairs in the hall. Some were parked in front of television sets or in front of windows looking out onto beautifully manicured gardens. A few residents walked up and down the halls with canes or walkers, seldom speaking, wrapped up in their own thoughts and anxieties.

"Hello, Mrs. Johnson. Hi, Pete." A friendly voice greeted them as they came even with the door to the crafts room. "Have you seen Pete's latest sculptures? It seems we've graduated from ducks and retrievers to airplanes." Helene, retired from the art department of the university, directed them over to the shelf where Pete's work was on display.

Hillary noted that his work, which only a year ago was very good, had become crude and juvenile. "I'll bet this plane is the one you flew in the war, isn't it, Pete?" She tried to be encouraging without fawning over the pieces. He'd see right through it if she was patronizing. He probably knew the work was not good and was frustrated that his hands wouldn't obey anymore.

Helene understood, too. "We've had a hard time keeping his pieces to display. Seems they get dumped in the floor more often than not. But accidents will happen, and Pete here is doing better than most of my residents. At least he concentrates very hard and he's organized in his work."

Hillary was happy to hear this evaluation. She hadn't been sure that he did, or could. Grasping for straws, she knew she just wanted to hear anything positive, then she would blow it all out of proportion.

At Pete's suppertime, Hillary gathered up her things to go home. It was almost sundown. Time for mothers to start supper for their children and husbands. That bittersweet time of day that brought back so many memories of other, happier, times.

And she was going home to feed the dog.

Hillary had thrown off her melancholy feelings and thrown herself into the preparation of snacks for the bridge game. She was humming a happy tune and remembering what fun they had all had at the party, the ball. It was so perfect, she recalled once again. The music was great. Everyone seemed to be happy, at least for that evening. And Sam and Jesse had come just for her.

She began to do a simple tap dance in her running shoes, which made it difficult. She still could hardly believe that she tap-danced so blatantly in front of all her friends. But she had, and enjoyed it thoroughly.

Tonight would be the first ever of four-person bridge for Hillary, Sharon, and Jane. They were all excited that Marianne would be joining them now that Hank worked out of town and got home so seldom. How long had they argued about the fourth for bridge and always vetoed any suggestions? But all had been thrilled that Marianne had consented to join them. They'd have such fun.

When the evening was over, Hillary was pleased at the good time and wild, outlandish conversation they'd enjoyed. Each needed some comic relief in her life, and if all the laughter heard tonight was any indication, they had certainly had their fill.

Jane had walked in without her cane, posing and posturing like a runway model. Of course they all noticed immediately how well she walked and bragged on her progress. She only mentioned Preston briefly, explaining that he didn't call very often, but she was obviously very interested in this tall, gray doctor from Temple.

Sharon tried to sound objective when she mentioned Charlie Hoelscher, their favorite veterinarian. She and Hillary made some comments about their upcoming trail ride, something they had yearned to do for years, but had been impossible until Charlie's generous offer to make it happen.

Marianne, of course, was the witty, cheerful person they expected and was grateful for the chance to get out of the house for an occasional evening. Her big house was very empty, she admitted, now that Hank was in Atlanta for the new job. Sharon and Marianne had kept up a running comedy act into which Hillary and Jane occasionally added their own appropriate zinger.

CHAPTER 21

"Officer Robinson please," Hillary said into her telephone. She wasn't sure whether she should waste his time with her silly little report. It was probably nothing. But if it were nothing, why did it set her pulse to racing and make her hyperventilate?

"Robinson here," he said in his deep baritone voice. "Yes, Mrs. Johnson. Good to hear from you. Is everything alright?"

"I really don't know," she began, hesitating. "Maybe it's nothing or maybe it's just a coincidence." She searched for the right words, not melodramatic, but not flippant either, she hoped. "Do you remember my telling you about the cigarette butts I found around my backyard bench?"

"Yes, Ma'am. Have you found some more?"

"Yes, a couple of times. It's as if someone were sitting there watching me. Or waiting for something." She paused, trying to grasp the significance herself. It seemed very different now that she actually put it into words. It was either nothing or something very strange. "But I haven't seen any strangers. No one has tried to bother me." She paused to let him speak. To determine whether he thought her a hysterical old woman.

"Mrs. Johnson, is there something else? Something besides the cigarettes?"

"Well, yes, there is." She felt her voice start to quiver. Her breathing became rapid and shallow. Hillary recognized the lightheadedness and took some slow deep breaths. "One day I found a tiny little house and thought it was just a coincidence. There had been no children in my yard for the longest time. But it could have been tossed over the fence, couldn't it?" She didn't expect him to answer. He encouraged her with his silences.

Remembering the past week, Hillary became animated. Her emotions had run like a roller coaster all week. And she couldn't sleep at night. She must slow down and tell everything in sequence so that it might make some sense to Officer Robinson.

"Over the past week I found more little figures. The second toy was a little car. Then a few days later I found two little dolls, a girl and a baby, or maybe a mother and a baby."

"Do you have them there? I'd like to see them."

"Yes, of course. Would you like me to bring them in to the station?"

"No, I'd like to see where they were found." He looked at his watch and added, "Mrs. Johnson, it's almost dark now, but I'd like to come by first thing in the morning. Is eight o'clock too early?"

"Eight o'clock will be fine," Hillary agreed. "I'm an early riser."

Officer Robinson was prompt, and Hillary directed him immediately to the backyard where she had found cigarette butts and the small toys. Lady nuzzled his hand, perhaps remembering the night a few months ago when the officer had come to their rescue. It occurred briefly to Hillary that Lady recognized the good guys and bristled whenever she sensed someone in the backyard who shouldn't be there.

"Your garden is really beautiful, Mrs. Johnson." His thumbs were hooked on his belt, and he took a deep breath of the spring fresh garden. "I smell the roses and something else I can't identify. Maybe several things." Sheepishly he turned the conversation back to the items Hillary had found near the bench.

Robinson examined the small objects without commenting. "What brand of cigarettes did you find?"

"I checked them out, thinking it might be important. There were two different brands, neither of them major brands. I'd just call them Brand X, but I wrote the names on my notepad in the kitchen. They're probably just the cheapest." Hillary relaxed now that Robinson had taken charge. "Can you tell me what you really think? Am I making a mountain out of a molehill? I go around edgy and half scared most of the day, and then I don't sleep well at night. I've even imagined that I saw a man's footprints in my grass several times. It could have some reasonable explanation."

"Mrs. Johnson, let's go into the house and talk. I'd like to see your note about the cigarettes. Say, do you make coffee?" He grinned that elusive smile that, to Hillary, made him appear to be about seventeen years old.

While the coffee was perking, Hillary retrieved her good china and put the creamer and sugar in front of the officer sitting at her kitchen table. He was making notes in his tablet, not talking while he worked. Hillary had noticed that about Robinson. He seemed to be all business and fairly short on words. "Are you friendly with your neighbors, Patrick's parents?"

"Well, I don't see them very much. You know they are both very busy professional people. And since the incident with Patrick, I see them even less. They seem to avoid me. Maybe they're just embarrassed, or maybe they feel that I'm to blame for his being institutionalized. Why?"

"Because I stay in touch with his case workers. He's actually doing very well. He's going to school and will be able to join his regular class one day, we hope."

"That's good to hear. Such a handsome young man, but he always looked so sad, or lonely."

"Mrs. Johnson, do you know a Farley Grubbs? Or sometimes he uses his middle name, Wayne. Farley Wayne Grubbs."

"I don't believe I've ever heard that name." Hillary was puzzled now.

"We have reason to believe that Farley Grubbs has been in this neighborhood and that he has some kind of grudge against Mr. Johnson." Hillary gasped, inaudibly. "He's a heavy drinker and has been in jail. Anyway, while he was in prison and, at least once that we know of, since he's been out, and while he's drinking, he's made some threats that we presume are against your husband, Peter Johnson."

"But why? What could he possibly have against Pete? I thought all of Pete's customers loved him. He was a real old-fashioned banker, always helping customers to work out their financial problems. We've had so many notes from his customers, thanking him for helping them through hard times." Hillary frowned, trying to make sense of what she had just been told.

"I don't want to scare you, Mrs. Johnson, but I do want you to be on your guard. Do you have a cell phone in your car?"

"Well, yes. You remember my husband is very ill in a nursing home, and I don't want to be out of touch if they should need me."

"That's good. Please let me know if you see someone in the neighborhood that looks the least bit suspicious. And don't open your door to anyone you don't know."

"Oh, I will, I mean I won't. Oh, I don't know what I mean."

Hillary's tranquillity was shattered. Long after Officer Robinson had gone, she kept going over in her mind all that he had said. And all that she felt he had left unsaid. But the question kept coming back:

Why?

"Sharon, Sweetheart," he began, speaking softly into the telephone. Sharon flinched but said nothing. "I need you more than I ever have. I know I've made lots of mistakes, but I know you, and you always do the right thing, the moral thing." He paused, and she wondered how many times he had rehearsed this speech.

"I've just gone over to the clinic at Temple for a second opinion, and they confirmed what the doctor here told me. It's cancer. I have to have radical surgery for cancer." Harvey paused for her reaction, hoping she'd be devastated, or at least sympathetic. He was scared, really scared, and he expected to play the situation for all it was worth. Maybe it would be a way to get Sharon back. He would be so needy, so docile. And she would be so concerned, so gentle, maternal even.

"Well, Harvey, I'm sorry to hear that. What are your plans then? When will you have the surgery?" Her voice was unemotional, straightforward. Not cold exactly, he admitted, just matter-of-fact. He was sure that she must be overwhelmed, but trying not to seem too shocked. Yes, that was it. She was good at masking her emotions but she still cared, he knew it.

"A week from Monday, here in Waco." He paused again for maximum effect. "I'd like for you to be by my side. I need you to be there for me. Please say you will. I couldn't bear it alone. It's all I can do to get through each day without you."

"Well, of course I will, Harvey. Just because we're no longer married doesn't mean that we can't be friends." Sharon was firm. "After all, you're my oldest friend in Waco. Just let me know the time, and I'll be with you when you go into surgery and when you come out of Intensive Care."

"Why don't you come over on the weekend so we can talk a little bit? I'm really apprehensive. The doctors have given me some good pre-operative instructions, but I need to talk with someone a little more personally."

"Nope, I'll be out of town on the weekend and can't change my plans. Sorry."

"Well, it must be something very important. More important than a life-threatening operation," Harvey flared.

"Harvey, you just said your surgery is not until Monday. And I'll be back Sunday evening. I'll give you a call before you go to sleep Sunday night. That's the best I can do."

"That's not good enough," Harvey argued. "Anyone would understand that I needed you at that time. What could be more important?"

Sharon didn't answer immediately. She flushed with anger. How easy it would be to just tell Harvey it was none of his business. "I'm going to take Major and go trail riding up the Bosque. Something I've wanted to do for years and we've finally gotten together a group. We're going to trailer the horses to a place near Valley Mills and ride up to a ranch west of there. I wouldn't change my plans for anything short of disaster."

"I'll bet that damn vet has something to do with this, doesn't he?" Harvey was getting louder and angrier.

"Well, Harvey, I'm glad you called. But of course I'm sorry to hear your news. And I will be there for your surgery. But since it's more than a week away, I'm sure we'll talk together before that time. Goodnight, and keep your spirits up. I'm confident the procedure will go very well and you will have a complete recovery." Sharon hung up, hoping she had not been too blunt, yet hoping she had been direct enough to discourage any thoughts of their getting back together.

Still sitting beside the phone, Sharon noticed her hands were shaking. Was she scared? she wondered. People shake when they're frightened. Or was she angry? Yes, she thought it was definitely anger. For how long had she been able to deliberately put Harvey out of her mind? She was doing it long before their divorce. Thoughts of Harvey were just too painful at one time. Where was he? What was he doing? Why had he stopped loving her? Everything she did was to please him, to make him love her. What was wrong with her? She tried to be attractive for him. Lots of people seemed to think she was pretty.

Here I go again, she thought. *This is where I decided to stop thinking destructive thoughts, and it worked.* She didn't know exactly when her love died, or was murdered. And it turned into a feeling that was sometimes apathy and sometimes anger. He was really a pathetic middle-aged man, trying to prove his virility with young women who probably hoped to steal a wealthy husband. She thought it was strange how many young women would compromise their values, or morals, if they had any, and throw themselves at a married man. *Don't they have any pride?* she wondered. Since she felt she could never behave this way, she sometimes wondered if perhaps the girls were "in love" with Harvey. Maybe, but probably not. Maybe it's the difference in generations. She had heard this behavior explained recently as a "nineties thing." As if immorality were just invented.

Once again Sharon willed her mind to turn to something pleasant, which had nothing to do with Harvey. She smiled to herself. "That darned vet" was definitely involved with her plans for the next weekend, and she could hardly wait.

CHAPTER 22

The sky was beginning to show a slight pink cast when Sharon drove into Hillary's driveway. She hopped out of the Suburban with a youthful spring in her step. "Hill," she shouted as she opened the back door. "I need some of your coffee. I was too excited to eat or even make coffee. Can you believe we're finally going to do this?" She picked up the carafe and poured a mug full of coffee.

Hillary was coming down the hall with saddlebags thrown across her shoulder. "I'm the same way. I've already been up for more than an hour. Look at these old saddlebags. I had forgotten we even had them. I've got some snacks in one side and my sleeping clothes and toiletries in the other side; it's just perfect."

"Yeah, just like real cowboys. They probably had some fat-free cookies and a lace nightie, too."

Driving out to the riding club, both women were going over their list of things they must have, hoping they didn't forget anything. Admitting they had no idea what they really needed and what they could do without. They knew that traveling light was the most important. But how nice it would be to have a cup of tea over a campfire at lunch. They continued their animated chatting till they drove into the gate at the Range Riders Club.

Sharon stopped in front of Queen's stall for Hillary to get out. Still no sign of Charlie. Maybe he had some trouble. How could he get in touch with them if something went wrong? Sharon parked and opened the tack room. The horses were finishing up their morning feed but stopped long enough to greet their owners. They both began stomping around as they ate, sensing that something was about to happen. Sharon opened the tack room and pulled out the grooming tray. She reached a halter and bridle and hung them on the fence. The western saddle with a breast collar was underneath the English saddle on the rack, and she took a few minutes to re-arrange the tack, still wondering if she should take anything else.

The saddle was heavy, but she lugged it outside the gate to be stored with the other tack in Charlie's truck. Sharon tipped the saddle up on its end in the grass and went back for the blanket, bridle, and breast collar. By then Major was finished with his hay and following her every step she took. She stopped to pet him and give him a good brushing, wondering if he really did know they were about to do something fun. As she was buckling the halter around his chin, she noticed a big pickup pulling into the front gate. Yes, it had a stock trailer on behind. *Wow, this is it*, she reminded herself, *show time!*

Hillary was having equally euphoric thoughts watching Charlie's pickup make the turns that would bring him over to the row of stalls where Queen was and then down farther to pick up Major. She giggled to herself, wondering how many of her friends would understand her feelings about this outing. Most of them would think she had lost her mind. Thank goodness for Sharon. And thank goodness for Charlie, too. Because without him neither of them would have dared a trip like this. What if something happened that they couldn't handle? She was confident that Charlie could handle anything. She chuckled again remembering her fantasy and the "True Grit" episode, but realized that her hands were trembly with excitement.

The three of them sat companionably in the front seat of Charlie's pickup truck. Although the sun was up, the morning was still cool and brisk. It would be a beautiful spring day with little chance of rain.

"Anyone for coffee?" Charlie asked. "There's a thermos in the back with some black coffee. I didn't think to put cream or sugar in it, sorry."

Sharon, sitting in the middle of the front seat, turned enough to reach the thermos and cups. "That's fine, Charlie. Neither of us use cream or sugar."

Hillary quietly savored the strong coffee and the company. What could make this outing more perfect? Well, maybe having Pete along with them. How many times had they discussed a trail ride, or perhaps a Louis L'Amour type adventure, watching your back trail, making a dry camp, the victory of good over evil. But since Pete could no longer enjoy this type of outing, she was going to have fun and no regrets.

"Charlie," Hillary began. "You can't imagine how grateful we are for this trip. Sharon and I have been talking about it for ages but didn't really believe it would ever happen. I was even scared the horses wouldn't load or wouldn't get along after they were loaded. But you just loaded them so smoothly and they act like they're as excited to be going as we are."

"Well, Hillary, it's my pleasure," Charlie drawled with a crooked grin and continued driving in silence.

After a few miles of driving west out of Waco Sharon broke the silence. "Hillary, tell Charlie about that man that may be stalking you. He might have some ideas. I know you don't want your kids to know in case it's a false alarm or something, but don't you think it would be okay to tell Charlie?"

"Well, okay. Actually I feel like maybe I've overreacted, but if Elizabeth knew about him, she might want me to move in with them or get someone to move in with me, and I'm just not willing to give up my independence." She tried to begin with her first suspicions and give an objective but complete picture of the events which had been giving her a scare.

Charlie listened to the entire story, nodding encouragement. "No, Hillary, I don't think you've overreacted at all. Officer Robinson is a good man. I've known him for several years. I think he's right about Lady being your best protection. But you be careful. Stay alert and don't let him sneak up on you. What do you have to defend yourself with? Do you have a gun or mace or what?"

"I've got a bar of soap." Hillary felt foolish admitting this. "I listened to a self-defense program on TV and this officer was telling women to put a bar of soap in a sock for protection when they go jogging. And if they're about to get mugged they can swing this sock and clobber the mugger."

Charlie laughed. "Good idea." They slowed at the Valley Mills city limit, and Charlie told them about how much longer they would drive. A few miles out of town, they turned off onto a gravel road and shortly pulled up in front of a set of weathered corrals.

"This is it, ladies. I know the people who own this place, and they know we're leaving the truck and trailer here." Charlie deftly unloaded the horses and tied each one on the side of the trailer for saddling. He reached into the bed of the pickup and handed out the saddles, bridles, and blankets.

Queen was alert but stood quietly through the brushing and saddling. Major was skittish and kept dancing around while Sharon tried to brush him down and place the blanket on his back. Charlie laughed and said, "Here, Sharon, let me give you a hand. You just hold the lead rope while I throw the saddle on."

Major was over sixteen hands tall, and Charlie gave Sharon a leg up and held a hand on Major's bridle while Sharon settled into the saddle. Her bundle with snacks and change of clothes was tied neatly behind the saddle, and she mentally went over her check list but couldn't think of anything she was forgetting. Major continued to dance around while she patted his neck and crooned encouraging words.

Hillary's old saddle bags fit snugly behind her saddle and, glancing around, she felt that they were a believable-looking trio in their riding clothes, boots, and hats.

Red had picked up some of Major's excitement and began to dance as Charlie prepared to saddle him. "We don't often get to go riding with pretty ladies. Like never, in fact. Anyway, not since Jenny got pregnant and quit riding."

Charlie finished saddling Red and reached into the bed of his pickup for the saddle bags. "Can't think of anything else we might need. The house is pretty well stocked. I just brought a few things for our lunch." Charlie swung up into his big hand-tooled roping saddle which had a patina of much use.

After opening one gate, the trio lined out onto a trail that ran beside the Bosque River, which was only a creek in this area. Red set the pace at a smooth, fast gait, wanting to lope, but Charlie held him in check for the ladies' comfort and because they had a long way to go and he didn't want to tire them.

Major, remembering his racing days, was trying to bolt, but was held back skillfully by Sharon, and finally, after a couple of miles, settled into a ground-covering trot. Queen and Hillary followed the long-legged geldings and sometimes had to break into a lope to catch up.

Traveling through a dense wooded area, Charlie became noticeably more alert, and both Sharon and Hillary saw him unsnap the strap on his saddle holster. Red's nostrils were flared and his ears forward. Major became hard to control, again trying to run and prancing sideways. No one spoke.

Coming out onto a long clearing, both horses and riders relaxed. "There's a good spot for a picnic up here a little way. We can make a fire and rest a little. I hope you're not too tired. I guess you'd let me know if you need to stop anytime?"

"We're fine, Charlie. At least I am. How about you, Hill? That old arthritis kicking up yet?"

Hillary laughed. "It's there alright. But I'm so pumped up with adrenalin that it doesn't have a chance. What happened back there, Charlie?"

"Cougar, maybe."

Men! thought Hillary, amazed. A woman could make a whole conversation out of "Cougar, maybe." Yes, maybe even a vocation. And it could grow into a wonderful adventure: "Did I ever tell you about the time we were trailriding up the Bosque and were attacked by a pack of cougars?..."

The picnic area was, indeed, well chosen. The live oaks were growing, as if planted, on a rise above the river. Several large stones surrounded a burned-out circle where campfires had been built before. The sun was bright and warm, but the breeze underneath the trees was welcomed.

"I know this isn't very fancy fare," apologized Charlie while toasting the weiners over the campfire. "It's just easy."

"Smells wonderful," Sharon said, smearing the first weiner with mustard and pickle relish. "I'm starved. I've got some fruit, too, for later."

Hillary, watching the horses graze, was enjoying a cool drink. "I'm already dreading for this trip to end, Charlie. I hope we're not almost there."

Charlie laughed his infectious laugh. "I was just kicking myself, thinking maybe I've made too long a trip and will wear out the ladies. You gals are tougher'n I thought. Tougher than lots of fellows I know, that's for sure. I think we can stop one more time at a place I know down by the river, not quite two hours ride, and then the next stop will be my place. If you're not too tired when we get there, I'll show you around the ranch." Hillary and Sharon looked at each other doubtfully, and Charlie added, "In the Jeep, of course."

The horses were ready to be caught up and continue the ride. The trail was up and down but gradually climbing to a slightly higher elevation. There were clusters of woods and open prairies. Along the river they could see strata of rocks in interesting layers. Charlie told the women about floods in this area and the devastation they brought. It seemed very unlikely today, the gently burbling stream making its way lazily toward the lake at Waco.

Major had finally settled into an ambling walk. He and Queen had not been ridden for long periods recently, and both horses were beginning to tire, as evidenced by their slower gait. Their riders began to feel tender areas on their backsides and muscles tightening in their backs.

The second rest area was very welcomed. The women found some shrubbery handy for their relief and didn't know where Charlie disappeared to. Men have such an advantage when it comes to relieving themselves, they agreed.

Walking felt stiff and unnatural. After all day on Major, Sharon felt short when she dismounted. She rubbed the circulation back into her gluteal muscles, trying not to attract Charlie's attention.

A snack of fruit and cookies washed down by coffee revived the trio somewhat. "I believe you girls are going to wear me out," Charlie confessed. "You know I don't do this often and I'm going to feel it tomorrow."

Hillary laughed. "I'm glad you mentioned it first. I didn't want to be the only tenderfoot in the crowd. However, it's not my foot that's feeling tender at the moment."

Sharon and Charlie laughed with Hillary. Sharon flushed at her own thoughts. Charlie was such good company. So natural and lots of fun. Yes, that too, but it was something else that was attractive about him. He was considerate. He was no one's doormat, but always congenial. *I wonder if I'm comparing him to my father*, Sharon worried. *Maybe it was his hands. The men I knew growing up had hands like that. Rough, weathered, with short nails. A working man's hands. Not manicured like Harvey's.* Sharon glanced up to see that both Hillary and Charlie were studying her. *Maybe they can read my thoughts.* "Well, this was a great rest stop. I have to admit I was beginning to get weary, too."

The last hour of the ride went quickly. Charlie pointed out his house high on a ledge from about a half mile away, and then it vanished from sight as they climbed steadily upward through the trees. As the trio came out into a clearing, Sharon was impressed by the neatness and simplicity of this modest ranch headquarters. On their right was a small barn and corral, toward which they were heading. On their left was a large mobile home and apparently the back door facing out to the barn.

Charlie was quick to pull the saddles off and hand over a tray of grooming tools to the women to brush down their horses. He then disappeared into what seemed to be a feed room/tack room combination and came back with grain for the three anxious mounts. Hillary and Sharon quickly unbuckled the bridles and laughed at the excitement all three horses were showing, as if they had not been fed for days. Before they knew it, Charlie had stowed the tack and had a large bundle of hay put in a manger for the horses to graze on through the evening.

Charlie led the way down a flagstone walk to the side of the house and around to the front porch. "Oh, mercy! Charlie, this is absolutely beautiful!" Hillary exclaimed. "I'll bet you did all this work, too, didn't you?"

Grinning modestly but proudly, Charlie admitted, "Well, yeah, most of it. But Jenny and Dick helped me a lot. Especially with the landscaping. I don't know a ligustrum from a crape myrtle, and Jenny knows about things like that."

"Well, you all did a beautiful job," Sharon added. "I've been on lots of ranches but I don't think I've seen anything like this. And look at those chairs on the porch. What do you call them, Adirondack chairs?"

Charlie laughed out loud. "Naw, I don't think I'd call them that. That's the kind my grandpa made, and we've always had some in the family. They're just comfortable. And Jenny made those cushions for them."

Hillary and Sharon stood quietly looking south and east over the river valley and the woods on the slope. In several places they were able to see the Bosque River for a short distance. Long shadows were beginning to cover the valley although the sun was still fairly high in the sky. They turned and realized that Charlie had unlocked the front door and was standing watching them, amused.

Charlie's furnishings were simple and chosen for comfort. The chairs and couch were of leather, and the women suspected that Jenny also had a hand in choosing the color scheme which carried into every room.

"So this is roughing it, Hill. Do you think we're tough enough?" Sharon was shaking her head and laughing.

"You girls look around while I start the fire in the barbecue pit. And then I'll give each of you a job to do."

Hillary and Sharon chose a bedroom each that shared a small but convenient bath. After snooping into closets and stowing their things, they came out to see what their instructions would be.

"Sharon, will you be in charge of the baked potatoes? We've got sour cream, butter, and bacon bits. You can chop up some of those little onions, too, if you want to. And Hillary, will you make a tossed salad? I think we've got all the fixings in the frig."

While the coals were heating in the pit and the potatoes on to bake, Charlie pulled the old Jeep out of the garage and offered the women the tour of his place that he had promised. The gravel road followed the ridge up to a higher elevation, and at the top they stopped to get a view all around. "You see, off to the north there's a high mesa, and my place doesn't go much beyond that. Over on the west you can't see my property line fence; it's in those trees over there, and I have improved grass in all the fairly level pastures. This old ridge isn't much good for anything, but I sure do love to come up here just to look around."

The breeze was cool on their faces, and the sunset was beginning to make a spectacular pattern with little puffs of cumulus clouds turning gold in color. "On the south our place goes down to the creek and over to the highway. You saw where our place began on the east when we came through that last gate." Charlie held out his hands, palms up. "So that's all there is to show, not a big place as ranches go, but with the improved pastures and cross fencing, I've got a herd of cattle that anyone would be proud of." He looked embarrassed. "Now listen to me bragging. I don't know what got into me."

"Oh, Charlie, that's not bragging. This place is beautiful. Are you going to show us your cattle?" Sharon asked.

"Sure, if you'd like to see them. They're down there in the woods on the west side." Charlie drove the Jeep skillfully down a rocky washed-out trail which finally leveled out onto a grassy pasture. White cattle began coming out of the trees on hearing the motor. Sharon knew that Charlie must feed them from his pickup by the way they were encircled by bellowing mother cows, most of which had calves at their sides.

"Are these Charolais, Charlie?"

"Yep. Most of 'em are first cross. I've experimented with several crosses and these look as good as any we've had. They have leaner meat, and that's what's selling."

Charlie looked over each cow briefly and drove along the edge of the woods till he spotted the bull and then turned back up the ridge toward his house. "The coals should be ready for the steaks by now."

The dinner was a huge success, every morsel eaten and the conversation animated. With the kitchen cleaned up and the dishes in the dishwasher, the three trailriders took their coffee out to the front porch and settled into the comfortable chairs.

"You should see the view from here when the moon is full. Sure is pretty. The sunrise is pretty too, on a clear day." Charlie was not into waxing poetic, just matter of fact, and Sharon and Hillary understood.

The conversation naturally gravitated to each one's favorite topic, their work. Sharon mentioned her childcare problems and some high points. She proudly recited cute things Tony had said or done recently as the others smiled encouragement. They had heard about Tony and felt they knew him.

Charlie was asked about the danger in his line of work. "Well," he said slowly, "I've learned to have a little more respect for my patients over the years. A jersey bull broke some ribs for me several years ago, and I've had to have stitches I can't remember how many times. You don't know anyone who's had any more tetanus shots than I have," he laughed.

"What about you, Hill? Tell us about the lives you saved in nursing." Sharon realized that she had heard very few stories about the hospital from Hillary. She always kept them to herself. *Must be a patient/nurse privacy thing*, Sharon admitted.

"I don't know how many I've saved," Hillary laughed. "You see, if nurses recognize when a patient is about to go bad and then do the proper, uh, *interventions,* they call them, then you may never know how many potential crises may have been avoided." She thought back. "There was a period, though, when we had a lot of laryngectomies, that I felt everything I did for them was important. It was a gratifying period." Hillary couldn't be serious for very long at a time. "I'll tell you a secret about nurses that I've discovered. My definition of nurses: people who can wade ankle deep through blood, emesis, and feces, but who run, retching and gagging at the sight of mucus."

She paused while Charlie and Sharon laughed at her description. "But those patients, with their new tracheostomies, needed immediate attention when they started gurgling. And suctioning a trach can be very tricky, but the nurses on that unit became pretty skilled. I don't know of any other type of patient who bonded with his nurses any tighter. And, of course, they can't speak, either. Now isn't this fine dinner party conversation?" After an hour of quiet visiting and lots of stifled yawns, Hillary looked at her watch. "My stars, I can't believe it's so early. I could have sworn it was nearly midnight, as tired as I am."

"I'm sitting here yawning myself. Charlie, I don't remember such a perfect day: the ride, the meal, the company. Thanks again. You've made a couple of women very happy."

Charlie grinned a mischievous smile. "It's been a long time since I made one woman happy, and when word gets out that I've made two happy, I guess my stock'll go up."

"Oh, you!" Sharon laughed and did not finish her sentence.

After the long day and unaccustomed activity, Sharon and Hillary felt happily exhausted and slept soundly.

Charlie was tired but did not feel sleepy. He went back to the front porch to look at the stars and organize his thoughts. He walked around the side of the house and out to the corral to check on the horses. They had finished up their hay and were dozing companionably.

How good it felt to have women in his house. He didn't have to entertain them; they both helped with all the chores and kept up some continual chatter interspersed with what must be some inside jokes that he didn't really understand. He was amused just listening to the chatter. He knew he wasn't good with small talk, and sometimes he even felt tongue-tied around pretty women, especially Sharon, whom he would like to impress favorably.

Turning out the lights Charlie listened for any sound from the bedrooms and was assured by the stillness that his guests were asleep. He made his way back to his bedroom beyond the kitchen and, after awhile, fell asleep himself.

Sharon opened her eyes and didn't know where she was. She lay still for a few minutes remembering the ride and being here on Charlie's ranch. Oh, murder, those sore muscles, but she smiled to herself even as she was checking them out. The room was still dark, but she was sure it was nearly morning. She slipped into the bathroom she would share with Hillary and brushed her hair smooth. With her big shirt over her pajamas, she quietly opened the bedroom door. Charlie had set up the coffee pot and deputized the first one awake to plug it in. Since she was the first up, she would do it, and then Charlie and Hillary would be happy to have a cup when they arose.

Her bedroom door squeaked slightly as she eased it open. The living room was dark, but Sharon noticed a faint glow coming from the eastern sky. As she tiptoed toward the kitchen, she heard the unmistakable pip-pop of the percolator. As her eyes adjusted to the darkness of the room, she saw Charlie standing in front of the double window studying her.

The sky was brightening by the second, and Sharon realized that Charlie had been standing by the window to watch the show of a promising sunrise. He held out his right arm as an invitation, and Sharon slipped under it as naturally as if she had done it many times. And maybe she had, in her imagination.

The pinks of the sunrise burst into silvers and golds, a kaleidoscope of colors, with no hint of what was coming next.

"Wups!" Hillary said, standing in her doorway, afraid that she had come upon a very private moment by accident.

Charlie grinned and held out his big left arm. Hillary happily accepted the invitation, and together the three of them watched the unfolding sunrise until it settled behind a cloud too thick to penetrate.

"How about a cup of coffee, ladies?" Charlie poured coffee into three mugs. "The horses are eating now, so they'll be ready when we are. Let's turn on the TV and check out the weather. I heard there's a chance of rain showers this afternoon. Did you bring slickers? I've got some extras I think, if you need them."

Both women assured him that they had come prepared for rain, sleet, snow, or gloom of night, and giggled.

Charlie made a big breakfast with both Hillary and Sharon helping where they could. Cleanup didn't take long, and each retired to the bedroom to finish dressing for the return trip.

As Charlie was locking up, Sharon and Hillary leaned over the porch rail and drank in the fresh smell of a spring morning, a slight odor of cedar trees mixed in with unidentifiable aromas.

The return ride back to the truck didn't take as long as the trip over. The horses were just as eager as before and seemed to know they were going home. The trio didn't stop at their first rest area, which had been their last stop the day before. After a hot lunch under the live oaks, they began to hear the distant roar of thunder. The wind picked up and there were occasional strong gusts which made the horses dance and snort.

"I don't think we can outrun the storm, but if we hurry maybe we won't have to be out in it for so long. Okay girls?" Charlie set the pace with an easy lope that covered the distance much faster than before. After about a mile, the first drops began peppering down like small rocks. They pulled up under a dense thicket to retrieve their slickers and put them on tightly.

Shortly after starting back on the trail, they each realized they were not completely waterproof, but remained fairly warm. Charlie stopped several times to ask whether Sharon and Hillary were okay and if they'd rather stop and make a fire. They denied being too uncomfortable. Charlie slowed his lead to a careful trot, knowing that it would be easy for the horses to slide in the mud and that might be dangerous.

Sharon was hunched down in her slicker, a stream of rainwater pouring off her hat, thinking about a hot bubble bath. Even with the slicker protecting most of her clothing, she felt water dripping into her lap and sometimes into her boot. She pulled up her leg so that she could reach the hem of her pants and pull it down over her boot top. Her gloves were saturated, her fingers stiff. She didn't realize that she chuckled aloud as she was thinking that she'd still rather be here than any other place she could think of.

"Did you say something, Sharon?" Charlie turned to look at her, a drowned caricature of the woman he had started with.

"No, I was just laughing."

"Oh, Sharon," Hillary said, understanding completely. "Isn't this wonderful? Have you ever been so wet and miserable? And horseback, besides." Hillary also laughed uncontrollably as Charlie, perplexed, looked from one to the other as if they had just lost their minds.

After another soggy mile, Charlie announced that they were almost back to the pickup, news that both Hillary and Sharon were beginning to doubt they'd ever hear.

With the horses loaded and the heater warming the trail riders, Charlie apologized that he only had a little coffee left in the thermos. They'd each have about half a cup, but he promised to stop at the cafe in Valley Mills for a refill. The half cup was only lukewarm but enjoyed nevertheless.

The ride back to Waco was quiet and comfortable. The rain was slow but steady and the windshield wipers set up a mesmerizing rhythm. Sharon was enjoying the big shoulder next to hers and hoping to repeat this nearness but, as usual, doubted whether Charlie would welcome an invitation from her. But she could try.

"I have tickets to the last concert of the season next week. Jane's going to be playing again. It's the first concert for her since she broke her hip. Would you two like to go with me?" She held her breath, fearing rejection.

"Yes, I'd love to," Hillary answered immediately. She didn't know what was going on between Sharon and Charlie but instinctively felt that they were both afraid of it. If she were along maybe they would feel "safe."

"Yeah, me too," Charlie answered unexpectedly. "They're having that Spaniard who plays the classical guitar, aren't they?"

After making their date to the symphony concert, Charlie delivered the horses and riders back to the riding club and then left to put Red away with a good reward of hay and oats. With the horses rubbed down and munching on their evening feed, Sharon drove quietly to Hillary's neighborhood. As soon as the motor was turned off, they could hear welcoming barks from Lady in the back yard. Hillary unpacked her things, most of which were stowed in her old saddle bags.

"Well, what else can I say?" Hillary began. "That Charlie. He made it happen for us, and you did, too. I'll always have these memories to treasure. But, hey, maybe we'll do it again someday." With that thought, she waved goodbye to Sharon and, smiling, she unlocked the back door, anxious to get to the noisy, exuberant Lady.

CHAPTER 23

The magazines in the waiting room held no interest for Sharon. Few were published this year, and she felt little excitement for the hunting and fishing issues strewn around, even less for automobile mechanics. How long had Harvey been gone? Only a little more than an hour. If she went for coffee would she miss the doctor? Yes, probably. But if she didn't it would be another two hours. Sharon had left home before breakfast because Harvey had made her promise she'd be here before they took him into surgery, and he was the first case, leaving the room about 6:30. She had arrived by 6:00 by way of the emergency entrance, the only door open at that hour.

She stood up and stretched, smiled at the other tense families in the waiting room and decided to chance a visit to the cafeteria.

All alone, she realized. Harvey had no children, no brothers or sisters. He didn't make close friends and now she was the only one waiting while he had surgery. How sad. He had reminded her, in his not-too-subtle style, that she had promised to love, honor, and cherish him, till death do us part, in front of God and all those people at the wedding. She snapped back that he also promised something about forsaking all others, didn't he?

"There you are," a familiar cheerful voice said. "I knew you'd be having a long day, so I brought you something to read. Waiting in the hospital can sure tire you out." Hillary pulled up a chair and put her bag with new issues of magazines into it. "I'll get some tea and be right back."

"How was Harvey this morning?" asked Hillary as she picked up the pink packet to sweeten her tea. "Was he very scared, or could you tell?"

"Yes, I think he was petrified. The doctor and his assistant have given him a lot of information to prepare him, but I'm not sure it helped. He wants to be real dependent on me, and I'm resisting. I thought we'd broken off our relationship long ago. And now he's giving me a guilt trip as if I were totally to blame for the breakup of our *happy home*."

"But Sharon, he should do just fine. After a few days he'll be able to get around okay. And he's got help at home, too. It's not as if you needed to sit and hold his hand."

"Yeah, tell *him* that," Sharon brooded.

"How long has he had this malignant tumor, do you know? And I wonder why they didn't suspect it when he had his tests last year."

"They didn't really explain it to my satisfaction. Maybe he didn't have any symptoms and they just missed it. I don't know. And for all I know they may have told him and for his own reasons just didn't want to do anything about it. You know, the impotence thing."

"He's got some good doctors, anyway," Hillary volunteered. "I've known them for a long time. Did he tell you what his schedule may be like?"

"No, he implied that I'll have to look after him for a long, long time."

"It's not like that, Sharon. Although it certainly is a serious procedure." Hillary frowned, thinking of a usual scenario. "He'll go home in four or five days with staples in his incision and his foley catheter. Then he may go back to the doctor to have the staples out in about ten days. After that the catheter will come out in two to three weeks. Most men complain more about the catheter than any other part of the surgery. You see, it causes bladder spasms. And after the catheter is out, he won't have control for awhile—two or three months, maybe. But I understand that there are some men who never completely regain their control."

Sharon was very quiet. "Wow, what a blow to his ego. Besides worrying whether he's cured of cancer, too. You know, Hillary, I was just wishing he had not sold his business. He's been so restless and unhappy since he doesn't have an office to go to and problems to solve." She drank the last of her coffee. "And now that I have a job and am very happy doing it, his unhappiness somehow seems to be my fault. And almost every time we talk, he has to say something about 'that damned vet.'"

Hillary said nothing, but Sharon squirmed uncomfortably. "I don't even answer that silly accusation."

Back in the waiting room, several members of the church were waiting to speak to Sharon. Hillary stayed another hour and then left to visit Pete.

Finally the doctor came out to give a report to Sharon. "Mrs. Butler," he said as if they were still married. Maybe Harvey told him they were. "Harvey is now in ICU and doing very well. They'll let you come in and see him as soon as they get him hooked up to the monitors and all the tubes doing what they're supposed to." He paused for any questions Sharon might have, and when she didn't ask anything, he continued, "We think that the surgery went well and that all the tumor is gone. We'll follow him closely for awhile, but he should do fine."

Harvey was still drowsy the first time Sharon visited but was wide awake and complaining of lots of pain when she returned for the next scheduled visit. "Harvey, they said you can press this little button when you feel you're having too much pain and you'll get some medicine in your IV line."

"Sharon, darling, will you press it for me?" Harvey whined.

"Look, it's right here. Just put your finger on this, see? I'm not going to be here all night and you'll have to do it yourself."

"Oh, no, you're not leaving me, are you?"

"This is the last visiting period they have till morning, Harvey. It wouldn't do anyone any good for me to spend the night here. And you certainly need your rest more than anything I could do for you anyway."

Harvey whimpered but said no more. Apparently the pain reliever had kicked in and he was comfortable. Sharon sat beside his bed for another few minutes. She stared at the balding, paunchy, past-middle-aged man in the bed wondering why she didn't feel something. She was very sorry for his pain. And she hoped that the cancer was gone. But shouldn't she feel something more?

Sharon walked out into the parking lot still wondering about her feelings. Most of the cars were gone by now. She appreciated the good lighting and looked around for any potential culprits hiding, determined that she would not be a victim of a mugging if she could help it. Next to her car there was a large pickup truck, and when the door opened a tall broad-shouldered man stepped out.

"Charlie!" Sharon stammered. "Did you come just to see that I got home safely?" she teased.

"Well, yeah, I did as a matter of fact." He grinned, seeing that she still had her sense of humor. "I figured you'd stay till they kicked you out and then it'd be dark and the parking lot would be deserted. How'd Harvey do?"

"They said he did very well and that they felt all the tumor was removed," she answered truthfully, still a little bit flustered at finding Charlie there.

"I'll bet you're tired after such a long day. Would you like for me to follow you home? To see that you get there okay?"

"Charlie, you can't imagine what this means to me, but no. I've got the automatic garage door opener, so I don't ever worry about coming home after dark." She felt weary but hated to send him away and didn't make a move toward her car. "Thanks for being here. For being such a good friend." As she said the words, she felt tears come to her eyes and was afraid she'd cry. Finally she did move to her car and unlocked the door. "Goodnight," she said simply, not knowing what else to say.

"Goodnight, Sharon."

The night was very dark, and Hillary was glad to have the night light glowing faintly in the dressing area, giving her just enough light to find her way to the bathroom without tripping on anything or stumbling into walls. She didn't know what awakened her but decided she should go to the bathroom since she was awake anyway.

As she pulled up her pajama bottoms, she heard a slight rustling on the other side of the window, on the patio. *The wind must be getting up*, she decided. *Maybe it's going to storm*. The next sound she heard was more like a clank and made her skin prickle. Wind wouldn't make anything on the patio clank.

Hillary quietly walked over to the window and cupped her hands around her eyes to block out any other light and peered out into the darkness. What she saw was what she feared she might see, but prayed she wouldn't see. Another face peering in at her.

She sat up in bed with a start, perspiring and pulse racing. Thank goodness it was only a dream. Nevertheless, Hillary jumped out of bed and turned on the patio lights. As she peered out the crack in the drapery, there was nothing menacing in her yard as far as the lights lit up. "Tomorrow I'm going to get more lights for the back yard," she promised herself.

Hillary was still happily reliving her trip up the Bosque, but she was also excited about the bridge party that Marianne would be hosting tonight. Driving over to the fine, big home, she was remembering how each day at the nursing home she would tell Pete a few more details about their ride. He responded by looking straight ahead with no expression. She would like to believe that he understood some of what she said and maybe he enjoyed her story. On the other hand, maybe he hated the fact that she could get out and do the things they had once done together and now here he was trapped in this useless body. No, Hillary didn't want to believe that. Besides, it was not like Pete. She could never believe that he would be resentful of her continuing to enjoy life. No, he would wish it. He would encourage her if he could speak.

Her thoughts were interrupted by the ringing of her mobile telephone. "Hill, this is Sharon. Dad gummit, I've had a flat. Will you pick up Jane? I've called my auto club and they should be here anytime. I just didn't want anyone to be waiting on me. See you in a little bit."

Hillary turned toward Jane's street, happy to have a diversion from her thoughts. She had talked with Jane Monday morning after the ride and told her all about the weekend. Jane had made a few droll comments, mostly wondering why any otherwise normal people would subject themselves to such a thing. And now Jane was getting ready to go to another rehearsal for Saturday's concert. They had both been in high spirits, and the conversation was animated.

Jane was out the door before Hillary fully stopped the car. She was walking with no limp and no cane, which Hillary, the nurse, took note of. But Hillary, the friend, jumped out to open the door for Jane. "You don't have to baby me anymore, Hill. I'm just about back to normal. I've even been doing some free throws lately; no more slam dunks for me, I'm afraid, and boy am I rusty! Speaking of rusty, you should have heard me on the cello when I started rehearsing for this last concert." Hillary was happy to listen to Jane and her non-stop chatter. How great it was to have her back.

Marianne's home was as beautifully appointed inside as out. "Hillary, you and Jane have never been over, have you? Would you like the grand tour?" She modestly took them room to room explaining how they came to get certain items and laughing at some mistakes they had made. "See, it's only four bedrooms, each with its own bath. But most of the size is in the big rooms—the library, game room, living room, even the kitchen with its sitting area."

"Don't forget to show them your utility room. It's to die for," Sharon added.

"You're too sweet, Sharon. But, yes, it is nice." They walked into an interesting area, which they soon discovered was a large room divided into niches. An area for sewing, washer and dryer with a countertop for folding, nearby a pulldown ironing board had its own small television set and radio. Another cabinet, next to the outside door, had a large stainless steel sink, and Marianne explained that she did her re-potting here or started seeds in the winter to transplant to her garden in the spring. There were cabinets for storage and closets filled with the usual clutter of mops, brooms, a vacuum, luggage, Christmas decorations, all nicely stored and easily visible.

"I can see you've thought of everything, Marianne. Is there any chance that you might stay here and retire?" Hillary asked.

"No. We don't even want to." She looked around fondly. "It was a great house and we've got some wonderful memories, but we've both decided that we could be happy in something much smaller and more modest. Well, maybe, not *too* modest." They all laughed, understanding. "To us this house represents all the best features of our building business. We were able to use lots of ideas that we couldn't get into our spec houses or even most of the customs, because everyone is on some kind of budget. But someone will come along and this house will fit them to a tee and we'll just be happy for them." She glanced around again. "There are a few things I'll miss, though. That's about it, how about some bridge?"

The four women took their coffee and iced tea to the game table, careful to bring a coaster to protect the beautiful woods in the parquet top. They had only played a few games together, but Marianne was a skilled player and had picked up on their personal nuances and imposed a few of her own.

"Okay, I was wrong," Jane said suddenly after the first game. The other three stared at her, wondering what she could mean. It certainly was not like Jane to ever admit to being wrong. "Marianne, we're glad you joined us. It was my fault that we played three-handed for so many years, but this is more fun. And we're especially glad to have found someone who'll put up with us." She pointed at Sharon and put on her pretend stern face. "You won't believe the under-handed, devious trick this woman played on me." And laughingly all three told how Sharon had subtly mentioned Marianne's name as a fourth for their bridge group.

After the first rubber, Marianne suggested they take their dessert and coffee out to the terrace beside the pool. The night was warm, and the moon, reflecting on the water, was almost full. The only other light was a mercury vapor security light, high on a utility pole. "I'll turn on some more lights if you want, but Hank and I always enjoyed sitting out here like this. Kind of romantic, don't you think?"

They chatted awhile, asking about Harvey and his progress, and Sharon informed them that he was in a private room now and apparently progressing nicely. Hillary asked Marianne, "How is your mother doing? Sunday's Mother's Day, I just remembered."

"She's great. She's got diabetes, hypertension, and arthritis, and doesn't let any of them get her down. Her group just got back not long ago from a bus trip down the azalea trail. And would you believe they're trying to get a group together for a cruise this fall."

"Funny about mothers," Jane said quietly, "I lost mine a long time ago, sixteen years, I think. And I still miss her a lot. Sometimes I think of something I need to tell her right away. Kind of like with Max."

"Do you remember that Mother's Day the preacher got his foot in his mouth?" Hillary asked, laughing.

"Yes, I remember," Jane answered. "The choir was outside the double doors waiting for the pastor to give the announcements, like we always did. And then we would march ceremoniously into the choir loft. Well, anyway, Chester was going to honor the mothers of the church and in his deep booming voice he says, 'Will every single mother please stand!'" They began to laugh at the memory. "The congregation started buzzing and the mothers weren't sure whether to stand up or not, since they weren't single, and then the choir just started howling. Poor Chester didn't know what to do because he didn't understand what he had said. But he's sharp, and when he realized his goof, he covered it very well. I've loved him for it ever since. Makes you know the guy is human after all."

"Why?" asked Marianne. "I didn't hear about it. You know, I go to the *other* church."

"He kind of looked embarrassed and then he said something like, 'You know, I haven't messed up this badly since one of my first marriage ceremonies when I pompously announced, 'What God hath joined asunder, let no man put together!' The whole congregation just nearly died laughing. And all through the rest of the service someone would burst out giggling, or trying to stifle their laughter."

"That ought to be written up in one of those 'Most Embarrassing Moments' books," Sharon responded. "Reminds me of the one I heard not long ago." And then they each had to tell a funny story about an embarrassing incident.

They were all chuckling as they returned to the game room to resume their bridge game. "Jane, what's the status on your move?" Marianne knew about the sale of Jane's house to Julian and Jasmine but didn't know when it would take place.

"We'll close at the end of the month, and then they've graciously given me an extra two weeks to get moved. I've rented an old house that's big enough for my furniture, what I want to keep anyway. Bruce and Chrissy have taken several things off my hands and that helps us both out. I've got a great builder, I think. He's found me a lot that I like, not too far from Sharon, and a plan that I just love. It's all barrier free. I insisted on that."

"How long does it take to build a house?" Hillary wondered.

"The builder said he could easily get it finished in five or six months. Does that sound reasonable, Marianne?"

"Sure, if he's got his subs all lined up. We used to finish spec houses in less time than that. But custom, well, that depends. You know some people will make changes or add things along the way and that takes time. And money. But I'm not saying you shouldn't do it. After all, you'll be living in your home a long time. We hope."

"What about Julian and Jasmine? I'll bet they're getting excited about the move. Are they going to remodel or redecorate?" Hillary wanted to know.

Jane pondered the question. "A funny thing is going on there. They're excited, I know, but their kids are giving them some flack. I think maybe the news is out that they're moving from their old neighborhood to a *white* neighborhood and they're catching all kinds of criticism. And there's another black doctor at the hospital, Jasmine told me, who's always calling Julian 'Uncle Tom' or 'Doctor Oreo,' things like that. And this move is adding fuel to the flame, so to speak. It's an interesting situation."

After discussing the sale a little longer, Jane changed the subject. "You know what? We haven't added anything to our gritch kitty in so long I'd almost forgotten about it. What do you suppose that means?" No one had an answer, but they all smiled.

At the end of the evening, Sharon promised to take Jane home, and Hillary was the first to leave, humming a happy tune. An evening with her friends was like a tonic to her. She was renewed, revived, or what would be a better description? "My batteries are re-charged," she said aloud and smiled.

CHAPTER 24

Pulling into her driveway, Hillary depressed the button on her garage remote control and noticed the light come on and the door begin to rise. She took note that the lights she had left on were still on, a habit she had unconsciously formed last winter when she found that Pete had walked from the nursing home. How many times had she replayed that evening? She admitted that she had said to herself many times, "If only I could have him back for just one day, just one night..." And then she did have him, if only for a few hours.

Hillary pulled her car up until she gently bumped the concrete curb that was built into the garage. She turned off the key, then the lights. She reached into her purse and turned off her cell phone so the battery would not run down. As she pressed the garage control and heard the door begin to lower Hillary reached for the door handle and did not see the person dressed in dark camouflage slide underneath the lowering garage door. She did not notice him crouch behind the car as she stepped out and turned back to reach down and pick up her purse.

Suddenly rough hands grabbed Hillary, pinning her arms to her side, slamming her head against the door liner as he dragged her out. The blow dazed her momentarily so that she could not move or protest. In one movement, it seemed, a dirty burlap bag was thrown over Hillary's head and her wrists were tied behind her with rough nylon rope. She had not seen a face or form, and the only impression she had was the strong smell of whisky.

Hillary found that her legs would not hold her up. As she was slowly sinking to the concrete floor, a loud string of profanity was directed at her, and the strong rough hands once again grabbed her. The back car door was opened, and Hillary was thrown into the floorboard in an awkward position, her nose against the back of the front seat and the hump in the floor cutting into her midsection. When she got her bearings she realized that the dirty sack made it hard to breathe. She might suffocate. "Slow and deep, slow and deep," she told herself because she recognized that she was about to panic and hyperventilate.

"Please, mister, whoever you are. Let me out of here. Besides, you must have the wrong person."

"Just shut up, Mrs. Johnson. I have the right person alright," he slurred. "Now you shut up or I'll shut you up. Bet you've never been pistol-whupped, have you? Usually fractures the skull." He laughed a high-pitched laughter that, to Hillary, sounded insane, or maybe he was just drunk. Or both?

Her kidnapper found the keys she had dropped when he grabbed her. With great difficulty he found the garage door control, raised the door, and backed the car out. Hillary felt a terrible pain as the driver ran over the curb, forcing the hump into her diaphragm. *Oh, dear Lord*, she prayed, *those knees and that elbow are on fire. And I can't even change my position.* She began to wonder if anyone ever died from arthritis pain and felt she just might be the first.

I've got to think of something, Hillary reasoned. *No one will even know I'm gone for hours, or days maybe. Oh, mercy, this must be that Grubbs guy, the one that Officer Robinson told me about.* "Mr. Grubbs," she tried and felt the car swerve and hit the curb a hard blow that once again pushed her face into the seat back and slammed the hump into her lower ribs.

"You shut up, and don't call me that!" Hillary heard him continue talking, as if to himself, but the words were muffled and she couldn't hear. His driving continued to be erratic, but Hillary didn't hear any other traffic on the road. They must be in the outskirts of town, maybe in the country. She was sure of it when they turned onto a gravel road that later gave way to what seemed to be a rutted trail.

Where could they be? Hillary wondered. If she could get to her cell phone and call 911... But what good would that do when she didn't have any idea where they were? Maybe he'd kill her before that anyway. No, he could have killed her in the garage. *He's using me to get to Pete, that's it. I'll tell him that Pete's dead. Or just imply that he's dead. Then maybe he'll release me. Or kill me?*

Pain shot through her sternum with every jolt of the car, and her right eye felt bruised. She tried to open it, but it would only open half way. No matter, there wasn't anything but blackness to see inside the tow sack. *Be calm, Hillary. Pretend this is one of your fantasies and you'll be some kind of big hero when it's over, like always.* She couldn't convince herself. Painful tears were escaping from her eyes, which she knew would just pick up the dust from the sack and she would have little mud balls all over her face. *Maybe when they find my body tomorrow or next week, the coroner will take note of mud balls all down my cheeks. I wonder just how he'd write that up and what he'd make of it. And who will take care of Pete if I'm gone?*

The nylon rope cut into Hillary's wrists. *If I were kidnapping someone I wouldn't use nylon rope*, she thought. *Never could get a real fast knot, it always seems to slip.* She had a momentary thought of telling Mr. Grubbs that it was a bad choice, and if she hadn't been in so much pain, might have laughed at the idea. It reminded her of an Aggie joke they had once laughed at: The Aggie told his executioner, "If you'll put some grease on that guillotine it'll work much better." She tried to move her wrists around, and even though the rope had cut into her skin, she did think the knots might be slipping. *At least that's something positive to think about.* She kept moving her fingers around till she had the knot under her right index finger. With only a slight range of motion, she could barely get her fingernail under one edge of the knot and pulled. Nothing happened. Wrong edge. She tried the other side and wasn't sure it moved but kept working on it. Little by little the two ends of the rope came apart only to find that there were more backup knots. He must have tied half a dozen knots, she fretted. The second was hard to find, but when it released the next knot was easy.

Just as Hillary began to unwind the last of the cord, the car braked to a sudden stop, causing her to cry out with pain. The rough hands once again grabbed her and shoved her to her feet. She hoped he didn't notice that the hands once tied behind her back were now in front of her. She kept her wrists together and the cord wrapped around them and held the ends firmly in her hands.

"Aren't those Hillary's glasses there on the rug?" Sharon and Jane were about to leave Marianne's house after the bridge party had broken up. When Hillary had gone, Marianne remembered that she wanted to show Sharon how her needlework was progressing and ask her advice on the next step.

"Yes, they are, and she can't see to read anything without them," Jane answered.

"Oh, dear, how can we get them to her?" asked Marianne. "I have to be at the library by 7:30 tomorrow. I know how lost I'd be without mine."

"I'll call her car phone; she may not be home yet." Sharon dialed and got the recorded message letting her know that the phone was turned off. Again she dialed and got Hillary's answering machine. "Hmmm, she's not home, either. Well, let's just swing by there, Jane, do you mind?"

Sharon wondered why Hillary's cell phone was turned off and there was no answer on her home phone. It wasn't like Hill. She was very conscientious about being reachable. In case something happened with Pete or the kids. She didn't mention this to Jane as they were driving over to Hillary's neighborhood, but they were quiet and didn't visit. Maybe Jane was concerned too. There was some very reasonable explanation. Hill was a very reasonable person.

"Oh, dear," Sharon gasped as they drove into Hillary's driveway. They saw an empty garage, the door raised and the automatic light had gone off, meaning it had been more than a few minutes since the car had left.

"Maybe she had to go back to the convenience store for milk or bread," Jane offered and then contradicted herself, as if in an argument. "Nah, she wouldn't go after 11:00 at night. Besides, she's too organized to forget something like that. And she'd put down the garage door anyway."

"Jane, did Hillary ever mention Farley Wayne Grubbs to you?"

"No, why?" Jane began to feel anxious.

"Well, it's not like Hillary to complain or even to admit being scared. She didn't even tell her kids. But there's this very nice officer that Hill visits with fairly often and he told her about Grubbs." Sharon started at the beginning and told Jane everything she knew about the insane alcoholic wanting to get even with Pete.

"Let's call Robinson, now. Even if there is some reasonable explanation. I know where there's a hidden key. Let's go in the house to make the calls and wait for Hill."

Hillary was thrown roughly into a chair with uneven legs. She was afraid it would dump her out if she moved too much. Finally she had it balanced so that with both feet on the floor the chair was steady. She still was fighting not to breathe too deeply inside the dirty sack.

The sounds from across the room made Hillary suspect that Grubbs was drinking from a bottle. Sometimes she would hear a loud burp. Once he broke out crying loudly and mumbling something she couldn't understand. Later, much later, it became very quiet. Hillary thought he may have fallen asleep. Now that her hands were in front of her, she didn't dare turn loose of the nylon cord, she could push up the edge of the sack and see what was happening.

As she peered out from under the edge of the filthy sack, Hillary took a deep breath of clean air. She looked at her surroundings in disgust. What a dump. Under the bare light bulb Grubbs had fallen asleep with his forehead resting on his arm. *Passed out, we call it, Hill*, she told herself.

She took the sack off her head completely and let it drop to the floor. As she unwound the nylon cord from her wrists and hands, the circulation returned with painful tingling. Hillary stood up slowly, knowing the boards of the rickety floor would creak. And they did, but quietly. Where was her purse and cell phone? The dim bulb didn't provide enough light for her to see all around the room. Maybe he left the purse in the car.

Hillary slowly made her way to the back door. She tried the handle and it didn't give. She then noticed the edge of the door had been nailed shut with large nails. It looked like the only way out of the cabin was right behind Grubbs. *Please, oh, please, let him sleep right through this.*

As she tiptoed past him, she got a better look at her kidnapper. He was skinny but with a large belly. Alcoholic cirrhosis, she suspected, with ascites making his abdomen resemble a pregnant woman's. *And maybe he really does have an alcoholic psychosis.* Her nurse's objectivity was tempered with some very real disgust at this dishevelled person in front of her, snoring loudly and drooling on his arm. A few more steps and she would reach the door. The wind outside was picking up and making very welcomed background noises. In the distance Hillary thought she heard thunder rumbling and hoped the outside noises would cover the opening of the door.

Holding her breath, she waited for another roar of thunder before slowly opening the door. She hadn't expected the loud screech of rusty hinges and was sure Grubbs would awaken. She stepped quickly over the threshold anyway without looking back. Hillary pulled the door nearly shut and stood just outside long enough to take a few slow deep breaths and wait for her heart to quit racing.

The night was entirely dark because of the cloud cover. The only light she could see was through the dirty window of the cabin. Peering into the darkness, Hillary guessed that the car would be out past the bushes somewhere. As her eyes became accustomed to the gloom, a distant flash of lightning gave her a brief glimpse of a car fender. She made her way carefully toward the car, stumbling on rocks and tripping on thorny weeds. If only he left the key in the ignition, she prayed.

As she opened the door to the driver's side she slid quickly behind the wheel. No key. Where is her purse? She hated to open the door again and would not turn on the dome light. Grubbs could wake up any minute from his drunken stupor and this would be the first place he would look for her.

With both hands, she felt along the seat and down into the floorboard on the passenger side, no purse. Then in the crack between the seats she felt something cold and hard—her cell phone!

She could hardly see to dial 911 in the black darkness and without her glasses. The faint light from the phone was hardly enough to assure a right number. After several attempts she finally reached the emergency number and, scared as she was, she became very matter-of-fact, trying to give as much information in as few words as possible. "Hello," she said breathlessly, "my name is Hillary Johnson and I've been kidnapped by Farley Wayne Grubbs. Please get in touch with Officer Robinson. I don't know where we are but it's a shack and only about fifteen minutes from town. My car is parked outside and, Yiiiii!!" The door across from Hillary flew open and long arms grabbed for her.

Hillary was out of the car and into the bushes before Grubbs could get out from behind the steering wheel. She tried to find some kind of trail, but the bushes were thick and their thorns tore at her skin. She ran until she could no longer get her breath and could feel her pulses pounding; she thought she might black out. Or stroke out, she worried. Backing into a large bush, she felt that she would be partially hidden for the time necessary to catch her breath.

As her breathing returned to nearly normal, Hillary was aware of no sound but the rain, which started out slowly and was now beginning to pour down. Had Grubbs gone away? Had he missed the trail? Another flash of lightning proved her mistaken. There, not twenty feet away, stood Farley Grubbs, immobilized in the light, looking around and listening for revealing sounds.

Hillary slowly slid to the ground. As she heard Grubbs going off down a trail to the left, she realized that he had been standing in something of a trail on her right which must lead back to the house. At any rate she wanted to be going in the opposite direction from her kidnapper.

As she crawled on her hands and knees, Hillary remembered this rocky terrain was well known for snakes—rattlesnakes in fact—scorpions, and tarantulas. "Ugh!" she said half aloud. Crawly things had always scared her, and now here she was, right in their habitat. As soon as she felt she had intercepted the trail, she tried to stand up.

The pain was so intense that she felt tears come to her eyes. Her knees were on fire and her back so stiff that it took several tries before she could stand upright. Her hands were aching, and she felt something crawling on the back of her left hand. She quickly brushed it away, not even wanting to know what it was.

A distant flash of lightning showed Hillary that she was on a trail of sorts, and then she could see the dim light through the dirty window of the cabin. She was careful not to get too near the house and be seen in the light by Grubbs. She started off down a rutted road which hopefully would lead her to the highway and help.

Hillary stayed in the edge of the road so that she could quickly duck into the bushes if she heard Grubbs nearby. She stopped often to listen for telltale sounds. She heard nothing, only the pelting of the rain and an occasional rumble of retreating thunder.

He must be trained as some kind of guerrilla, Hillary guessed, *since he gets around fast without making a sound*. When the road came to a Y, Hillary finally chose the one on the right because it seemed to be more heavily traveled, realizing that in the deep darkness and pouring rain she could easily be wrong.

The road was winding downward, and Hillary slipped and stumbled, almost falling, on the rain-slicked gravel. She found a gnarled stick that she used for a walking cane and brandished it at the darkness; it might be a good weapon, too, if she needed one.

In the darkness Hillary did not see the pier until she stumbled against it. When she realized what it must be she heard the gentle waves lapping against the shore in the aftermath of the storm. *There must be a boat*, she reasoned. *If only I can get away from this area I'll be safe. Even if I have to stay in the middle of the lake all night. Until Officer Robinson finds me.* She was confident that he would find her.

The pier was in bad repair, and Hillary stepped cautiously from one board to the next, sure that any minute a rotted board would splinter, dumping her into the lake. She bumped a foot against a cleat on the side of the pier and found that there was a rotted rope, or painter as she was taught to say, tied to it. Her eyes were becoming slightly more accustomed to the darkness, and the rain seemed to be letting up a little. She could see the outline of a small rowboat and hear it bumping rhythmically against the dock.

Now, what if it's full of water and sinks as I step into it? What if it's got spiders in it, or worse yet, a snake? Quickly she decided that snakes and spiders were only a vague possibility, but Farley Grubbs was real and he was after her. She pulled on the painter till the boat was alongside the pier, and untying the frayed rope, she stepped off into the boat and sat with a thud in the bottom with the plank seat scraping her back. "Oof!!" escaped her lips unexpectedly. She hadn't made much noise, but if Grubbs were nearby, he would have heard the ungraceful entry into the rowboat.

Knowing she had little time to waste, Hillary began feeling around for oars. What she found was a small paddle and began to make good use of it.

"I see you out there and I'm coming to get you!"

Hillary heard a great splash and knew Grubbs had dived in after her. But she didn't slow down her paddling. *Where is he? I hear splashing and he's coming this direction. He can hear me paddling, too.* She tried to paddle without splashing the water but knew she wasn't making good time.

She stopped briefly to listen for his location and heard nothing. She was totally unprepared when he surfaced right at the boat and grabbed onto the side, almost turning it over. Hillary grabbed the sides of the boat to keep from being thrown out and dropped her paddle into the bottom of the boat. *He's trying to climb into the boat*, she realized in her hysteria. *Then he'll kill me for sure.*

Just as Hillary picked up her paddle, the clouds parted, and an almost full moon gave light onto the lake. Not two feet away from her was the insane face smiling with psychotic glee that he had captured his helpless prey and knew what he expected to do to her now. He had the impression of her standing but was not prepared for the full force of a wooden paddle coming down on his head.

Grubbs disappeared from sight into the blackness of Lake Waco. "Oh, dear. Oh, my!" Hillary kept repeating. "Mr. Grubbs, where are you? Mr. Grubbs!" She cupped her hands around her mouth and shouted, "Help me somebody. Help!"

Hillary felt a soft thump against the boat and braced for another attack. When none came, she carefully looked over the side of the boat, and there was the huddled body of her assailant, bleeding from a scalp wound and about to go under the water again. "No, no. Don't drown. Please don't die!" She reached over and got a grip on the collar of his shirt and tugged him toward the bow of the boat. With the painter she did a figure eight under each arm and around his chest. When she secured him well enough she gave another big tug to ensure that his head would stay above the water and began yelling again.

Over and over she yelled for help, sometimes adding, "Call the police." Hillary couldn't remember being this tired, ever. Her knuckles were painful, and a moan escaped her lips every time she readjusted the rope around Grubbs. An occasional moan also came from Grubbs, who was not yet entirely conscious. The night became dark again, and Hillary was dozing and did not hear the helicopter as it circled overhead with its searchlight sweeping the lake.

Later the sound of a motor awakened Hillary. A loudspeaker seemed to be shouting her name.

"Mrs. Johnson! Mrs. Johnson, this is the police! Are you okay?"

Hillary was dazed. She didn't know where she was or what all the commotion was about. Gradually she took note of her surroundings. She was in a rickety rowboat, and her right hand was wound tightly with a rotted rope. She looked over the side of the boat to see what she was tied onto. Farley Grubbs was making incoherent sounds and rolling his head from side to side, still kept afloat by Hillary's wraps around his chest and under his arms.

Finally Hillary raised her eyes to the oncoming motorboat, unable to focus her eyesight without her glasses. She just waited till they approached. As the driver cut the power back, another officer spoke to Hillary, not needing the bullhorn, "Mrs. Johnson, this is Officer Robinson. Are you okay?" He waited for the smile that broke across Hillary's face as his answer. "Your family is all gathered at your house worried about you." Here he chuckled. "But it looks like you've got everything under control."

The other officer was struggling to get Grubbs into the patrol boat, and when he had done so, was quick to snap the handcuffs on his wrists. Robinson had gently assisted Hillary into the patrol boat and explained that he had to make a phone call. "Yes, she's right here and seems to be okay. Do you want to talk with her?"

"Hello? Yes, dear." Hillary held the phone away from her ear. "It's my daughter," she explained, "she's pretty excited." After a few more minutes of listening, Hillary said, "Yes, I'll be home right away." Robinson quickly took the phone from Hillary.

"Hello, this is Robinson again. Mrs. Johnson is not coming directly home. She is going to the emergency room first to be checked over. We should be there in about twenty minutes; there's an ambulance waiting at the marina. Yes, yes, I'm sure everything will be alright." He smiled at Hillary. "Your daughter was really worried about you. That's nice. You're a lucky woman."

She had her eyes closed, but smiled. *Yes, I'm a lucky woman.*

Hillary felt warm and loved being back in her Sunday School class with the women she had known so long and with whom she had shared so much.

They had all been incensed learning she had been maltreated in such a way. They oohed and aahed about her two black eyes. They were so sympathetic that she had to stay in the hospital overnight for observation. When they learned she had a cracked rib, they all wanted to help her walk or carry her purse and Bible.

During the opening prayer, Hillary couldn't resist the temptation to open her eyes and study her friends. There they were, with hair in so many shades of gray, and some in colors that neither God nor nature had given them. Their faces relaxed in the grumpy expressions that gravity had produced, and that were so contradictory to their true natures. *But aren't they beautiful*, she marveled. Hillary quickly closed her eyes before Martha, their teacher, said the "Amen."

And then Martha, surveying the group with love and caring, smiled her mischievous grin and asked, "Well, girls, have you claimed your joy this week?"

Printed in the United States
65549LVS00005B/277-282